HOUSE OF MIRRORS

Justin Trudeau's Foreign Policy

Yves Engler

BLACK ROSE BOOKS

Montréal, Chicago, London

Copyright © 2020 Yves Engler

All rights reserved. No part of this book may be reproduced or transmitted in any form by any means without permission in writing from the publisher, except by a reviewer, who may quote brief passages in a review.

Black Rose Books No. UU415

Cover by Frank Myrskog
Printed and bound in Canada
by Marquis Printing
A co-publication of
RED Publishing
203 32nd Street West
Saskatoon, SK
S7L 0S3 and

Black Rose Books
C.P. 35788
Succ. Léo Pariseau
Montréal, QC
H2X 0A4
CANADA
www.blackrosebooks.com

BLACK ROSE BOOKS

Library and Archives Canada Cataloguing in Publication

Title: House of mirrors : Justin Trudeau's foreign policy / Yves Engler.
Names: Engler, Yves, 1979- author.
Description: Includes bibliographical references.
Identifiers: Canadiana (print) 20200181157 | Canadiana (ebook) 20200181165 | ISBN 9781551647494 (softcover) | ISBN 9781551647517 (hardcover) | ISBN 9781551647531 (PDF)
Subjects: LCSH: Trudeau, Justin. | CSH: Canada—Foreign relations—21st century. | CSH: Canada— Politics and government—2015-
Classification: LCC FC655 .E54 2020 | DDC 971.07/4—dc23

Ordering Information

USA/INTERNATIONAL	CANADA	UK/EUROPE
University of Chicago Press	University of Toronto Press	Central Books
Chicago Distribution Center	5201 Dufferin Street	Freshwater Road
11030 South Langley Avenue	Toronto, ON	Dagenham
Chicago, IL 60628	M3H 5T8	RM8 1RX
(800) 621-2736 (USA)	1-800-565-9523	+ 44 (0) 20 8525 8800
(773) 702-7000 (World))	utpbooks@utpress.utoronto.ca	contactus@centralbooks.com
orders@press.uchicago.edu		

Table of Contents

The Ugly Canadian II
Introduction ... 5
1. The Sun Never Sets on Canadian Military
Hard Power ... 9
2. The Canadian Monroe Doctrine
Interfering Down South ... 22
3. Loving Monarchies, Hating Palestinians
Middle East ... 68
4. Commies No More, But ...
Russian Bogeyman ... 112
5. The Asian Contradiction
China and North Korea ... 124
6. Buddies With Africa's Most Ruthless Dictator
Curious Case of Kagame ... 134
7. Climate Criminal
Spewing Carbon Dioxide ... 139
8. Same Old, Same Old
Business Above All Else ... 144
9. Ugly Canadian Abroad
Mining Exploitation ... 156
10. House of Mirrors
Judge What I Say, Not What I Do ... 168
11. It's the System Dummy
Conclusion ... 179

Glossary

Acronyms

ATT	Arms Trade Treaty
ALBA	Bolivarian Alliance for the Peoples of our America
CCC	Canadian Commercial Corporation
CF	Canadian Forces
CSE	Communications Security Establishment
DND	Department of National Defence
EDC	Export Development Canada
FIAP	Feminist International Assistance Policy
FIPA	Foreign Investment Promotion and Protection Agreement
GCC	Gulf Cooperation Council
IMF	International Monetary Fund
IRBO	International Rules Based Order
JCPOA	Joint Comprehensive Plan of Action
LAV	Light Armored Vehicle
OAS	Organization of American States
PDAC	Prospectors and Developers Association of Canada
TCS	Trade Commissioner Service

Justin Trudeau's Senior Cabinet Ministers

Foreign Minister

November 2015 – January 2017	Stéphane Dion
January 2017 – November 2019	Chrystia Freeland
November 2019 – Today	François-Philippe Champagne

Defence Minister

November 2015 – Today	Harjit Singh Sajjan

International Development Minister

November 2015 – February 2019	Marie-Claude Bibeau
March 2019 – November 2019	Maryam Monsef
November 2019 – Today	Karina Gould

Trade Minister

November 2015 – January 2017	Chrystia Freeland
January 2017 – July 2018	François-Philippe Champagne
July 2018 – Today	Jim Carr

The Ugly Canadian II — Introduction

> "Many of you have worried that Canada has lost its compassionate and constructive voice in the world over the past 10 years. Well, I have a simple message for you: on behalf of 35 million Canadians, we're back."
> —**Justin Trudeau**, *following 2015 election*

> "We're Canada and we're here to help."
> —**Justin Trudeau**, *2016 address to UN General Assembly*

> "I guess the lesson is we shouldn't be fooled by good-looking Liberals no matter how well-spoken they are."
> —**Jane Fonda**, *Actress and activist, January 2017*

Justin Trudeau presents himself as "progressive" on foreign affairs. The Liberals claim to have brought Canada "back" after the disastrous Stephen Harper government. But, this book will demonstrate the opposite.

While promising to "make a real and valuable contribution to a more peaceful and prosperous world", Trudeau has largely continued the Conservatives pro-corporate/empire international policies.[1] The Liberals have followed the previous government's posture on a wide range of issues from Russia to Palestine, Venezuela to the military.

In 2017 the Liberals released a defence policy that called for 605 more special forces, which have carried out numerous violent covert missions abroad.[2] During the 2015 election campaign defence minister Jason Kenney said if re-elected the Conservatives would add 665 members to the Canadian Armed Forces Special Operations Command.[3] The government's defence policy also included a plan to acquire armed drones, for which the Conservatives had expressed support. Additionally, the Liberals re-stated the previous government's commitment to spend over one hundred billion dollars on new fighter jets and naval ships.

The Harper regime repeatedly attacked Venezuela's elected government and the Liberals ramped up that campaign. The Trudeau government launched an unprecedented, multipronged, effort to overthrow Nicolás Maduro's government. As part of this campaign, they aligned with the most reactionary political forces in the region, targeting Cuba and recognizing a Honduran president who stole an election he shouldn't have participated in. Juan Orlando Hernández' presidency was the outgrowth of a military coup the Conservatives tacitly endorsed in 2009.

In Haiti the Liberals propped up the chosen successor of neo-Duvalerist President Michel Martelly who Harper helped install. Despite a sustained popular uprising against Jovenel Moïse, the Liberals backed the repressive, corrupt and illegitimate president.

The Trudeau government continues to justify Israeli violence against Palestinians and supports Israel's illegal occupation. Isolating Canada from world opinion, they voted against dozens of UN resolutions upholding Palestinian rights backed by most of the world.

Initiated by the Conservatives, the Liberals signed off on a $14 billion Light Armoured Vehicle sale to Saudi Arabia. The Liberals followed Harper's path of cozying up to other repressive Middle East monarchies, which waged war in Yemen. They also contributed to extending the brutal war in Syria and broke their promise to restart diplomatic relations with Iran, which the Conservatives severed.

The Liberals renewed Canada's military "training" mission in the Ukraine, which emboldened far-right militarists responsible for hundreds of deaths in the east of that country. In fact, Trudeau significantly bolstered Canada's military presence on Russia's doorstep.

Simultaneously, the Trudeau government expanded Harper's sanctions against Russia.

On China the Liberals were torn between corporate Canada and militarist/pro-US forces. They steadily moved away from the corporate sphere and towards the militarist/US Empire standpoint. (During their time in office the Conservatives moved in the opposite direction.) Ottawa seemed to fear that peace might break out on the Korean Peninsula.

Trudeau backed Africa's most bloodstained politician.

Unlike his predecessor, Trudeau didn't sabotage international climate negotiations. But the Liberals flouted their climate commitments and subsidized infrastructure to expand heavy emitting fossil fuels.

Ignoring global inequities, the Liberals promoted the interests of corporations and wealth holders in various international forums. They backed corporate interests through trade accords, Export Development Canada and the Trade Commissioner Service. Their support for SNC Lavalin also reflected corporate influence over foreign policy.

In a stark betrayal of their progressive rhetoric, the Trudeau regime failed to follow through on their promise to rein in Canada's controversial international mining sector. Instead they mimicked the Conservatives' strategy of establishing a largely toothless ombudsperson while openly backing brutal mining companies.

To sell their pro-corporate/empire policies the Liberals embraced a series of progressive slogans. As they violated international law and spurned efforts to overcome pressing global issues, the Liberals crowed about the "international rules-based order". Their "feminist foreign policy" rhetoric rested uneasily with their militarism, support for mining companies and ties to misogynistic monarchies.

Notwithstanding the rhetoric, the sober reality is that Trudeau has largely continued Harper's foreign policy. The "Ugly Canadian" continued to march across the planet, but with a prettier face at the helm.

My 2012 book *The Ugly Canadian: Stephen Harper's Foreign Policy* detailed the first six and a half years of Harper's rule. This book looks at the first four years of Trudeau's reign. I will discuss the many ways Canadian foreign policy under Conservative and Liberal governments remained the same. Support for empire and a pro-corporate neoliberal economic order is the common theme that links the actions of conservative and self-described "progressive" prime ministers. I will conclude with an attempt to answer the question of why this is.

Introduction Notes

1 Prime Minister announces Canada's Growth and Investment Strategies, Nov 15 2015 (https://pm.gc.ca/en/news/news-releases/2015/11/15/prime-minister-announces-canadas-growth-and-investment-strategies)

2 Yves Engler, War Crimes in the Dark: Inside Canada's Special Forces, Oct 2 2015 (https://www.counterpunch.org/2015/10/02/war-crimes-in-the-dark-canadas-special-forces/)

3 Jason Kenney says Conservative government will boost special forces, Sep 26 2015 (https://www.cbc.ca/news/canada/saskatchewan/conservative-jason-kenney-regina-special-forces-1.3245266)

1. The Sun Never Sets on Canadian Military — Hard Power

Does a country with a "progressive" foreign policy use military might to get its way in the world? Does it send troops, planes and ships thousands of kilometres away to the borders of countries with which it has disagreements? Does it vastly expand military spending, including the number of specially trained soldiers whose use is kept secret? Does it train with and serve under the world's No. 1 military power that has nearly a thousand bases across the planet to protect its empire?[1]

As this book went to print, Canada was not formally at war, but had more than 2,100 troops sprinkled across the globe.[2] According to the Armed Forces, these soldiers were engaged in 28 international missions.[3] The two most significant missions instigated by the Liberals were on Russia's doorstep and in Iraq.

The scope of the military's international footprint was hard to square with the idea of a force defending Canada. That's why military types promote so called "forward defence". The Liberals June 2017 "Strong, Secure, Engaged: Canada's Defence Policy" said Canada had to "actively address threats abroad for stability at home" and that "defending Canada and Canadian interests … requires active engagement abroad."[4] That logic, of course, can be used to justify participating in endless US-led military endeavors.

In a major foreign policy speech the day after the launch of the defence policy, Chrystia Freeland said Canada required "hard power" and a readiness to fight wars to maintain the North American-led "world order". "To put it plainly: Canadian diplomacy and development sometimes require the backing of hard power," explained the foreign minister. "Principled use of force, together with our allies and governed by international law, is part of our history and must be part of our future."[5]

In the speech Freeland also praised the US's "outsized role" in world affairs since World War II. "Canada is grateful, and will always be grateful, to our neighbour for the outsized role it has played in the world," she noted. "And we seek and will continue to seek to persuade our friends that their continued international leadership is very much in their national interest — as well as that of the rest of the free world."[6]

The Liberals 2017 defence policy called for a 70-per-cent increase in military spending over a decade.[7] It re-stated the previous government's commitment to spend more than one hundred billion dollars on new fighter jets and naval ships. Purchasing 15 surface-combat vessels was alone expected to cost over $60 billion ($100 billion over their lifecycle), making it the largest single taxpayer expense in Canadian history.[8]

These funds could pay for dozens of light rail lines across the country and other infrastructure required to shift off of fossil fuels. In that vein Canadian Voice of Women for Peace board member, Tamara Lorincz, pointed out that the Liberals committed $553 billion in federal money to maintaining Canada's "high-end warfighting" capabilities in their defence policy while the 2016 Pan-Canadian Framework for Clean Growth and Climate Change budgeted $132 billion of new federal and provincial funds over eleven years.[9]

"Strong, Secure, Engaged" included a plan to acquire armed drones. It also called for adding 605 members to the special forces, which have carried out numerous violent covert missions abroad.[10] The defence review committed $1.5 billion in long-term equipment projects for the special forces.

Paralleling the rise of the US Cyber Command to formal command status, the Liberals' defence policy called for expanding the Canadian Forces Intelligence Command's (CFINTCOM) scope and adding 300 intelligence positions. It described the need to "build CFINTCOM's capacity to provide more advanced intelligence support to operations, including through an enhanced ability to forecast flashpoints and emerging threats, better support next generation platforms and understand rapid developments in space, cyber and other emerging domains."[11]

Unlike the Communications Security Establishment or CSIS, no legislation spells out the parameters of CFINTCOM's operations. Nor is there civilian oversight.[12] The Chief of Defence Staff and military leaders are responsible for monitoring Canadian Forces intelligence activities.

The defence policy lauded the North American Aerospace Defense Command (NORAD). A Cold War agreement supposed to defend the two countries from an invasion by Soviet bombers coming from the north, NORAD's political implications are vast. The accord impinges on Canadian sovereignty, influences weapons procurement and ties Canada to US belligerence. Through NORAD the CF has provided logistical support to US air strikes in Iraq, Afghanistan and elsewhere.[13]

"Strong, Secure, Engaged" cited the importance of being "interoperable"/"interoperability" with US and NATO forces at least 19 times. At its most basic "interoperability" means the ability for military forces to act together seamlessly because doctrines, processes and equipment are compatible. But, the political implications of this fairly elastic military buzzword are significant. The search for interoperability has been used to justify participating in belligerent US-led missions.[14]

The defence policy also promoted <u>NATO</u>, which currently encompasses 29 states. NATO intensified pressure on Ottawa to increase military spending and participate in wars. As its Cold War pretext faded further from view, NATO became more belligerent. In 1999 Canadian fighter jets dropped 530 bombs in NATO's illegal 78-day bombing of Serbia. During the 2000s tens of thousands of

Canadian troops fought in a NATO war in Afghanistan while in 2011 a Canadian general led NATO's attack on Libya in which seven CF-18 fighter jets and two Canadian naval vessels participated. In a dangerous game of brinksmanship, NATO massed troops and fighter jets on Russia's border.

After French President Emanuel Macron criticized NATO in November 2019 Trudeau immediately defended the alliance and a month later declared, "for 70 years, NATO has been fundamental to Canada's security and defence, and we remain committed to this alliance. In recent years, Canada has strengthened its engagement in NATO, taking on vital leadership roles. Today, Canada is leading NATO missions in Latvia, Iraq, and NATO maritime forces in the Mediterranean Sea and the Black Sea."[15]

The Trudeau government announced that Canada will add six fighter jets and a frigate to bolster NATO's High Readiness Forces. In total Canada has committed 12 CF-18 fighter jets, an expeditionary air task force, a maritime patrol aircraft, three frigates, a submarine, a mechanized infantry battalion, a mobile hospital and a platoon for chemical, biological, radiological and nuclear decontamination to this NATO force.[16]

The Trudeau government has empowered the DND-run Communications Security Establishment (CSE). They authorized CSE to carry out offensive operations "to degrade, disrupt, influence, respond to or interfere with the capabilities, intentions or activities" of foreign actors.[17] In effect, the intelligence agency could seek to take a government offline, shutter a power plant, knock a drone out of the sky, or interfere in court proceedings and elections in countries Ottawa didn't deem "democratic." The Liberals restricted CSE from offensive cyber activities that could cause injury or death or "obstruct, pervert or defeat the course of justice or democracy."[18] But, these limitations wouldn't apply if CSE receives approval from the foreign minister or conducts its cyber-attacks on behalf of a Canadian military operation. And CSE was allowed to do "anything that is reasonably necessary to maintain the covert nature of the activity."[19]

Incredibly, CSE's mandate was expanded only two years after former National Security Agency (NSA) contractor Edward Snowden's revelations prompted US decision-makers to rein in its US counterpart (2015 USA Freedom Act). Instead of facing more stringent rules, CSE brought in a series of measures to avoid what the *Toronto Star* labeled a "Canadian Snowden".[20] According to a document that newspaper uncovered, the signals intelligence agency spent $45 million to upgrade the federal government's Top Secret network to avoid "insider threats".[21] In addition to expanding CSE's powers, the Liberals put up $500 million in 2017 to create a federal "cybersecurity" centre run by CSE.[22]

Supposed to be foreign-focused, CSE monitors phone calls, radio, microwave and satellite signals, emails, chat rooms and other forms of Internet exchanges. It engages in various forms of data hacking, sifting daily through millions of videos and online documents. Or as Vice reporter Patrick McGuire put it, CSE "listens in on phone calls and emails to secretly learn about things the Canadian government wants to secretly learn about."[23]

Snowden revealed that CSE hacked Mexican computers and spied on Brazil's Department of Mines and Energy.[24] CSE also planted sophisticated malware on mobile phones and hacked into computers abroad to attack targets without being detected.[25]

The agency's website says it played a "vital role" in the 2001-14 occupation of Afghanistan, and CSE head John Adams boasted that the agency was responsible for more than half the "actionable intelligence" Canadian soldiers used in Afghanistan. CSE also aided the deployment to Iraq and Syria that began in 2014.[26]

In April 2018 Trudeau labeled CSE "an extraordinary institution".[27] He did so after revealing a meeting of Five Eyes, the Canadian, US, UK, Australian and New Zealand intelligence sharing arrangement.[28] CSE is Canada's main contributor to the Five

Eyes arrangement that monitors billions of private communications worldwide. Trudeau claimed the Five Eyes "keeps all of our citizens safe" and the 2017 defence policy labeled it "central to protecting Canada's interests."[29]

The Five Eyes accords are ultra-secretive and operate with little oversight. Snowden labeled it a "supra-national intelligence organisation that doesn't answer to the known laws of its own countries."[30] In addition to sharing information they've intercepted, collected, analysed and decrypted, the five signals intelligence agencies exchange technologies and tactics. They also cooperate on targeting and "standardize their terminology, codewords, intercept–handling procedures, and indoctrination oaths, for efficiency as well as security."[31] CSE Special Liaison Officers are embedded with Five Eyes counterparts while colleagues from the US, Britain, Australia and New Zealand are inserted in CSE.

Five Eyes agencies help each other skirt restrictions on spying on their own citizenry. Former Solicitor-General Wayne Easter told the *Toronto Star* it was "common" for NSA "to pass on information about Canadians" to CSE.[32] Conversely, former CSE officer Michael Frost said NSA asked the agency to spy on US citizens.[33]

The Liberals seem indifferent to other damaging aspects of the military and militarism. They failed to stop the navy from conducting live fire exercises in areas protected for endangered killer whales. "They closed down this area to recreational fishing to save the whales, and then the navy sets off phosphorus bombs and 50 caliber guns," said Paul Pudwell, a whale-watching captain in Sooke, BC, in November 2018. "They do it 20, 30 times a year. We can't fish there, but you can go shoot it up?"[34]

Despite campaigning from animal rights activists, DND continues to employ animals in training and testing. In 2018 DND used 882 live animals, mostly rodents, for research and an undisclosed number of larger animals to train battlefield doctors.[35] Goats and pigs were employed to simulate blast trauma and amputations.[36]

Then there are the Liberals' sins of omission. Trudeau's government failed to close a loophole in Canada's appropriating legislation for the Convention on Cluster Munitions. It allowed the Canadian Forces to participate in joint military missions alongside allies (the US) that use cluster bombs, which often leave unexploded bomblets that later wreak havoc on unintended targets. When he was the party's foreign affairs critic Liberal MP Marc Garneau criticized the loophole, proclaiming "you're either against cluster bombs or you're not."[37] The Liberals amended the Export and Import Permits Act to make Canada eligible to join the Arms Trade Treaty (ATT). But, the new arms control legislation failed to require the tracking and publication of the value of weapons shipments to the US. Some claimed this was contrary to the principles of the ATT. Irrespective of the treaty, the omission was significant since most Canadian arms exports go to the US and it's "the most warlike nation in the history of the world", in the words of former president Jimmy Carter.[38] During discussion of the legislation the Liberals defeated an NDP motion to establish an oversight committee to review arms exports modeled after a similar body in the UK.[39] The Trudeau government also rejected a June 2018 Senate human rights committee report that recommended additional controls on the transfer of arms by foreign customers to third parties and to give greater weight to human rights and international humanitarian law in the arms-export control system. In response Freeland wrote, "taking unilateral measures not aligned with the export controls of our allies and partners could severely limit the impact we can have in protecting international human rights and humanitarian law, while putting legitimate Canadian exporters at a significant competitive disadvantage."[40]

The Liberals hid behind multilateral action to justify inaction on arms controls. They also deflected criticism of their light armoured vehicle sales to Saudi Arabia by touting their promise to accede to the ATT.[41] But, the legislation they adopted to accede to the

ATT would probably allow another major human rights trampling armoured vehicle sale to the Saudi monarchy.[42]

In fact Trudeau's Liberals have promoted the arms industry in various ways. "Strong, Secure, Engaged" called weapons manufacturing a "vital sector".[43] It noted: "Defence industry employees' average annual salaries are almost 60 percent above the average of other manufacturing sector employees and close to 60 percent of defence sector sales are exports. This vital sector also helps keep Canada's economy vibrant and innovative with over 30 percent of defence occupations in innovation-relevant science and technology-related fields."

The Liberals funded previously established arms industry subsidy programs and initiated at least one significant new one. In 2018 they launched the Innovation for Defence Excellence and Security (IDEaS) program. Framed as a new way to "solve specific defence and security challenges", IDEaS supported the development of solutions from their conceptual stage, through prototype testing and capability development.[44] IDEaS is set to pump $1.6 billion into military research initiatives over 20 years.[45]

Sajjan repeatedly spoke at the CANSEC arms bazar in Ottawa. The annual Canadian Association of Defence and Security Industries (CADSI) conference brought together representatives of arms companies, DND, other federal government departments and dozens of foreign governments.

The Liberals deployed ministers, diplomats, trade commissioners and military members to promote international arm sales.[46] They also maintained the Defence Attaché program. Based in 30 diplomatic posts around the world (with cross-accreditation to many neighbouring countries), Defence Attachés assist "Canadian defence manufacturers in understanding and accessing foreign defence markets ... support Canadian industry at key defence industry events in accredited countries."[47] In other words, business as usual in the arms selling business.

But the hypocrisy of the Trudeau government has been even worse. More than any element of their militarism, the Liberals' nuclear weapons policy demonstrates the emptiness of their "rules-based international order" and "progressive" foreign affairs rhetoric. The Liberals said they sought nuclear disarmament while largely ignoring international nuclear arms control efforts and promoting a nuclear alliance. The Liberals have ignored nuclear disarmament efforts supported by most countries. In July 2017 they refused to join 122 countries represented at the UN Conference to Negotiate a Legally Binding Instrument to Prohibit Nuclear Weapons, Leading Towards their Total Elimination.[48]

In June 2019 Swedish foreign minister Margot Wallström hosted a high-level meeting to reinvigorate nuclear disarmament commitments made by states party to the Nuclear Non-Proliferation Treaty (NPT).[49] While most of the 16 countries invited were represented by their foreign ministers, Freeland did not attend. Instead, the government dispatched Parliamentary Secretary for Consular Affairs, Pamela Goldsmith-Jones, to Stockholm.[50]

Similarly, they showed little interest in a November 2019 Nonproliferation Conference in Moscow. Despite high-level representation from many quarters, including Russian Foreign Minister Sergey Lavrov, no one from either the Canadian Embassy in Moscow or Global Affairs attended.[51]

Reducing or eliminating the threat of nuclear weapons wasn't mentioned in the Liberals 2017 defence policy (North Korean nukes received one mention). Instead, "Strong, Secure, Engaged" made two dozen references to Canada's commitment ("unwavering") to the North Atlantic Treaty Organization. Ghastly nuclear weapons were fundamental to NATO's strategic planning. According to the official description, "nuclear weapons are a core component of the Alliance's overall capabilities."[52]

Through NATO Canada has effectively committed to fighting a nuclear war if any country breaches its boundaries. Additionally, the alliance does not restrict its members from using nuclear weapons first. Canada participated in the NATO Nuclear Planning Group and contributed personnel and financial support to NATO's Nuclear Policy Directorate.[53]

While NATO maintained nuclear weapons in Turkey and various European countries, Canadian officials blamed Russia for the arms control impasse and the demise of the Intermediate-Range Nuclear Forces (INF) Treaty, which banned an entire class of nuclear weapons.[54] In April 2019 Director General of International Security Policy at Global Affairs, Cindy Termorshuizen, said, "we call on Russia to return to compliance with the INF Treaty."[55] But, it's not clear Russia violated one of the most significant nuclear accords ever signed.[56] The Donald Trump administration, on the other hand, began to develop new ground-launched intermediate-range missiles prohibited under the pact long before it formally withdrew from the INF. US military planners wanted to deploy intermediate-range missiles against China, which is not party to the INF.

In December 2018 Canada voted against a UN General Assembly resolution for "Strengthening Russian-United States Compliance with Intermediate-Range Nuclear Forces Treaty."[57] At that vote Canada's representative said Moscow's position on the INF reflected its "aggressive actions in neighbouring countries and beyond." But, it is Washington that broke its word in expanding NATO into Eastern Europe, withdrawing from the Anti-Ballistic Missile treaty in 2001 and establishing missile 'defence' systems near Russia.[58] As part of NATO, Canadian troops have been stationed on Russia's border in Latvia and Ukraine, which isn't conducive to nuclear retrenchment.

A look elsewhere also demonstrates the Liberals' ambivalence to nuclear disarmament. They strengthened the Stephen Harper government's agreement to export nuclear reactors to India, even though New Delhi refused to sign the NPT (India developed atomic weapons with Canadian technology).[59] The Liberals didn't mention Israel's 100+ nuclear bombs or endorse a nuclear free Middle East.

While Canada has never been an antinuclear country, governments from the 1970s through the 1990s expended some political capital on nuclear non-proliferation. While the follow-through was disappointing, Trudeau Père at least spoke about "suffocating" the nuclear arms race.[60]

His son, on the other hand, responded to a call to participate in a widely endorsed nuclear disarmament initiative by stating "there can be all sorts of people talking about nuclear disarmament, but if they do not actually have nuclear arms, it is sort of useless to have them around, talking."[61] Justin Trudeau also refused to congratulate Canadian campaigner Setsuko Thurlow, a survivor of the atomic bombing of Hiroshima, who accepted the 2017 Nobel Peace Prize on behalf of the International Campaign to Abolish Nuclear Weapons.[62]

Trudeau does not even talk the talk, let alone walk the walk when it comes to ending the threat of nuclear annihilation.

Chapter 1 Notes

1 David Vine, The United States Probably Has More Foreign Military Bases Than Any Other People, Nation, or Empire in History, Sept 14 2015 (https://www.thenation.com/article/archive/the-united-states-probably-has-more-foreign-military-bases-than-any-other-people-nation-or-empire-in-history/)

2 Nick Westoll, Thousands of cards arrive for Canadian Armed Forces troops after social media appeal, Nov 28 2019 (https://globalnews.ca/news/6227418/canadian-armed-forces-holiday-cards-letters-cfb-trenton/)

3 Ibid

4 Strong, Secure, Engaged: Canada's Defence Policy, June 2017 (http://dgpaapp.forces.gc.ca/en/canada-defence-policy/docs/canada-defence-policy-report.pdf)

5 Address by Minister Freeland on Canada's foreign policy priorities, Global Affairs Canada, June 6 2017 (https://www.canada.ca/en/global-affairs/news/2017/06/address_by_ministerfreelandoncanadasforeignpolicypriorities.html)

6 Ibid

7 Murray Brewster, More soldiers, ships and planes for military in Liberal defence plan, Jun 7 2017 (https://www.cbc.ca/news/politics/liberal-sajjan-garneau-defence-policy-1.4149473)

8 Steven Chase, New warships to cost more than $100-billion, Ottawa estimates, Nov 13 2013 (https://www.theglobeandmail.com/news/politics/ottawa-estimates-new-warships-to-cost-more-than-100-billion/article15407360/)

9 Tamara Lorincz, NATO is the enemy when it comes to fighting climate change, Dec 6 2019 (https://www.saltwire.com/opinion/local-perspectives/tamara-lorincz-nato-is-the-enemy-when-it-comes-to-fighting-climate-change-385022/?location=corner-brook)

10 Yves Engler, War Crimes in the Dark: Inside Canada's Special Forces, Oct 2 2015 (https://www.counterpunch.org/2015/10/02/war-crimes-in-the-dark-canadas-special-forces/)

11 Strong, Secure, Engaged: Canada's Defence Policy, June 2017 (http://dgpaapp.forces.gc.ca/en/canada-defence-policy/docs/canada-defence-policy-report.pdf)

12 More stringent oversight of military intelligence at DND in limbo, Canadian Press, Jan 18 2015 (https://www.thespec.com/news-story/5263606-more-stringent-oversight-of-military-intelligence-

at-dnd-in-limbo/)

13 Yves Engler, Long past time for Canada to exit NORAD, May 11 2018 (https://yvesengler.com/2018/05/11/long-past-time-for-canada-to-exit-norad/)

14 Jim Cox, A military perspective of Canada's mission in Iraq, Mar 30 2015 (http://thevimyreport.com/2015/03/a-military-perspective-of-canadas-mission-in-iraq/)

15 Prime Minister concludes productive NATO Leaders Meeting, Dec 4 2019 (https://pm.gc.ca/en/news/news-releases/2019/12/04/prime-minister-concludes-productive-nato-leaders-meeting)

16 Ibid

17 Foreign Cyber Operations (https://www.cse-cst.gc.ca/en/cse-act-loi-cst/cyberop)

18 Ibid

19 First Session, Forty-second Parliament, 64-65-66 Elizabeth II, 2015-2016-2017 HOUSE OF COMMONS OF CANADA BILL C-59 An Act respecting national security matters FIRST READING, June 20 2017 (https://www.parl.ca/DocumentViewer/en/42-1/bill/C-59/first-reading)

20 Alex Boutilier, A Canadian Snowden? CSE warns of "insider threats", July 26 2015 (https://www.thestar.com/news/canada/2015/07/26/a-canadian-snowden-cse-warns-of-insider-threats.html)

21 Ibid

22 Stuart Thomson, Federal budget invests $500 million over five years to battle cyber crime, Feb 27 2018 (https://nationalpost.com/news/politics/federal-budget-invests-500-million-over-five-years-to-battle-cyber-crime)

23 Patrick McGuire, Is CSEC, the Canadian Version of the NSA, Trustworthy?, Sep 4 2013 (https://www.vice.com/en_ca/article/jmkbjd/is-csec-the-canadian-version-of-the-nsa-trustworthy)

24 Colin Freeze and Stephanie Nolen, Charges that Canada spied on Brazil unveil CSEC's inner workings, Oct 7 2013 (https://www.theglobeandmail.com/news/world/brazil-spying-report-spotlights-canadas-electronic-eavesdroppers/article14720003/)

25 Matthew Braga, How, when and where can Canada's digital spies hack?, Jun 20 2017 (https://www.cbc.ca/news/technology/bill-c59-cse-act-spies-canada-hacking-foreign-cyber-ops-1.4169689)

26 Colin Freeze, Canada's little-known spy agency comes out into the open, Dec 22 2010 (https://www.theglobeandmail.com/news/national/canadas-little-known-spy-agency-comes-out-into-the-open/article4260580/)

27 Trudeau talks Russian cyberattacks with Five Eyes counterparts, Canadian Press, Apr 18 2018 (https://www.cbc.ca/news/politics/trudeau-five-eyes-russia-cyberattacks-1.4625386)

28 Lee Berthiaume, Justin Trudeau attending 'Five Eyes' intelligence briefing in London, Russia and Syria likely on agenda, Canadian Press, Apr 18 2018 (https://globalnews.ca/news/4152387/justin-trudeau-five-eyes-intelligence-briefing-london/)

29 Canada's Trudeau to continue sharing intelligence despite leaks, May 25 2017 (https://www.reuters.com/article/us-usa-trump-nato-trudeau/canadas-trudeau-to-continue-sharing-intelligence-despite-leaks-idUSKBN18L1MK)

30 Pat Kane, Wikileaks is providing post-indy food for thought, Mar 10 2017 (https://www.thenational.scot/politics/15149341.pat-kane-wikileaks-is-providing-post-indy-food-for-thought/)

31 Intelligence/Parapolitics, Issues 54-71, 1984 (https://books.google.ca/books?id=YaNCAQAA-IAAJ&q=standardize+their+terminology,+code-words,+intercept–handling+procedures,+and+indoctrination+oaths,+for+efficiency+as+well+as+security.&dq=standardize+their+terminology,+code-words,+intercept–handling+procedures,+and+indoctrination+oaths,+for+efficiency+as+well+as+security.&hl=en&sa=X&ved=0ahUKEwiTlsLrqsraAhUN3YMKHZhoDccQ6AEIKTAA)

32 Bill Robinson, More on CSE and the monitoring (or not) of Canadians, June 12 2013 (https://luxexumbra.blogspot.com/2013/06/more-on-cse-and-monitoring-or-not-of.html)

33 Michael Frost, Spyworld: Inside the Canadian and American Intelligence Establishments

34 Canada: locals angry after navy holds live fire exercises in orca habitat, Nov 23 2018 (http://thevictoriapost.com/canada-locals-angry-after-navy-holds-live-fire-exercises-in-orca-habitat/)

35 Animal experiments on the Wane, DND says, National Post, Jan 8, 2019

36 Ibid ; Lee Berthiaume, Military uses thousands of live animals every year for training, testing, July 23 2013 (canada.comhttps://o.canada.com/news/military-uses-thousands-of-live-animals-every-year-for-training-testing)

37 Mike Blanchfield, Liberals criticized for inaction on cluster bomb treaty loophole, Sep 11 2016 (https://ipolitics.ca/2016/09/11/liberals-criticized-for-inaction-on-cluster-bomb-treaty-loophole/)

38 Brent Patterson, Canada-US trade rules promote Canadian military exports, May 18 2009 (https://canadians.org/fr/node/4816) ; Brett Wilkins, Jimmy Carter: US 'Most Warlike Nation in History of the World', Apr 18 2019 (https://www.commondreams.org/views/2019/04/18/jimmy-carter-us-most-warlike-nation-history-world)

39 Marco Vigliotti, Liberals accused of misrepresenting arms export control regime, Oct 12 2016 (https://www.hilltimes.com/wp-content/uploads/2016/10/101216_ht.pdf)

40 Steven Chase, Ottawa rejects senators' demand to give greater weight to human rights in arms deals, Nov 6 2018 (https://www.theglobeandmail.com/politics/article-ottawa-rejects-senators-plea-to-prioritize-human-rights-over-saudi/)

41 Norman Hillmer and Philippe Lagassé, Justin Trudeau and Canadian Foreign Policy, 219

42 Ibid, 220

43 Brett Boudreau, Representing Canada in the UAE IDEX, FrontLine, Vol 16, No 1 (https://defence.frontline.online/article/2019/1/11186-Representing-Canada-in-the-UAE)

44 Understanding IDEaS (https://www.canada.ca/en/department-national-defence/programs/defence-ideas/understanding-ideas.html)

45 Ibid

46 Yves Engler, Canada's defence minister promoting arms sales to anti-democratic, repressive regimes, May 10 2019 (https://canadiandimension.com/articles/view/canadas-defence-minister-promoting-arms-sales-to-anti-democratic-repressive)

47 Support for Canadian defence and security exporters (https://www.canada.ca/en/department-national-defence/services/doing-business-with-foreign-defence-markets/support-canadian-defence-security-exporters.html)

48 Conference to Negotiate Legally Binding Instrument Banning Nuclear Weapons Adopts Treaty by 122 Votes in Favour, 1 against, 1 Abstention, DC/3723, July 7 2017 (https://www.un.org/press/en/2017/dc3723.doc.htm)

49 FM Freeland's disarmament no-show and latest on Iran–USA confrontation, June 14 2019 (https://www.ceasefire.ca/fm-freelands-disarmament-no-show-and-latest-on-iran-usa-confrontation/)

50 Ibid

51 2019 Moscow Nonproliferation Conference: The big losers were the no-shows, Nov 11 2019 (https://www.ceasefire.ca/2019-moscow-nonproliferation-conference-the-big-losers-were-the-no-shows/)

52 NATO's nuclear deterrence policy and forces, Oct 25 2019 (https://www.nato.int/cps/en/natohq/topics_50068.htm)

53 Ernie Regehr, Canadian Defence Policy and NATO's Nuclear Weapons The Canadian Defence Policy Review Briefing papers, Simons Foundation, Aug 23 2016 (http://www.thesimonsfoundation.ca/sites/default/files/Canadian%20Defence%20Policy%20and%20NATO's%20Nuclear%20Weapons%2C%20Defence%20Policy%20Review%20briefing%20paper%20-%20Aug%2023%2C%202016.pdf)

54 Adam Taylor, Canadian senator's NATO report accidentally reveals location of U.S. nuclear weapons in Europe, July 16 2019 (https://nationalpost.com/news/world/canadian-senators-nato-report-accidentally-reveals-location-of-u-s-nuclear-weapons-in-europe) ; Without arms control, hypersonic weapons will magnify already growing nuclear dangers July 12 2019 (https://www.ceasefire.ca/without-arms-control-hypersonic-weapons-will-magnify-already-growing-nuclear-dangers/)

55 Third session of the Preparatory Committee for the 2020 Review Conference of the Parties to the Treaty on the Non-Proliferation of Nuclear Weapons General Debate Statement delivered by Cindy Termorshuizen Director General, International Security Policy, Global Affairs Canada New York, April 29 2019 (http://statements.unmeetings.org/media2/21491824/canada.pdf)

56 Farewell to the INF-Treaty (III) (https://www.german-foreign-policy.com/en/news/detail/7998/)

57 General Assembly Rejects Resolution Calling for Strengthening Russian-United States Compliance with Intermediate-Range Nuclear Forces Treaty, GENERAL ASSEMBLY PLENARY SEVENTY-THIRD SESSION, 64TH & 65TH MEETINGS, GA/12116 21, Dec 2018 (https://www.un.org/press/en/2018/ga12116.doc.htm)

58 Von Uwe Klußmann, Matthias Schepp, Klaus Wiegrefe, Did the West Break Its Promise to Moscow?, DER SPIEGEL, Nov 26 2009 (https://www.spiegel.de/international/world/nato-s-eastward-expansion-did-the-west-break-its-promise-to-moscow-a-663315.html) ; David Axe, THAAD Missile Defense Systems Are Coming to Russia's Doorstep, May 21 2019 (https://nationalinterest.org/blog/buzz/thaad-missile-defense-systems-are-coming-russias-doorstep-58667)

59 India-Canada Joint Statement: Partnership for Security and Growth, Feb 23 2018 (https://pm.gc.ca/en/news/backgrounders/2018/02/23/india-canada-joint-statement-partnership-security-and-growth)

60 Paul Meyer, Pierre Trudeau and the "suffocation" of the nuclear arms race, International Journal, Aug 15 2016 (https://journals.sagepub.com/doi/abs/10.1177/0020702016662798?journalCode=ijxa)

61 Marie-Danielle Smith, 'Astonishing': Justin Trudeau criticized for not congratulating Nobel Peace Prize winners, keeping Canada out of nuclear treaty, Oct 26 2017 (https://nationalpost.com/news/politics/astonishing-justin-trudeau-criticized-for-not-congratulating-nobel-peace-prize-winners-keeping-canada-out-of-nuclear-treaty)

62 Ibid

2. The Canadian Monroe Doctrine — Interfering Down South

Unfortunately, a lack of commitment to any real progressive foreign policy has not been confined to militarism. As we shall see in this chapter, rather than a turn to the left, Trudeau's Liberals have continued an empire-like "diplomatic" policy towards *Norte Americanos'* "backyard".

The obvious questions to pose before getting into the sordid details are: Is it progressive to interfere in the political affairs of other countries? Should the Canadian government provide resources to political parties in foreign countries? If a foreign diplomat in Ottawa offered money and other resources to a Canadian political party how would we respond? Why does Canada support right wing dictators in Latin America but claim to "promote democracy" elsewhere?

Venezuela

The Trudeau government has engaged in a brazen effort to overthrow Venezuela's government. In a bid to elicit "regime change", Ottawa worked to isolate Caracas, imposed illegal sanctions, took that government to the International Criminal Court, financed an often-unsavoury opposition and decided a marginal opposition politician was the legitimate president.

For nearly two decades the Hugo Chavez led Bolivarian revolution empowered Venezuela's poor and working class. During its first 15 years substantial gains were made in public health, reducing illiteracy and lessening inequality.[1] Even amidst a severe economic downturn, Nicolás Maduro's government built three million units of social housing.[2]

The Chavez-led government/movement massively increased democratic space through community councils, new political parties, grassroots media and worker cooperatives. Between 1998 and 2018 the Bolivarian Revolution won 19 elections.[3] After almost every defeat, large swaths of the opposition cried foul and sought to oust the president through unconstitutional means. US and Canadian officials largely sided with the opposition.

Taking advantage of Chavez' death in 2013 and a huge drop in the price of oil, the Barrack Obama administration instigated sanctions on Venezuela. Washington labeled the South American country a threat to US "national security".[4] Donald Trump ramped up sanctions and repeatedly threatened to invade.[5] Concurrently, the opposition attempted to assassinate Maduro.[6]

The Bolivarian revolution and Maduro, of course, deserve criticism for some actions/inactions. The failure to overcome the country's dependence on oil is an obvious one. Another is the Chavez/Maduro governments' failure to address startling levels of insecurity and police violence. After a presidential recall referendum was scuttled in 2016 and the Constituent Assembly usurped the power of the opposition-dominated National Assembly, there were also questions about Maduro's electoral bonafides.[7] (Government supporters retort that when the opposition took control of the national assembly in January 2016 they sought to paralyze the government and openly defied the Supreme Court all the while backing violent anti-government protests and economic sabotage.)

The May 2018 presidential election demonstrated that Maduro and his PSUV party maintained considerable support. Despite the opposition boycott, the turnout was 40% and Maduro received a higher proportion of the overall vote than leaders in the US, Canada and elsewhere. (In 2019 Trudeau's Liberals received 33% of the vote with 66% of eligible voters casting their ballots, which amounted to 22% of the adult population. Maduro received 67% of votes cast with 41% of eligible voters participating, which equaled 27% of the population.)

Despite the complicated political situation, Liberal officials leveled over-the-top criticism against Venezuela's government. Trudeau repeatedly called Maduro a "brutal dictator" while Freeland said he was "robbing the Venezuelan people of their fundamental democratic rights."[8] The Liberals supported efforts to condemn Venezuela at the Organization of American States (OAS) and in September 2018 Ottawa requested the International Criminal Court (ICC) investigate the Maduro government. Supported by five like-minded South American nations, it was the first time a member state was brought before the ICC's chief prosecutor by other members.[9]

The Liberals backed Peru's decision to block Maduro from attending the April 2018 Summit of the Americas in Lima. "As Venezuela slides deeper into dictatorship, and as Venezuelans continue to suffer, Maduro's participation at a hemispheric leaders' summit would have been farcical," Freeland noted.[10] But, Canada's foreign minister had no problem with the presence of Brazilian President Michel Temer, who didn't have any pretence of electoral legitimacy. Nor did she oppose the participation of Honduran president Juan Orlando Hernandez who defied that country's constitution in running for a second term and then 'won' a highly questionable election.[11] (Ottawa also stayed mum about far worse human rights violations in Mexico, Honduras and Colombia.[12])

At the same time Freeland put forward impossible-to-meet conditions regarding the presidential election in Venezuela. After demanding new elections, she declared that Canada wouldn't recognize the Spring 2018 presidential election "as they do not give a reasonable amount of time to ensure free and fair elections" and then three weeks later "demand[ed] that presidential elections be called with sufficient advance notice."[13] When the opposition and government agreed to push back the presidential election from April 22 to May 20, Freeland responded by tweeting "Maduro regime's decision to postpone Venezuela's elections until May changes nothing."[14]

Another demand Freeland made of the Venezuelan authorities was that international observers be allowed to monitor the election. Yet, the Venezuelan government's vocal request for UN observers was opposed by the country's opposition alliance.[15] Behind the scenes the US undoubtedly lobbied the international body to reject Caracas' request. (Notwithstanding the partisan attacks, Venezuela has had among the world's most efficient, secure and transparent electoral systems.[16] In 2012 former US President Jimmy Carter, then head of the Carter Center, stated, "as a matter of fact, of the 92 elections that we've monitored, I would say the election process in Venezuela is the best in the world."[17])

The third condition Freeland imposed for respecting the election was "that all Venezuelan political players be included in the election."[18] But, the Maduro government wasn't in a position to release all those found guilty of crimes or repatriate political figures who fled the country to avoid criminal charges.

Ottawa founded the anti-Maduro Lima Group coalition with Peru. Amidst discussions between the two countries' foreign ministers in Spring 2017, Trudeau called his Peruvian counterpart, Pedro Pablo Kuczynski, to "stress the need for dialogue and respect for the democratic rights of Venezuelan citizens, as enshrined in the charter of the Organization of American States and the Inter-American Democratic Charter."[19] But the Lima Group was established in August 2017 as a structure outside of the OAS largely because that organization's members refused to back Washington and Ottawa's bid to interfere in Venezuelan affairs, which they believed defied the OAS' charter.

Canada was maybe the most active member of the coalition of governments opposed to Venezuela's elected government. Freeland participated in a half dozen meetings of the Lima Group and she repeatedly prodded Caribbean and Central American countries to join the Lima Group's anti-Maduro efforts.[20] The second Lima Group meeting held in Toronto in October 2017 urged regional governments to take steps to "further isolate" Venezuela.[21]

The Liberals even backed talk of an invasion other members opposed. Eleven of the 14 members of the Lima Group backed a September 2018 statement distancing the alliance from "any type of action or declaration that implies military intervention" after OAS chief Luis Almagro stated: "As for military intervention to overthrow the Nicolás Maduro regime, I think we should not rule out any option ... diplomacy remains the first option but we can't exclude any action."[22] Canada, Guyana and Colombia refused to criticize the head of the OAS' musings about an invasion of Venezuela.

Canadian diplomats played an important role in uniting large swaths of the Venezuelan opposition behind a US-backed plan to ratchet up tensions by proclaiming the new head of the opposition-dominated National Assembly, Juan Guaidó, president. The Canadian Press quoted a Canadian diplomat saying they helped Guaidó "facilitate conversations with people that were out of the country and inside the country" while the *Globe and Mail* reported that "Freeland spoke with Juan Guaidó to congratulate him on unifying opposition forces in Venezuela, two weeks before he declared himself interim president" in January 2019.[23] Canadian diplomats spent "months", reported the Canadian Press, coordinating the plan with the hardline opposition. In a story titled "Anti-Maduro coalition grew from secret talks", the Associated Press reported on Canada's "key role" in building international diplomatic support for claiming a relatively marginal National Assembly member was Venezuela's president.[24] Alongside Washington and a number of right-leaning Latin American governments, Ottawa immediately recognized Guaidó after he proclaimed himself president at a rally. At the opening of the Lima Group meeting in Ottawa after Guaidó's presidential declaration Trudeau declared, "the international community must immediately unite behind the interim president."[25]

The PM called the leaders of France, Spain, Paraguay, Ireland and Italy, International Monetary Fund and European Union to convince them to join Canada's campaign against Venezuela.[26] In a May 2019 conversation with Spanish Prime Minister Pedro Sánchez, Venezuela was the only subject mentioned in the official press release about the call.[27] Venezuela was also on the agenda during Japanese Prime Minister Shinzo Abe's visit to Ottawa in April 2019. The post meeting release noted, "during the visit, Prime Minister Abe announced Japan's endorsement of the Ottawa Declaration on Venezuela."[28] Produced at a February 2019 meeting of the Lima Group, the "Ottawa Declaration" called on Venezuela's armed forces "to demonstrate their loyalty to the interim president" and remove the elected president.[29]

On April 30 Guaidó, convicted opposition politician Leopoldo Lopez and others sought to stoke a military uprising in Caracas. Hours into the early morning effort Freeland tweeted, "watching events today in Venezuela very closely. The safety and security of Juan Guaidó and Leopoldo López must be guaranteed. Venezuelans who peacefully support Interim President Guaidó must do so without fear of intimidation or violence."[30] She followed that up with a statement to the press noting, "Venezuelans are in the streets today demonstrating their desire for a return to democracy even in the face of a violent crackdown. Canada commends their courage and we call on the Maduro regime to step aside now."[31] Then Freeland put out a video calling on Venezuelans to rise up and requested an emergency video conference meeting of the Lima Group.[32] Later that evening the coalition issued a statement labeling the attempted putsch an effort "to restore democracy" and demanded the military "cease being instruments of the illegitimate regime for the oppression of the Venezuelan people."[33]

Two weeks after he was officially dethroned as leader of Venezuela's national assembly (the matter was contested), in January 2020, Guaidó sought to reaffirm his international backing. Guaidó was fêted in Ottawa, meeting the prime minister, international development minister and foreign minister. Trudeau declared, "I commend Interim President Guaidó for the courage and leadership he has shown in his efforts to return democracy to Venezuela, and I offer Canada's continued support."³⁴

Over a two-year period, Ottawa severed diplomatic relations with Caracas. In December 2017 Venezuela declared Canada's chargé d'affaires in Caracas, Craib Kowalik, persona non grata. In making the announcement, the president of the National Constituent Assembly, Delcy Rodriguez, denounced Kowalik's "permanent and insistent, rude and vulgar interference in the internal affairs of Venezuela."³⁵ Ottawa declared Venezuela's top diplomat persona non grata in response. In June 2019 Canada's resident embassy in Caracas was closed.

Following Washington's lead, Ottawa imposed four rounds of sanctions on Venezuelan officials.³⁶ In September 2017 the elected president, vice president, head of the electoral board and 37 other officials had their assets in Canada frozen and Canadians were barred from having financial relations with these individuals. On April 15, 2019, Freeland announced the fourth round of sanctions. Forty-three individuals were added to the list of 70 leaders Canada had already sanctioned. CBC reported that the latest round of sanctions were designed to "punish Venezuelan judges who rubber-stamped Maduro's moves" and "lower-ranking police officials who took prominent roles in suppressing the attempt by Venezuela's opposition to bring humanitarian aid into the country on February 23."³⁷ But, the real objective of the sanctions was to help squeeze the economy to precipitate regime change. While ostensibly targeted at individuals, Canadian sanctions deterred companies from doing business in Venezuela. They also helped legitimate more devastating US actions.

The Venezuelan government responded to Canadian sanctions by denouncing Ottawa's "alliance with war criminals that have declared their intention to destroy the Venezuelan economy to inflict suffering on the people and loot the country's riches."³⁸ A Center for Economic and Policy Research report gave credence to this perspective. Written by Jeffrey Sachs and Mark Weisbrot, "Economic Sanctions as Collective Punishment: The Case of Venezuela" concluded that 40,000 Venezuelans may have died in 2017 and 2018 as a result of US sanctions.[39] A July 2019 *Financial Times* story titled "Venezuela sanctions fuel famine fears" and a *New York Times* op-ed that month titled "Misguided sanctions hurt Venezuelans" highlighted their growing impact.

Unilateral sanctions violate the UN charter and the UN Human Rights Council passed a resolution condemning the economic sanctions the US and Canada adopted against Venezuela.[40] It urged "states to refrain from imposing unilateral coercive measures (and) condemns the continued unilateral application and enforcement by certain powers of such measures as tools of political or economic pressure."[41] For its part, Caracas called Canada's move a "blatant violation of the most fundamental rules of International Law."[42]

After a meeting with Canadian officials in August 2019 Donald Trump's special representative for Venezuela, Elliott Abrams, told CBC's Power & Politics they strategized on how to convince the European Union to impose sanctions. "We both agreed that it would be really helpful if the EU would follow Canada and the U.S. in imposing sanctions on the Maduro regime," Abrams said.[43]

Throughout their time in office the Liberals have encouraged Canadian diplomats to play up human rights violations in Venezuela. A 27-page Global Affairs report uncovered by the *Globe and Mail* noted, "Canada should maintain the embassy's prominent position as a champion of human-rights defenders." Alluding to the hostility engendered by its interference in that country's affairs, the partially redacted 2017 report recommended that Canadian officials also "develop and implement strategies to minimize the impact of attacks by the government in response to Canada's human rights statements and activities."[44]

Ottawa worked to amplify oppositional voices inside Venezuela. In August 2017 outgoing Canadian ambassador Ben Rowswell told the *Ottawa Citizen*: "We established quite a significant internet presence inside Venezuela, so that we could then engage tens of thousands of Venezuelan citizens in a conversation on human rights. We became one of the most vocal embassies in speaking out on human rights issues and encouraging Venezuelans to speak out."[45] (Can you imagine the hue and cry if a Russian ambassador said something similar about Canada?)

During Rowswell's tenure at the embassy Canada financed NGOs with the expressed objective of embarrassing the government internationally. According to the government's response to a July 2017 Standing Senate Committee on Foreign Affairs and International Trade report on Venezuela, "CFLI [Canadian Funding to Local Initiatives] programming includes support for a local NGO documenting the risks to journalists and freedom of expression in Venezuela, in order to provide important statistical evidence to the national and international community on the worsening condition of basic freedoms in the country."[46] Another CFLI initiative funded during Rowswell's tenure in Caracas "enabled Venezuelan citizens to anonymously register and denounce corruption abuses by government officials and police through a mobile phone application."[47]

In line with its policy of amplifying oppositional voices, the Canadian Embassy in Caracas co-sponsored an annual Human Rights Award with the Centro para la Paz y los Derechos Humanos whose director, Raúl Herrera, repeatedly denounced the Venezuelan government. In late 2017 Herrera said, "the Venezuelan State systematically and repeatedly violates the Human Rights of Venezuelans and political prisoners."[48]

The "Human Rights Prize" was designed to amplify and bestow legitimacy on anti-government voices. The winner received a "tour of several cities in Venezuela to share his or her experiences with other organizations promoting human rights" and a trip to Canada to meet with "human rights authorities and organizations."[49] They generally presented to Canadian Parliamentary Committees and garnered media attention. The Venezuelan NGOs most quoted in the Canadian media criticizing the country's human rights situation — Provea, Foro Penal, CODEVIDA, Observatorio Venezolano de la Conflictividad, Observatorio Venezolano de Prisiones, etc. — had been formally recognized by the Canadian embassy.

In March 2018 the embassy gave its human rights prize to Francisco Valencia, director of the Coalición de Organizaciones por el Derecho a la Salud y la Vida (CODEVIDA). Numerous media outlets reported on the award given to an aggressive opponent of the Venezuelan government.[50] "I believe that we are facing a criminal State", Valencia told Crisis en Venezuela.[51] In July 2018 Valencia spoke in Ottawa and was profiled by the *Globe and Mail*. "Canada actually is, in my view, the country that denounced the most the violation of human rights in Venezuela … and was the most helpful with financing towards humanitarian issues," explained Valencia, who also told that paper he was "the target of threats from the government."[52]

In another example of an anti-government figure invited to Ottawa, the former mayor of metropolitan Caracas, Antonio Ledezma, called for "humanitarian intervention" before the Subcommittee on International Human Rights of the Standing Committee on Foreign Affairs and International Development.[53] In September 2018 Ledezma said, "if the international community does not urgently activate the principle of humanitarian intervention for Venezuela — which developed the concept of the responsibility to protect — they will have to settle for sending Venezuelans a resolution of condolence with which we will not revive the thousands of human beings who will lose their lives in the middle of this genocide sponsored by Maduro."[54] In November of the previous year Ledezma escaped house arrest and fled the country.[55]

Ottawa allied with some of the most anti-democratic, hardline and electorally marginal elements of Venezuela's opposition. Guaidó's Voluntad Popular (VP) party repeatedly instigated violent protests. Not long after the Democratic Unity Roundtable opposition coalition presidential candidate Henrique Capriles effectively conceded defeat in January 2014, VP leader Leopoldo López launched La Salida (exit/departure) in a bid to oust Maduro. VP activists formed the shock troops of "guarimbas" protests that left 43 Venezuelans dead, 800 hurt and a great deal of property damaged in 2014.[56] Dozens more were killed in a new wave of VP-backed protests in 2017.

Effective at stoking violence, VP failed to win many votes. It took eight per cent of the seats in the 2015 elections that saw the opposition win control of the National Assembly.[57] With 14 out of 167 deputies in the Assembly, it won the fourth most seats in the Democratic Unity Roundtable coalition.[58] In the December 2012 regional elections VP was the sixth most successful party and did little better in the next year's municipal elections.

VP was founded at the end of 2009 by López who "has long had close contact with American diplomats", reported the *Wall Street Journal*.[59] A great-great-grand nephew of independence leader Simón Bolívar, grandson of a former cabinet member and great-grandson of a president, López was schooled at Harvard's Kennedy School of Government.[60] Between 2000 and 2008 López was the relatively successful and popular mayor of the affluent 65,000 person Caracas municipality of Chacao.

During the 2002 military coup López "orchestrated the public protests against Chávez and he played a central role in the citizen's arrest of Chavez's interior minister."[61] He was given a 13-year jail sentence for inciting and planning violence during the 2014 "guarimbas" protests.[62]

Canadian officials had significant contact with López's emissaries and party. The Canadian embassy in Caracas worked with VP officials pushing for the overthrow of the elected government. The leader of VP in Yaracuy state, Gabriel Gallo, was runner-up for the embassy's 2015 human rights award.[63] A coordinator of the Foro Penal NGO, Gallo was also photographed with ambassador Ben Rowswell at the embassy's 2017 human rights prize ceremony.[64]

Throughout the Liberals' time in office a slew of VP representatives came to Ottawa. In May 2017 Trudeau met Lilian Tintori, wife of VP leader López. Tintori acted as an emissary for Lopez who couldn't travel to Ottawa because he was convicted of inciting violence during the "guarimbas" protests in 2014.

Three months earlier Tintori met US President Donald Trump and *The Guardian* reported on her role in building international support for the plan to anoint VP deputy Guaidó interim president.[65]

In response, Venezuela's foreign affairs minister Delcy Rodríguez described Tintori as an "agent of intervention" who claims the "false position of victim" while she's aligned with "fascist" forces in Venezuela.[66] According to a series of reports, Lopez was the key Venezuelan organizer of the plan to anoint Guaidó interim president.[67]

Canada strengthened VP's hardline position within the opposition. A February *Wall Street Journal* article titled "'What the Hell Is Going On?' How a Small Group Seized Control of Venezuela's Opposition" noted that leading opposition figures on stage with Guaidó when he declared himself interim president had no idea of his plan despite it being reliant on the Democratic Unity Roundtable's agreement to rotate the National Assembly presidency within the coalition.[68] (VP's turn came due in January 2019).

Presumably, Canada's "special coordinator for Venezuela" worked with the opposition. Canadian taxpayers paid hundreds of thousands of dollars to a hardline pro-corporate, pro-Washington, former diplomat to coordinate the Liberal government's bid to oust Venezuela's government.

In 2019 Global Affairs Canada tendered an 11-month $200,000 contract for an individual to coordinate its bid to oust Maduro. According to buyandsell.gc.ca, the Special Advisor on Venezuela needs to be able to: "Use your network of contacts to advocate for expanded support to pressure the illegitimate government to return constitutional order. Use your network of civil society contacts on the ground in Venezuela to advance priority issues (as identified by civil society/Government of Canada). Must have valid Government of Canada personnel TOP SECRET security clearance."[69]

From fall 2017 through 2019 Allan Culham was the Liberals' Special Advisor on Venezuela. Culham was a former Canadian ambassador to Venezuela, El Salvador, Guatemala and the Organization of American States. During his time as ambassador to Venezuela from 2002 to 2005 Culham was hostile to Hugo Chavez's government. According to a WikiLeaks publication of US diplomatic messages, "Canadian Ambassador Culham expressed surprise at the tone of Chavez's statements during his weekly television and radio show 'Hello President' on February 15 [2004]. Culham observed that Chavez's rhetoric was as tough as he had ever heard him. 'He sounded like a bully,' said Culham, more intransigent and more aggressive."[70]

The US cable quoted Culham criticizing the national electoral council and speaking positively about the group overseeing a presidential recall referendum targeting Chavez. "Culham added that Súmate is impressive, transparent, and run entirely by volunteers", it noted. The name of then head of Súmate, Maria Corina Machado, was on a list of people who endorsed the April 2002 military coup against Chavez, for which she faced charges of treason.[71] She denied signing the now infamous Carmona Decree that dissolved the National Assembly and Supreme Court and suspended the elected government, attorney general, comptroller general, and governors as well as mayors elected during Chavez's administration.[72] It also annulled land reforms and reversed increases in royalties paid by oil companies.

After retiring from the civil service in 2015 Culham described his affinity for another leading hard-line opposition leader. Canada's Special Advisor on Venezuela wrote, "I met [Leopoldo] López when he was the mayor of the Caracas municipality of Chacao where the Canadian Embassy is located. He too became a good friend and a useful contact in trying to understand the many political realities of Venezuela."[73] But, López also endorsed the failed 2002 coup against Chavez and was convicted of inciting violence during the deadly 2014 "guarimbas" protests that sought to oust Maduro.

In his role as Canada's ambassador to the OAS Culham repeatedly took positions viewed as hostile by the Chavez/Maduro governments.[74] When Chavez fell gravely ill in 2013, he proposed the OAS send a mission to study the situation, which then Vice-president Maduro described as a "miserable" intervention in the country's affairs.[75] Culham's comments on the 2014 "guarimbas" protests and support for Machado speaking at the OAS were also unpopular with Caracas.[76]

At the OAS Culham criticized other left-of-centre governments. He blamed elected President Rafael Correa for supposedly closing "democratic space" in Ecuador, not long after a failed coup attempt in 2010. When describing the Honduran military's overthrow of social democratic president Manuel Zelaya in 2009 Culham refused to employ the term coup and instead described it as a "political crisis".[77]

In June 2012, the left-leaning president of Paraguay, Fernando Lugo, was ousted in what some called an "institutional coup". Upset with Lugo for disrupting 61-years of one-party rule, Paraguay's ruling class claimed he was responsible for a murky incident that left 17 peasants and police dead and the senate voted to impeach the president. The vast majority of countries in the hemisphere refused to recognize the new government. The Union of South American Nations (UNASUR) suspended Paraguay's membership after Lugo's ouster, as did the MERCOSUR trading bloc. A week after the coup Culham participated in an OAS mission that many member countries opposed.[78] Largely designed to undermine those countries calling for Paraguay's suspension from the OAS, delegates from the US, Canada, Haiti, Honduras and Mexico traveled to Paraguay to investigate Lugo's removal from office. The delegation concluded that the OAS should not suspend Paraguay, which displeased many South American countries.

Four years later Culham still blamed Lugo for his ouster. He wrote: "President Lugo was removed from office for 'dereliction and abandonment of duty' in the face of rising violence and street protests (that his government was itself instigating through his inflammatory rhetoric) over the issue of land rights. Violence in both the countryside and the streets of Asunción threatened to engulf Paraguay's already fragile democratic institutions. Lugo's impeachment and removal from office by the Paraguayan Congress, later ratified by the Supreme Court, launched a firestorm of protest and outrage amongst the presidents of Paraguay's neighbours. Presidents Rousseff of Brazil, Hugo Chavez of Venezuela and Cristina Kirchner of Argentina, were the chief defenders of Lugo's right to remain in office."[79]

After retiring from the civil service Culham became more candid about his hostility to those trying to overcome extreme power imbalances in the hemisphere, decrying "the nationalist, bombastic and populist rhetoric that many leaders of Latin America have used to great effect over the last 15 years."[80] For Culham, "the Bolivarian Alliance … specialized in sowing its own divisive ideology and its hopes for a revolutionary 'class struggle' across the hemisphere."[81]

Culham praised the defeat of Cristina Kirchner in Argentina and Dilma Rousseff Brazil. In a 2015 piece titled "So long, Kirchners" he wrote, "the Kirchner era in Argentine politics and economics is thankfully coming to an end."[82] (Kirchner won re-election as vice president in October 2019.) The next year Culham criticized Brazilian President Dilma Rousseff's bid to have UNASUR challenge her impeachment, which he celebrated as "a sign of change in Latin America".[83]

Culham denounced regional integration efforts. In a long February 2016 Senate foreign affairs committee discussion of Argentina, he denounced diplomatic forums set up by Brazil, Ecuador, Bolivia, Argentina, Venezuela and others to break from US domination of the region.[84] "Since I'm no longer a civil servant", Culham stated, "I will say that CELAC [Community of Latin American and Caribbean States] is not a positive organization within the Americas. Mainly because it's built on the principle of exclusion. It purposefully excludes Canada and United States. It was the product of President Chavez and the Chavista Bolivarian revolution."[85] Every single country in the hemisphere except for Canada and the US were members of CELAC.

Culham criticized left-wing governments' positions at the US dominated OAS. Culham bemoaned the "negative influence ALBA [Bolivarian Alliance for the Peoples of our America] countries have brought to the OAS" and said Argentina "often sided with Bolivarian revolution members" in their "negative agenda" at the OAS, which he called "very close to my heart".[86] In his comments to the Senate committee Culham criticized Kirchner for failing to pay the full price to US "vulture funds", which bought up the country's debt at a steep discount after it defaulted in 2001. He described Kirchner's refusal to bow down to highly predatory hedge funds as a threat to the "Toronto Stock Exchange" and labeled a Scotia Bank claim from the 2001 financial crisis a "bilateral irritant" for Canada.[87]

Culham presumably coordinated with the Venezuela Task Force at Global Affairs. In a further sign of the brazenness of their campaign to oust Maduro's government, the Professional Association of Foreign Service Officers gave Patricia Atkinson, Head of the Venezuela Task Force at Global Affairs, its Foreign Service Officers award in June 2019.[88] The write-up explained, "Patricia, and the superb team she assembled and led, supported the Minister's engagement and played key roles in the substance and organization of 11 meetings of the 13 country Lima group which coordinates action on Venezuela. She assisted in developing three rounds of sanctions against the regime."[89]

House of Mirrors— 37

As part of their campaign against Maduro Canadian officials echoed the language of the US Monroe Doctrine. Freeland justified Canada's aggressive interference in Venezuela's affairs by saying "this is our neighbourhood" while Trudeau's personal representative for the G7 Summits and appointee to the Senate, Peter Boehm told CBC, "this is our backyard, the Western hemisphere. We have a role here."[90]

Describing Latin America as "our backyard" is the language favoured by so-called Ugly American politicians seeking to assert the Monroe Doctrine. Latin Americans should beware of the emergence of Ugly Canadians promoting the "Trudeau Doctrine".

***

The Liberal government's hypocrisy regarding "democracy promotion" in Latin America has been head spinning. On numerous occasions Trudeau officials cited "the need to respect the Venezuelan Constitution" to justify their campaign to recognize Guaidó as Venezuela's president. Trudeau even responded to someone who yelled "hands off Venezuela" at a town hall by lecturing the audience on article 233 of the Venezuelan constitution, which the PM claimed made the head of the National Assembly president.[91] It didn't.[92]

As Trudeau lectured audiences on the need to uphold Venezuela's constitution, the Liberals recognized a completely illegitimate president in Honduras. What's more, they formally allied with that government in demanding Venezuela's president follow their erroneous reading of that country's constitution.

In November 2017 Ottawa's Lima Group ally Juan Orlando Hernandez (JOH) defied the Honduran constitution to run for a second term. At Hernandez' request the four Supreme Court members appointed by his National Party overruled an article in the constitution explicitly prohibiting re-election.[93]

(In 2009 Ottawa backed the Honduran military's removal of elected president Manuel Zelaya, which was justified on the grounds he was seeking to defy the constitution by running for a second term.[94] In fact, the social democratic president simply put forward a plan to hold a non-binding public poll on whether to hold consultations to reopen the constitution.)

JOH then 'won' a highly questionable poll.[95] With 70 per cent of votes counted opposition candidate Salvador Nasralla led by five-points.[96] The electoral council then went silent for 36 hours and when reporting resumed JOH had a small lead.

In the three weeks between the election and JOH's official proclamation as president, government forces killed at least 30 pro-democracy demonstrators in the Central American country of nine million.[97] More than a thousand were detained under a post-election state of emergency. Many of those jailed for protesting the electoral fraud, including prominent activist Edwin Espinal, who married Canadian human rights campaigner Karen Spring, remained in jail for over a year.

Ottawa immediately endorsed the electoral farce in Honduras. Following Washington, Global Affairs tweeted that Canada "acknowledges confirmation of Juan Orlando Hernandez as President of Honduras."[98] Tyler Shipley, author of *Ottawa and Empire: Canada and the Military Coup in Honduras*, responded: "Wow, Canada sinks to new lows with this. The entire world knows that the Honduran dictatorship has stolen an election, even the OAS (an organization which skews right) has demanded that new elections be held because of the level of sketchiness here. And — as it has for over eight years — Canada is at the forefront of protecting and legitimizing this regime built on fraud and violence. Even after all my years of research on this, I'm stunned that Freeland would go this far; I expected Canada to stay quiet until JOH had fully consolidated his power. Instead Canada is doing the heavy lifting of that consolidation."[99]

After JOH stole an election that he shouldn't have been able to participate in the Trudeau government continued to work with his government. I found no indication that Canadian aid — Ottawa's largest bilateral aid program in Central America — had been reduced and Canadian diplomats repeatedly met Honduran representatives.[100] JOH's foreign minister, Maria Dolores Aguero, attended the September 2018 Women Foreign Ministers' Meeting the Liberals organized in Montreal.[101] For his part, Trudeau was photographed with the Honduran foreign minister at the February 2019 Lima Group meeting in Ottawa.[102]

Canadian diplomats lauded the "bonds of friendship between the governments of Canada and Honduras" and "excellent relations that exist between both countries."[103] Canadian ambassador James K. Hill retweeted a US Embassy statement noting, "we congratulate the President Juan Orlando Hernandez for taking the initiative to reaffirm the commitment of his administration to fight against corruption and impunity" through an OAS initiative.[104]

(Honduran officials spoke of the legitimacy they gained from Canadian support. When an Al Jazeera documentary maker questioned the Honduran Attorney General's office about why it refused to agree to a truly independent investigation into the 2016 murder of world-renowned Indigenous leader Berta Cáceres the official replied: "Many governments do trust the work that we're doing. The EU trusts us, the US trusts us, Canada trusts us. They're supporting us in the technical parts of the investigation and with funds. So we believe that if all these governments and agencies believe in us, it's because we're doing things well."[105])

While they praised JOH's supposed fight against impunity, Trudeau officials refused repeated requests by Canadian activists and relatives to help secure Edwin Espinal's release from prison. In response to their indifference to Espinal's plight, Rights Action director Grahame Russell wrote, "have the Canadian and U.S. governments simply agreed not to criticize the Honduran regime's appalling human rights record … in exchange for Honduras agreeing to be a 'democratic ally' in the U.S. and Canadian-led efforts at forced government change in Venezuela?"[106]

Why the great concern for Venezuela's constitution and indifference to that of Honduras? Why didn't Trudeau recognize Salvador Nasralla as president of Honduras? Nasralla's claim to his country's presidency was far more legitimate than Guaidó's.

If it didn't put lives at risk, the blatant hypocrisy in Trudeau allying with the illegitimate president of Honduras to demand Venezuela succumb to their interpretation of that country's constitution would be amusing.

***

In their campaign against Venezuela's government the Liberals were willing to squeeze Cuba. In May 2019 the Canadian Embassy in Havana closed its Immigration, Refugees and Citizenship section. This forced most Cubans wanting to visit Canada or get work/study permits to travel to a Canadian embassy in another country to submit their documents. In some cases, Cubans had to travel to another country twice to submit information to enter Canada.[107] The draconian measure immediately undercut cultural exchanges and family visits.[108]

It's rare for an embassy to simply eliminate visa processing, but what prompted the measure was the stuff of science fiction. Canada's embassy staff was cut in half in January 2019 after diplomats became ill following a mysterious ailment that felled US diplomats sent to Cuba after Donald Trump's election.[109] Four months after the first US diplomats (apparently) became ill US ambassador Jeffrey DeLaurentis met his Canadian, British and French counterparts to ask if any of their staff were sick. According to a *New York Times Magazine* story, "none knew of any similar experiences afflicting their officials in Cuba. But after the Canadian ambassador notified his staff, 27 officials and family members there asked to be tested. Twelve were found to be suffering from a variety of symptoms, similar to those experienced by the Americans."[110]

With theories ranging from "mass hysteria" to the sounds of "Indies short-tailed crickets" to an "outbreak of functional disorders", the medical questions remained largely unresolved.[111] The politics of the affair were far clearer. In response, the Trump Administration withdrew most of its embassy staff in Havana and expelled Cuban diplomats from Washington. They rolled back measures the Obama administration instituted to re-engage with Cuba and then implemented an extreme measure even the George W. Bush administration shied away from.

Ottawa followed along partly because it committed to overthrowing Venezuela's government and an important talking point of the anti-Maduro coalition was that Havana propped him up. On May 3, 2019, three days after a failed military uprising in Venezuela, Trudeau called Cuban president Miguel Díaz-Canel to pressure him to join Ottawa's effort to oust President Maduro. The release noted, "the Prime Minister, on behalf of the Lima Group, underscored the desire to see free and fair elections and the constitution upheld in Venezuela."[112] Four days later Freeland added to the diplomatic pressure on Havana. She told reporters, "Cuba needs to not be part of the problem in Venezuela, but become part of the solution."[113] A week later Freeland visited Cuba to discuss Venezuela.

In an article titled "Canada at odds with Cuban 'ally' over Maduro's fate" Freeland told CBC that Cuba's role in Venezuela was "concerning" and that "we have heard directly from the Venezuelan opposition that they're concerned by the role that some Cubans are playing in their country."[114]

In May 2019 Freeland talked with US Secretary of State Mike Pompeo about Venezuela and Cuba. Afterwards the State Department tweeted, "Secretary Pompeo spoke with Canada's Foreign Minister Freeland to discuss ongoing efforts to restore democracy in Venezuela. The Secretary and Foreign Minister agreed to continue working together to press the Cuban regime to provide for a democratic and prosperous future for the people of Cuba."[115]

Ottawa supported putting pressure on Cuba in the hopes of further isolating/demonizing the Maduro government. But, the

Trudeau government was simultaneously uncomfortable with how the US campaign against Cuba threatened the interests of some Canadian-owned businesses.

The other subject atop the Liberal agenda with regards to Havana was Washington's decision to allow lawsuits for property confiscated after the 1959 Cuban revolution. In mid-2019 the Trump Administration activated a section of the Helms-Burton Act that permitted Cubans and US citizens to sue foreign companies doing business in Cuba over property nationalized decades ago.[116] The move could trigger billions of dollars in legal claims in US courts against Canadian and European businesses operating on the island.

Obviously, Canadian firms that extract Cuban minerals and deliver over a million vacationers to the Caribbean country each year don't want to be sued in US courts.[117] They want Ottawa's backing, but the Trudeau government's response to Washington's move was relatively muted, which spoke to Ottawa's commitment to overthrowing Venezuela's government.

In October 2019 the *Toronto Star* reported on a "Toronto food truck caught up in Trump's battle with Cuba."[118] Little Havana sold Cuban coffee purchased in Canada to Canadians. But, its payment processing firm had an account with US-based bank J.P. Morgan Chase so it suddenly stopped receiving its electronic payments. The legal battle cost the small food truck $14,000.

***

The contrast between the Liberals response to the governments in Haiti and Venezuela also highlights the Trudeau government's pro-empire hypocrisy.

Venezuela was a deeply divided society. Maybe a quarter of Venezuelans wanted the president removed by (almost) any means. A similar proportion backed Maduro. A larger share of the population oscillated between these two poles, though generally preferring the president to opposition forces that supported economic sanctions and a possible invasion.

Unlike Venezuela, Haiti was not divided. Basically, everyone wanted president Jovenel Moïse to go. Reliable polling was limited, but an October 2019 poll found that 81% of Haitians wanted the president to leave.[119] Many were strongly committed to that view, which is why the country's urban areas were paralyzed by a half dozen general strikes between July 2018 and late 2019.

So what was Ottawa's response to the popular protests in Haiti? Did Global Affairs release statements supporting the will of the people? Did Canada build a regional coalition to remove the president? Did Canada's PM call other international leaders to lobby them to join his effort to remove Haiti's president? Did they make a major aid announcement designed to elicit regime change? Did they ask the International Criminal Court to investigate the Haitian government? Did Trudeau call the Haitian president a "brutal dictator"?

In fact, it was the exact opposite to the situation in Venezuela. The only reason the Haitian president was able to hang on was because of support from Canada, the US and other members of the so-called "Core Group" of "Friends of Haiti" (France, Brazil, Germany, the EU and OAS).

Canada provided financial, diplomatic and policing assistance to the neo-Duvalerists subjugating Haiti's impoverished masses. In October 2019 *Le Devoir* reported that Canada had given $702 million in "aid" to Haiti since 2016.[120] Earlier in 2019 international development minister Marie-Claude Bibeau, who traveled to Haiti on multiple occasions, said "Haiti is one of the biggest development programs we have. Our ambassador in Port-au-Prince is in constant contact with the government."[121]

Alongside financial support, the Liberals provided diplomatic backing. Trudeau met Moïse at the Summit of the Americas in April 2018 and Moïse's Prime Minister Jean Henry Céant in Ottawa in December 2018.[122] According to the post-meeting press release, Trudeau "took the opportunity to convey his support for current efforts of the Haitian government to promote political dialogue."[123]

Before leaving on a February 2018 trip, which included a meeting with Moïse, Bibeau told CBC, "it's a new president and we want to support him."[124]

In January 2017 Dion and Bibeau "warmly congratulated Jovenel Moïse on his election" and declared it "essential that the Haitian political actors respect the definitive results of the presidential election."[125] But, the president's claim to legitimacy was paper-thin. Moïse assumed the job through voter suppression and electoral fraud.[126] Barely one in five eligible voters took part in the 2016 presidential election and, even according to official figures, Moïse only received 600,000 votes in a country of over 10 million.[127]

Canada's ambassador in Port-au-Prince visited Moïse when the president faced massive pressure to resign.[128] While a strike paralyzed the capital in November 2018 André Frenette met Céant with other Core Group diplomats to "express their support to the government."[129] During an even more intense upsurge in protest in October 2019, a new Canadian ambassador, Stuart Savage, was accredited and reportedly "renewed Canada's commitment to continue to accompany President Jovenel Moïse."[130]

Canadian officials put out a stream of statements defending Moïse. In November 2018 Bibeau declared a desire to "come to the aid" of the Haitian government and three months later she attacked the popular revolt.[131] When asked by TVA "the demonstrators demand the resignation of the president. What is Canada's position on this issue?" Bibeau responded, "the violence must stop; we will not come to a solution in this way."[132] But, the violence was overwhelmingly meted out by the Canadian-backed regime.

Through Core Group statements Ottawa backed Moise, blaming the protesters for Canadian trained and financed police firing on them. A November 2018 statement read, "the group recalls that acts of violence seeking to provoke the resignation of legitimate authorities have no place in the democratic process."[133] Their declaration continued, "the members of the group recall the democratic legitimacy of the government of Haiti and elected institutions and that in a democracy, change must be through the ballot box and not by violence."

Canadian officials regularly promoted and applauded a police force that was responsible for many abuses. During his first year as ambassador beginning in late 2017 Frenette attended more than a half dozen of their events and repeatedly tweeted praise for the police. "Canada has long stood with the HNP [Haitian national police] to ensure the safety of Haitians and we are very proud of it," Frenette noted in April 2018.[134] In another tweet he wrote, "very proud to participate today in the Canadian Armed Forces Ballistic Platelet Donation to the Haitian National Police."[135]

But, the police killed dozens, probably over 100, during the popular uprising between July 2018 and November 2019.[136] Videos of police beating protesters, violently arresting individuals and firing live ammunition during protests circulated widely. Amidst a month-long general strike at the end of October 2019 Amnesty International reported, "during six weeks of anti-government protests ... at least 35 people were killed, with national police implicated in many of the deaths."[137] A UN report confirmed government involvement in a massacre that left at least 26, and possibly as many as 71, dead in the Port-au-Prince neighborhood of La Saline in mid-November 2018.[138] Residents said men in police uniforms began the killing. A year later 15 people were massacred in a nearby slum, reported the Institute for Justice and Democracy in Haiti, "in politically backed gang attacks intended to force residents of Bel-Air to remove protest barricades."[139]

Frenette and the Core Group all but ignored the police and regime's violence against protesters.

On top of diplomatic cover, Trudeau's government provided various forms of support to the repressive force that maintained Moïse's rule. Ottawa paid for Haitian police buildings, vehicles, beds, etc.[140] Much to the delight of the country's über class-conscious elite,

Ottawa took the lead in strengthening the repressive arm of the Haitian state after the US, France and Canada ousted President Jean Bertrand Aristide and thousands of other elected officials in 2004. Since then a Canadian generally led the UN police contingent in Haiti and officers from this country staffed its upper echelons. Until October 2019 RCMP officer Serge Therriault led the 1,200-person police component of the Mission des Nations unies pour l'appui à la Justice en Haïti (MINUJUSTH). In June 2019 Ambassador Frenette tweeted, "one of the best parts of my job is attending medal ceremonies for Canadian police officers who are known for their excellent work with the UN police contingent in Haiti."[141] At the time there were a few dozen Canadian police officers in the country who assisted their Haitian counterparts.[142]

Canadian officials led the push to extend the 15-year old UN occupation that took over from the US, French and Canadian troops that overthrew Aristide's government and was responsible for introducing cholera to the country, which killed over 10,000 and made one million ill.[143] In May 2019 Canada's ambassador to the UN, Marc-André Blanchard, led a United Nations Economic and Social Council delegation to Haiti. Upon his return to New York Blanchard proposed creating a "robust" mission to continue MINUJUSTH's work after its conclusion in October 2019.[144] Five months later Canadian officials chaired a special UN Economic and Social Council meeting on Haiti as part of the newly formed Bureau Intégré des Nations Unies en Haïti.[145]

Canadian troops were deployed to the Port-au-Prince airport in February 2019.[146] There wasn't any public announcement, but the Haiti Information Project photographed/videoed a handful of heavily armed Canadian troops patrolling the Toussaint Louverture airport.[147] A knowledgeable source I emailed the photos to said they were probably special forces. The Haiti Information Project reported that they may have helped family members of Moïse's unpopular government flee the country.

Two days after Canadian troops were spotted at the airport five heavily armed former US soldiers were arrested. The next day the five Americans and two Serbian colleagues were quickly shuttled to the US where they did not face charges.[148] One of them, former Navy SEAL Chris Osman, posted on Instagram that he provided security "for people who are directly connected to the current President" of Haiti.[149]

Was the Canadian deployment in any way connected to the US mercenaries? While it may seem far-fetched, it's not impossible considering the politically charged nature of deployments to Haiti. (The night president Aristide was forced onto a plane by US Marines, JTF2 soldiers "secured" the airport and two thousand Canadian troops were deployed after a deadly 2010 earthquake out of fear of a "popular uprising".[150])

The Liberals supported the violent suppression of the popular will in Haiti. They continued a two-decade old Canadian policy of undercutting Haitian sovereignty and democracy.

In response, demonstrators repeatedly speechified against Canadian "imperialism". On a number of occasions protesters threw rocks at the Canadian Embassy in Port-au-Prince and in October 2019, reported Voice of America, "attempted to burn down the Canadian Embassy."[151]

So much for the idea, popular during the Trudeau senior era, that wearing a Canadian flag makes a backpacker safe from being perceived as a North American imperialist. In fact, the Liberal government has acted like Uncle Sam, prioritizing the interests of the corporate elite over democracy or the vast majority of people in the Caribbean, Central and South America. Events in the largest Portuguese-speaking country in the world confirm this.

***

In 2016 Brazilian Workers' Party President Dilma Rousseff was impeached through a "soft coup". A little more than a year into her second four-year term, parliamentarians voted Rousseff out.

They found her guilty of breaking Brazil's budget laws. The impeachment was sparked by an economic downturn and the massive "car wash" corruption probe that targeted various politicians, including her Workers' Party predecessor. There was no evidence Rousseff was corrupt and the case against former president, Lula da Silva, was flimsy. The lead prosecutor, who under the Brazilian system also acts as a judge, Sérgio Moro, later became justice minister in the Jair Bolsonaro government and in mid 2019, The Intercept released a trove of communications from Moro, confirming the political nature of the charges against Lula, which weakened Rousseff.[152]

While they made dozens of statements criticizing Venezuela, the Trudeau government remained silent on Rousseff's ouster and persecution of the left. The only comment I found was a Global Affairs official telling Sputnik that Canada would maintain relations with Brazil after Rousseff was impeached.[153] Soon after, Canada began negotiating to join the Brazilian-led MERCOSUR trade bloc (just after Venezuela was expelled).[154] They also held a Canada Brazil Strategic Dialogue Partnership.[155] In October 2018 Freeland met her Brazilian counterpart to discuss, among other issues, pressuring the Venezuelan government. She tweeted, "Canada and Brazil enjoy a strong friendship and we are thankful for your support in defending the international rules-based order and holding the Maduro regime in Venezuela to account."[156] Brazil joined the Lima Group after Rousseff was ousted.

In 2018 openly sexist, racist, anti-environmental politician Jair Bolsonaro won the presidential election largely because the front runner in the polls was in jail. Former Workers' Party president Lula da Silva, who ended his second term with an 83% approval rating, was blocked from running due to politically motivated corruption charges.[157] The Trudeau government was publicly silent on Lula's imprisonment. The night before the Supreme Court was set to determine Lula's fate the general in charge of the army hinted at military intervention if the judges ruled in favour of the popular former president.[158] Not even that was criticized by Ottawa.

At the G20 in June 2019 Trudeau warmly welcomed Bolsonaro and Canada continued negotiating the Canada-Mercosur Free Trade Agreement with the new right wing government.[159]

With over $10 billion invested in Brazil, corporate Canada appeared excited by the prospects of a right wing president.[160] After his election CBC reported, "for Canadian business, a Bolsonaro presidency could open new investment opportunities, especially in the resource sector, finance and infrastructure, as he has pledged to slash environmental regulations in the Amazon rainforest and privatize some government-owned companies."[161]

***

The Liberals also aligned with the Trump administration's regime change effort in Nicaragua. Ottawa criticized Managua, severed aid and sanctioned officials from a government that US national security adviser John Bolton listed as part of a "troika of tyranny" (Venezuela, Cuba and Nicaragua).

Daniel Ortega's government was part of the Venezuela-led Bolivarian Alliance for the Peoples of our America (ALBA), which was a response to North American capitalist domination of the hemisphere. Since the Sandinistas won power in 2007 poverty rates dropped substantially in the nation of six million.[162] The government expanded access to electricity in rural areas and doubled the proportion of electricity from renewable sources to over half.[163] Access to drinking water increased and health indicators improved.[164] Women's role in parliament grew sharply and Nicaragua's murder rate remained a fraction of its northern neighbours.[165] According to a July 2019 UN report, there were 8.3 murderers per 100,000 Nicaraguans compared with nearly 70 murders per 100,000 in El Salvador and Honduras.[166]

In March 2016 the *New York Times* reported, "Mr. Ortega enjoys strong support among the poor" while eight months later *The Guardian* noted he "cemented popular support among poorer Nicaraguans."[167] At the end of 2016 Ortega was re-elected with 72% of the vote in an election some in the opposition boycotted.[168]

A little more than a year after his third consecutive election victory a protest movement challenged Ortega's presidency. Ostensibly what unleashed the uprising was a social security reform pushed by the International Monetary Fund. But, pension benefits were largely maintained with the government offloading most of the cost on to employers. Despite a relatively working-class friendly reform, many student organizations and NGOs aligned with the major employer federation, the wealthiest Nicaraguans and the conservative Catholic church to oppose the government.[169] Many of these groups were financed and trained by the US government's National Endowment for Democracy, USAID and Freedom House, which is close to the CIA.[170] The movement was greatly influenced by Washington, which has long been powerful in the small, impoverished, country.

The protests quickly turned violent. At least 22 police officers were killed and as many as 300 lost their lives in politically related violence during 2018.[171] The North American media and internationally connected NGOs blamed the government for all the rights violations. But, this was absurd, as the death toll of police highlight. It was also public knowledge that opposition rebels had been attacking government supporters for years. In March 2016 the *New York Times* published a long sympathetic story headlined "Ortega vs. the Contras: Nicaragua Endures an '80s Revival" about a small number of anti-government rebels targeting police stations and Sandinistas in rural areas.[172]

Still, Canadian officials blamed the government — either implicitly or directly — for the violence. Between April 23 and July 18, 2018, Global Affairs put out at least four press releases critical of the situation in Nicaragua. Freeland's statements became steadily stronger with the foreign minister eventually demanding an immediate end to the "violence, repression, arbitrary detentions and human rights violations" and for "the government of Nicaragua to help create the conditions for safe, peaceful, and constructive discussions."[173] Subsequently Canada's foreign minister questioned Ortega's democratic legitimacy. In June 2019 Freeland declared, "Canada will continue to stand with the people of Nicaragua and their legitimate demands for democracy and accountability."[174] But, Ortega won the election in a landslide and it's hard to imagine that he suddenly lost all support.

The Liberals raised the conflict in Nicaragua in international forums. At a Women Foreign Ministers' Meeting in Montréal in September 2018 Freeland said "Nicaragua" was one of "the pressing issues that concern us as foreign ministers."[175] The "situation in Nicaragua" was discussed between Freeland and foreign minister Aloysio Nunes at the third Canada-Brazil Strategic Partnership Dialogue a month later.[176]

Ottawa supported a number of OAS resolutions and initiatives targeting Ortega. Along with the US, Paraguay, Jamaica and Argentina, Canada was part of the 2019 OAS High-Level Diplomatic Commission on Nicaragua, which Managua blocked from entering the country.[177] The commission claimed there was an "alteration of constitutional order that seriously affects the democratic order" in Nicaragua.[178] But, the group failed to win majority support at the OAS General Assembly.[179]

In August 2018 the Liberals officially severed aid to Nicaragua. Canadian funding for five major government backed projects was withdrawn.[180]

Ten months later Canada sanctioned nine Nicaraguan government officials, including ministers and the president of the National Assembly. Individuals' assets were frozen and Canadians were prohibited from dealing with said persons.[181] The sanctions were adopted in co-ordination with Washington. "United States and Canada Announce Financial Sanctions to Address the Ongoing Repression in Nicaragua", noted the US State Department's release.[182]

This Liberal government stance towards Nicaragua contrasts sharply with its words and actions towards its Central American neighbour Honduras. While Canada condemned Ortega, severed aid and sanctioned officials, it maintained friendly relations and aid spending after Juan Orlando Hernandez defied the constitution by running for a second term as president and then brazenly stole the election.

***

Next up on the pro-empire Liberal agenda was the Trudeau government's support for the ouster of President Evo Morales in November 2019. An alliance of economic elites, Christian extremists and security forces backed by Washington deposed Bolivia's first Indigenous president.

Morales was replaced by a politician whose party won 4% of the vote.[183] The unconstitutional post-coup government immediately attacked Indigenous symbols and the army perpetrated a handful of massacres of anti-coup protesters that left at least 32 dead.[184] Hundreds were also arrested in political repression with many journalists detained and media outlets such as Telesur, RT en Español and dozens of local and community-based radio stations shuttered.[185]

The "caretaker" regime expelled 700 Cuban doctors, returned USAID to the country, restarted diplomatic relations with Israel and joined the anti-Venezuela Lima Group. These moves were made during what should have been the two final months of Morales' 2015 election mandate, which no one seriously disputed.

As this book goes to press, repression against Indigenous and left wing organizations continues.

The pretext for Morales' overthrow was a claim that the October 20, 2019 presidential election was flawed. Few disputed that Morales won the first round of the poll, but some claimed that he did not reach the 10% margin of victory, which was the threshold required to avoid a second-round runoff. The official result was 47.1 per cent for Morales and 36.5 per cent for right-wing US-backed candidate Carlos Mesa.

Hours after the military command forced Morales to resign as president of the most Indigenous nation in the Americas, Freeland endorsed the coup. The foreign minister released a statement noting, "Canada stands with Bolivia and the democratic will of its people. We note the resignation of President Morales and will continue to support Bolivia during this transition and the new elections."[186] Freeland's statement had no hint of criticism of Morales' ouster while leaders from Argentina to Cuba, Venezuela to Mexico, condemned Morales' forced resignation.

Ten days earlier Global Affairs bolstered right-wing anti-Morales protests by echoing the Trump administration's criticism of Morales' first round election victory. "It is not possible to accept the outcome under these circumstances," said a Global Affairs statement.[187] "We join our international partners in calling for a second round of elections to restore credibility in the electoral process."[188]

At the same time, Trudeau raised concerns about Bolivia's election with other leaders. During a phone conversation with Chilean president Sebastián Piñera the PM criticized "election irregularities in Bolivia."[189] Ottawa also promoted and financed the OAS' effort to discredit Bolivia's presidential election. After the October 20 presidential poll, the OAS immediately cried foul. The next day the organization released a statement expressing "its deep concern and surprise at the drastic and hard-to-explain change in the trend of the preliminary results [from the quick count] revealed after the closing of the polls."[190] Two days later they followed that statement up with a preliminary report that repeated their claim that "changes in the TREP [quick count] trend were hard to explain and did not match the other measurements available."[191]

But, the "hard-to-explain" changes cited by the OAS were entirely expected, as detailed in the Washington-based Centre for Economic Policy Research's report "What Happened in Bolivia's 2019 Vote Count? The Role of the OAS Electoral Observation Mission". The CEPR analysis pointed out that Morales' percentage lead over the second place candidate Carlos Mesa increased steadily as votes from rural, largely Indigenous, areas were tabulated.[192]

Additionally, the 47.1% of the vote Morales garnered aligned with pre-election polls and the vote score for his Movement toward Socialism party. The hullabaloo about the quick count stopping at 83% of the vote was preplanned and there was no evidence there was a pause in the actual counting.

But, the OAS' statements gave oxygen to opposition protests. Their unsubstantiated criticism of the election was also widely cited internationally to justify Morales' ouster. In response to OAS claims, protests in Bolivia and Washington and Ottawa saying they would not recognize Morales's victory, the Bolivian president agreed to a "binding" OAS audit of the first round of the election. Unsurprisingly the OAS' preliminary audit report alleged "irregularities and manipulation" and called for new elections overseen by a new electoral commission. Immediately after the OAS released its preliminary audit US Secretary of State Mike Pompeo went further, saying "all government officials and officials of any political organizations implicated in the flawed October 20 elections should step aside from the electoral process."[193] What started with an easy-to-explain discrepancy between the quick count and final results of the actual counting, spiraled into the entire election is suspect and anyone associated with it must go.

At a Special Meeting of the OAS Permanent Council on Bolivia the representative of Antigua and Barbuda criticized the opaque way in which the OAS electoral mission to Bolivia released its statements and reports.[194] She pointed out how the organization made a series of agreements with the Bolivian government that were effectively jettisoned. A number of Latin American countries echoed this view. For his part, Morales said the OAS "is in the service of the North American empire."[195]

US and Canadian representatives, on the other hand, applauded the OAS' work in Bolivia. Canada's representative to the OAS boasted that two Canadian technical advisers were part of the audit mission to Bolivia and that Canada financed the OAS effort that discredited Bolivia's presidential election.[196] Canada was the second largest contributor to the OAS, which received half its budget from Washington.[197]

In a statement titled "Canada welcomes results of OAS electoral audit mission to Bolivia" Freeland noted, "Canada commends the invaluable work of the OAS audit mission in ensuring a fair and transparent process, which we supported financially and through our expertise."[198]

***

At the same time the Liberals backed the ouster of Morales, Trudeau supported the most embattled right-wing leader in the region. Two weeks into massive demonstrations against Sebastián Piñera's government, the PM held a phone conversation with the Chilean president who had a 14% approval rating.[199] According to Amnesty International, 19 people had already died and dozens more were seriously injured in protests that began against a hike in transit fares and morphed into a broader challenge to economic inequality.[200] A couple thousand were also arrested by a government that declared martial law and sent the army onto the streets.[201]

According to the published report of the conversation, Trudeau criticized "election irregularities in Bolivia" and discussed their joint campaign to remove Venezuela's president.[202] A Canadian Press story noted, "a summary from the Prime Minister's Office of Trudeau's phone call with Piñera made no direct mention of the ongoing turmoil in Chile, a thriving country with which Canada has negotiated a free trade agreement."[203] Despite appeals from Canada's Chilean community and others, the Liberals stayed quiet in subsequent months concerning the fiercest repression in Chile since Augusto Pinochet's dictatorship.

Trudeau met Piñera at a number of summits in 2018. The prime minister and billionaire president "praised … the benefits" of a "free trade" economic model Chileans later protested against in the millions.[204]

Across the region the Liberals largely ignored human rights violations committed by pro corporate/Washington governments. They said little about hundreds of killings by regimes they backed in Haiti, Honduras, Bolivia, Chile and Colombia.

The Liberals promoted President Iván Duque who *Le Soleil* labeled "le champion du retour de la droite dure en Colombie" (champion of the return of the hard right in Colombia).[205] After Duque won a close election Freeland "congratulated" him and said, "Canada and Colombia share a commitment to democracy and human rights."[206] In August 2018 Trudeau tweeted, "today, Colombia's new President, Iván Duque, took office and joins Swedish PM, Norway PM, Emmanuel Macron, Pedro Sánchez, and others with a gender-equal cabinet. Iván, I look forward to working with you and your entire team."[207] A month later he added, "thanks to President Iván Duque for a great first meeting at UNGA this afternoon, focused on growing our economies, addressing the crisis in Venezuela, and strengthening the friendship between Canada & Colombia."[208]

In subsequent months the PM had multiple phone conversations with his close ally in their campaign to oust Venezuela's government.

As Trudeau got chummy with Duque, the Colombian president undercut the peace accord the previous (right, but not far right) government signed with the Revolutionary Armed Forces of Colombia (FARC) to end Colombia's 50-year civil war, which left some 220,000 dead. Duque's policies increased violence towards the ex-rebels and social activists. Seventy-seven former FARC members were killed in 2019.[209] Even more human rights defenders were murdered. The United Nations High Commissioner for Human Rights found that 107 Colombian, mostly Indigenous, rights defenders were killed in 2019 (another 13 deaths had yet to be conclusively investigated).[210] The pace of the killing increased during early 2020.[211]

From the start of his mandate Trudeau bolstered governments that undercut the socialistic, regional integration efforts that shaped Latin America's politics in the early 2000s. The Liberal PM backed Mauricio Macri, visiting Argentina twice and meeting with the South American country's president on the sidelines of multiple summits.[212] The objective of a November 2016 trip, according to the Canadian Press, was to assist "the political shift that is underway in Argentina, something that's being mirrored in neighbouring countries." According to CP, "Macri is moving the country to the political centre after years of populist, nationalistic governments" and "is looking to make it easier for mining firms to operate in the country."[213]

During their meeting Trudeau and Macri jointly decried anti "trade" policies. But, this was effectively a Canadian endorsement of Argentina succumbing to the wolves of Wall Street. While the previous government resisted the extortion, Macri dished out US$8 billion to US "vulture funds", which bought the country's debt at a steep discount after Buenos Aires defaulted in 2001. Macri's transfer of Argentinian wealth to the US billionaire class set a terrible precedent, giving hard-line creditors greater incentive to hold out against debt restructuring.

Despite paying off the "vulture funds" to gain better access to international capital markets, Macri's pro-rich policies led to economic collapse. Buenos Aires was forced to turn to the International Monetary Fund to stabilize its currency and economy in what became the IMF's largest-ever bailout in 2018.

Amidst negotiations over a $50 billion IMF line of credit, Trudeau sought to boost Macri — the IMF was highly unpopular in Argentina — by inviting him to the G7 in Québec City. "By having Argentina present," noted iPolitics in June 2018, "Canada and the G7 may have helped President Macri regain added credibility at home where efforts to modernize the economy face tough opposition."[214]

Fortunately, Macri was handily defeated in the 2019 presidential election, which CBC labeled, "a loss for the Trudeau government."[215] The staying power of Nicolás Maduro was another setback for the Liberals. Despite their best efforts, a number of governments continued to challenge North American capitalist domination of the region.

Unless one believes it is "progressive" to side with the US Empire, support extreme right governments, prioritize Canadian business interests over democracy, and interfere in other country's domestic affairs, the record of the Trudeau government over its first four years in "our backyard" shouldn't be described as progressive.

As we shall see in subsequent chapters, Trudeau's claim-one-thing-and-do-another approach to foreign affairs was also on display elsewhere.

Chapter 2 Notes

1 Greg Shupak, US Media Erase Years of Chavismo's Gains, Feb 20 2019 (https://fair.org/home/us-media-erase-years-of-chavismos-gains/)

2 Venezuela: Social Program Meets Goal, Delivers 3 Million Homes, Dec 27 2019 (https://www.telesurenglish.net/news/Venezuela-Social-Program-Meets-Goal-Delivers-3-Million-Homes-20191227-0001.html)

3 Tamara Pearson, Municipal Election Results: Venezuela Winning the War Waged against It, Dec 9 2013 (https://venezuelanalysis.com/analysis/10232)

4 Jeff Mason and Roberta Rampton, U.S. declares Venezuela a national security threat, sanctions top officials, Mar 9 2015 (https://www.reuters.com/article/us-usa-venezuela/u-s-declares-venezuela-a-national-security-threat-sanctions-top-officials-iduskbn0m51ns20150310)

5 Julian Borger, Trump repeatedly suggested Venezuela invasion, stunning top aides – report, Jul 5 2018 (https://www.theguardian.com/us-news/2018/jul/04/trump-suggested-invading-venezuela-report)

6 Marilia Brocchetto, Jonny Hallam, Joe Sterling and Stefano Pozzebon, Venezuela makes six arrests in alleged Maduro assassination attempt CNN, Aug 6 2018 (https://www.cnn.com/2018/08/05/americas/venezuela-maduro/index.html)

7 Ryan Mallett-Outtrim, Venezuela's Constituent Assembly Assumes Parliamentary Powers, Aug 18 2017 (https://venezuelanalysis.com/news/13322) ; Ryan Mallett-Outtrim, The Curious Case of Venezuela's Recall Referendum: Murder … or Suicide?, Jan 9 2017 (https://venezuelanalysis.com/analysis/12875)

8 Levon Sevunts, Canada condemns Venezuela's 'undemocratic' vote but is not ready to follow U.S. sanctions yet, Radio Canada International, Jul 31 2017 (https://www.cbc.ca/news/politics/venezuela-sanctions-regime-vote-1.4229930)

9 Venezuela: Six States Request ICC Investigation Sept 26 2018 (https://www.hrw.org/news/2018/09/26/venezuela-six-states-request-icc-investigation)

10 Feb 14 2018 (https://twitter.com/cafreeland/status/963784113873412097)

11 Honduras President Seeks 2nd Term Despite Constitutional Ban, Nov 23 2017 (https://www.usnews.com/news/world/articles/2017-11-23/honduras-president-seeks-2nd-term-despite-constitutional-ban)

12 Daniel Joloy, Ten years of militarised drug policies in Mexico: more violence and human rights violations, May 7 2017 (https://www.opendemocracy.net/en/ten-years-of-militarised-drug-policies-in-mexico-more-violence-and-human-rights-violati/)

13 Canada supports decision that President Maduro of Venezuela not welcome at Summit of the Americas, Global Affairs Canada, Feb 14 2017 (https://www.canada.ca/en/global-affairs/news/2018/02/canada_supports_decisionthatpresidentmaduroofvenezuelanotwelcome.html)

14 Paul Dobson, Venezuela: Presidential Elections Moved to May, Falcon & Maduro Agree to Electoral Guarantees, Mar 2 2018 (https://venezuelanalysis.com/news/13695) ; Mar 1 2018 (https://twitter.com/CanadaFP/status/969325647620386816)

15 Venezuela in plea to UN to send observers for election, Mar 13 2018 (http://www.jamaicaobserver.com/latestnews/Venezuela_in_plea_to_UN_to_send_observers_for_election?profile=1228) ; Venezuelan opposition urges UN not to attend presidential election, Mar 13 2018 (https://www.theweek.co.uk/92255/venezuelan-election-opposi-

tion-boycott)

16 Lauren Carasik, Venezuela's electoral system is being unfairly maligned, Nov 30 2015 (http://america.aljazeera.com/opinions/2015/11/venezuelas-electoral-system-is-being-unfairly-maligned.html)

17 Carter States That the Election Process in Venezuela is "the Best in the World", Sept 21 2012 (https://www.businesswire.com/news/home/20120921005758/en/Carter-States-Election-Process-Venezuela-"the-World")

18 Feb 14 2018 (https://twitter.com/cafreeland/status/963784113873412097)

19 Prime Minister Justin Trudeau speaks with President of Peru, Pedro Pablo Kuczynski, May 1 2017 (https://pm.gc.ca/en/news/readouts/2017/05/01/prime-minister-justin-trudeau-speaks-president-peru-pedro-pablo-kuczynski)

20 Statement of the fifth meeting of the Lima Group on the situation in Venezuela, Spanish version, Feb 13 2018 (https://www.international.gc.ca/world-monde/international_relations-relations_internationales/latin_america-amerique_latine/2018-02-13-lima_group-groupe_lima.aspx?lang=eng) ; Yves Engler, Ottawa is trying to interfere in Venezuela's election, Apr 1 2018 (https://rabble.ca/blogs/bloggers/yves-englers-blog/2018/04/ottawa-trying-interfere-venezuelas-election)

21 Lucas Koerner, Venezuela Rejects Lima Group Statement Urging Further Isolation of Caracas, Oct 30 2017 (https://venezuelanalysis.com/news/13473)

22 Lima Group rules out military intervention in Venezuela, Sept 17 2018 (https://www.aljazeera.com/news/2018/09/lima-group-rejects-military-intervention-venezuela-180917061724188.html) ; Canada, Latin American allies at odds over Venezuela intervention pledge, Sep 19 2018 (https://www.cbc.ca/news/politics/canada-venezuela-military-intervention-1.4829074)

23 Mike Blanchfield, Canada's recognition of Juan Guaido as true Venezuelan leader was months in the making, Jan 26 2019 (https://globalnews.ca/news/4892715/canada-juan-guaido-venezuela-juan-guaido/) ; Michelle Carbert, Freeland spoke to Venezuelan opposition leader two weeks before he declared himself interim president, source says, Jan 24 2019 (https://www.theglobeandmail.com/politics/article-freeland-spoke-to-venezuelan-opposition-leader-two-weeks-before-he/)

24 Joshua Goodman, Luis Alonso Lugo and Rob Gillies, Anti-Maduro coalition grew from secret talks, Jan 25 2019 (https://apnews.com/d548c6a958ee4a1fb8479b242ddb82fd)

25 Feb 4 2019 (https://twitter.com/davidakin/status/1092430179970867201)

26 Yves Engler, Is Trudeau's Venezuela policy the Monroe Doctrine reborn?, Feb 20 2019 (https://canadiandimension.com/articles/view/is-trudeaus-venezuela-policy-the-monroe-doctrine-reborn)

27 Prime Minister Justin Trudeau speaks with Prime Minister Pedro Sánchez of Spain, May 9 2019 (https://pm.gc.ca/en/news/readouts/2019/05/09/prime-minister-justin-trudeau-speaks-prime-minister-pedro-sanchez-spain)

28 Prime Minister of Canada announces closer collaboration with Japan, Apr 28 2019 (https://pm.gc.ca/en/news/news-releases/2019/04/28/prime-minister-canada-announces-closer-collaboration-japan)

29 Peter Zimonjic, Lima Group embraces Venezuelan opposition leader Guaido, calls on military to quit Maduro, Feb 4 2019 (https://www.cbc.ca/news/politics/lima-group-declaration-venezuela-1.5005559)

30 Terry Glavin, Venezuelans are forced to fight on, alone, against Maduro Something big was happening in the broken country this week, May 1 2019 (https://ottawacitizen.com/opinion/columnists/glavin-venezuelans-are-forced-to-fight-on-alone-against-maduro)

31 Angus Berwick, Vivian Sequera, Corina Pons, Mayela Armas, Deisy Buitrago, and Luc Cohen, Chaos in the streets as Venezuela's Guaido launches military uprising to oust Maduro, Reuters, Apr 30 2019 (https://globalnews.ca/news/5220106/venezuela-military-coup-juan-guaido/)

32 May 1 2019 (https://twitter.com/cafreeland/status/1123758508573372417) ; Canada requests emergency meeting of Lima Group to discuss Venezuela, Reuters, Apr 30 2019 (http://news.trust.org/item/20190430181904-9uqf2/)

33 Guaido calls for more street protests Apr 30 2019 (https://apnews.com/1b271ef1f15940f394343dd2027a23e2)

34 Interim President of Venezuela Juan Guaidó to visit Canada, Prime Minister's Office, Jan 26 2020 (https://www.newswire.ca/news-releases/interim-president-of-venezuela-juan-guaido-to-visit-canada-830507706.html)

35 Venezuela Ejects Top Canadian and Brazilian Diplomats, Dec 24 2017 (https://www.telesurenglish.net/news/Venezuela-Ejects-Top-Canadian-and-Brazilian-Diplomats-20171224-0008.html)

36 David Ljunggren, Canada to impose sanctions on Venezuela's Maduro and top officials, Sept 22 2017 (https://ca.reuters.com/article/topNews/id-CAKCN1BX2PV-OCATP)

37 Evan Dyer, Canada expands Venezuela sanctions, adds 43 people close to Maduro, Apr 15 2019 (https://www.cbc.ca/news/politics/venezuela-sanctions-canada-1.5098288)

38 Venezuela accuses Canada of supporting Trump's 'war adventure', AFP, Apr 16 2019 (https://www.france24.com/en/20190416-venezuela-accuses-canada-supporting-trumps-war-adventure)

39 Mark Weisbrot and Jeffrey Sachs, Economic Sanctions as Collective Punishment: The Case of Venezuela, Apr 2019 (http://cepr.net/publications/reports/economic-sanctions-as-collective-punishment-the-case-of-venezuela)

40 Rahmat Mohamad, Unilateral Sanctions in International Law: A Quest for Legality, Economic Sanctions under International Law, Mar 4 2015

(https://link.springer.com/chapter/10.1007%2F978-94-6265-051-0_4) ; TeleSur English, UN Human Rights Council Condemns Sanctions Against Venezuela, Mar 26 2018 (https://venezuelanalysis.com/news/13737)

41 Ibid

42 Telesur, Trudeau Endorses Trump: Canadian Sanctions against Venezuela Violate 'International Law', June 3 2018 (https://www.globalresearch.ca/trudeau-endorses-trump-canadian-sanctions-against-venezuela-violate-international-law/5642871)

43 Brennan MacDonald and Katie Simpson, Canada, U.S. working to move EU toward sanctions on Venezuela, says top U.S. official, Aug 1 2019 (https://www.cbc.ca/news/politics/powerandpolitics/canada-us-talks-eu-sanctions-maduro-1.5233774)

44 Michelle Carbert, Canada encouraged diplomats to defend human rights in Venezuela, July 16 2018 (https://www.theglobeandmail.com/politics/article-canada-encouraged-diplomats-to-defend-human-rights-in-venezuela-amid/)

45 Peter Hum, Choosing danger, Ottawa Citizen, Aug 19 2017 (https://www.pressreader.com/canada/ottawa-citizen/20170819/282230895807092)

46 GOVERNMENT RESPONSE TO THE JULY 2017 REPORT OF THE STANDING SENATE COMMITTEE ON FOREIGN AFFAIRS AND INTERNATIONAL TRADE: THE DEEPENING CRISIS IN VENEZUELA: CANADIAN AND REGIONAL STAKES, Mar 19 2018 (https://sencanada.ca/content/sen/committee/421/AEFA/reports/2018_03_19_GovResponse(Venezuela)_e.pdf)

47 Foreign Affairs, Trade and Development Canada, Government of Canada, Catalogue Number: FR2-16E-PDF, International Standard Serial Number (ISSN): 2368-5778, Departmental Performance Report 2014-15 (https://www.international.gc.ca/gac-amc/publications/plans/dpr-rmr/dpr-rmr_1415.aspx?lang=eng_)

48 Ramón Antonio Pérez, Venezuela: La dura denuncia de un jesuita sobre la violación de los DDHH, Aleteia, Sep 22 2017 (https://es.aleteia.org/2017/09/22/venezuela-la-dura-denuncia-de-un-jesuita-sobre-la-violacion-de-los-ddhh/)

49 Embassy of Canada and the Center for Peace and Human Rights announce a call for the 8th edition of the Human Rights Award in Venezuela (https://www.canadainternational.gc.ca/venezuela/highlights-faits/2016/2016-11-8thHRA_PDP.aspx?lang=eng)

50 Valentina Rodríguez Rodríguez, Director de Codevida gana premio Derechos Humanos que otorga embajada de Canadá, TalCual, Mar 7 2018 (https://talcualdigital.com/director-de-codevida-gana-premio-derechos-humanos-que-otorga-embajada-de-canada/)

51 Francisco Valencia, director de Codevida: Estamos frente a un Estado criminal, Crisis en Venezuela (https://crisisenvenezuela.com/project/entrevista-francisco-valencia-codevida-estamos-frente-un-estado-criminal/)

52 Michelle Carbert, Venezuelan human-rights advocate applauds Canada's leadership in denouncing Nicolas Maduro regime, July 4 2018 (https://www.theglobeandmail.com/politics/article-venezuelan-human-rights-advocate-applauds-canadas-leadership-in/)

53 Antonio Ledezma pidió en Canadá intervención humanitaria para rescatar a Venezuela, Diario Las Américas, Sept 20 2018 (https://www.diariolasamericas.com/america-latina/antonio-ledezma-pidio-canada-intervencion-humanitaria-rescatar-venezuela-n4162779)

54 Ibid

55 Rachael Boothroyd Rojas, Opposition Former Mayor Antonio Ledezma Breaks House Arrest, Flees to Colombia, Nov 17 2017 (https://venezuelanalysis.com/news/13506)

56 Tamara Pearson and Ryan Mallett-Outtrim, Venezuelan Guarimbas: 11 Things the Media Didn't Tell You, Feb 16 2015 (https://venezuelanalysis.com/analysis/11211)

57 Popular Will (https://en.wikipedia.org/wiki/Popular_Will)

58 Ibid

59 David Luhnow, Juan Forero and José de Córdoba, 'What the hell is going on?' How a tiny cabal galvanised Venezuela's Opposition, Feb 7 2019 (https://www.wsj.com/articles/what-the-hell-is-going-on-how-a-tiny-cabal-galvanized-venezuelas-opposition-11549555626)

60 5 Things To Know About Venezuela's Protest Leader, Feb 20 2014 (https://www.npr.org/sections/thetwo-way/2014/02/20/280207441/5-things-to-know-about-venezuelas-protest-leader)

61 Ibid

62 Tamara Pearson and Ryan Mallett-Outtrim, Venezuelan Guarimbas: 11 Things the Media Didn't Tell You, Feb 16 2015 (https://venezuelanalysis.com/analysis/11211)

63 Yves Engler, Canada's Trudeau Government Supportive of Venezuela Anti-democratic Hardline Elements, Global Research, May 31 2019 (https://www.globalresearch.ca/ottawa-anti-democratic-hardline-venezuelas-opposition/5679142)

64 Feb 3 2017 (https://twitter.com/VoluntadPopular/status/827525918805598208)

65 Lucas Koerner, Trump Meets with Venezuela's Lilian Tintori, Demands Release of Leopoldo Lopez, Feb 16 2017 (https://venezuelanalysis.com/news/12934) ; Joe Parkin Daniels, Tom Phillips and Sabrina Siddiqui, This man plotted Guaidó's rise – and still dreams of leading Venezuela, Feb 7 2019 (https://www.theguardian.com/world/2019/feb/06/this-man-plotted-guaidos-rise-and-still-dreams-of-leading-venezuela)

66 Yves Engler, Ottawa in bed with anti-demo-

cratic, hardline part of Venezuela's opposition, May 30 2019 (https://yvesengler.com/2019/05/30/ottawa-has-aligned-with-the-most-hardline-anti-democratic-elements-of-venezuelas-opposition/)

67 Joe Parkin Daniels, Tom Phillips and Sabrina Siddiqui, This man plotted Guaidó's rise – and still dreams of leading Venezuela, Feb 7 2019 (https://www.theguardian.com/world/2019/feb/06/this-man-plotted-guaidos-rise-and-still-dreams-of-leading-venezuela)

68 David Luhnow, Juan Forero and José de Córdoba, 'What the hell is going on?' How a tiny cabal galvanised Venezuela's Opposition, Feb 7 2019 (https://www.wsj.com/articles/what-the-hell-is-going-on-how-a-tiny-cabal-galvanized-venezuelas-opposition-11549555626)

69 Special Advisor on Venezuela (18-142300), Reference number PW-18-00824282 (https://buyandsell.gc.ca/procurement-data/tender-notice/PW-18-00824282)

70 DAS DESHAZO'S MEETING WITH AMBASSADORS ON 2/16/2004, Canonical ID:04CARACAS628_a (https://wikileaks.org/plusd/cables/04CARACAS628_a.html)

71 Maria Corina Machado (https://en.wikipedia.org/wiki/Mar%C3%ADa_Corina_Machado)

72 Carmona Decree (https://en.wikipedia.org/wiki/Carmona_Decree)

73 Allan Culham, Venezuela, after midnight, May 24 2016 (https://www.opencanada.org/features/venezuela-after-midnight/)

74 Luisana Solano, Actualizado hace 6 años EEUU, Canadá y Panamá disconformes con la declaración de la OEA, solidaria con Venezuela, Infobae, Mar 8 2014 (https://runrun.es/internacional/internacionales/107050/eeuu-canada-y-panama-disconformes-con-la-declaracion-de-la-oea-solidaria-con-venezuela/)

75 Daniel L. Rodriguez, Venezuelan Crisis: Venezuelan Vice-President Describes Canadian Proposal At OAS As 'Miserable', Jan 18 2013 (https://www.huffingtonpost.ca/daniel-l-rodriguez/venezuelan-crisis-canadian-proposal_b_2501152.html)

76 Una dividida OEA pide calma a gobierno y oposición en Venezuela, NOTIMEX, Feb 19 2014 (https://www.20minutos.com.mx/noticia/b118982/una-dividida-oea-pide-calma-a-gobierno-y-oposicion-en-venezuela/) ; La OEA decide cerrar a la prensa la sesión en la que prevé intervenir María Corina Machado, EFE, Mar 21 2014 (https://www.emol.com/noticias/internacional/2014/03/21/651106/la-oea-decide-cerrar-a-la-prensa-la-sesion-en-la-que-preve-intervenir-maria-corina-machado.html)

77 Todd Gordon and Jeffery R. Webber, The Cartagena Accord: A Step Forward for Canada in Honduras, July 13 2011 (https://socialistproject.ca/2011/07/b526/)

78 OAS Mission Concludes Visit to Paraguay, Reference: E-243/12, July 3 2012 (https://www.oas.org/en/media_center/press_release.asp?sCodigo=E-243/12)

79 Allan Culham, Is Rousseff's likely ouster a sign of change in Latin America?, May 3 2016 (https://www.opencanada.org/features/rousseffs-likely-ouster-sign-change-latin-america/)

80 Ibid

81 Allan Culham, So long, Kirchners, Nov 26 2015 (https://www.opencanada.org/features/so-long-kirchners/)

82 Ibid

83 Allan Culham, Is Rousseff's likely ouster a sign of change in Latin America?, May 3 2016 (https://www.opencanada.org/features/rousseffs-likely-ouster-sign-change-latin-america/)

84 In committee from the Senate of Canada, Foreign Affairs Feb 3 2016 (https://www.cpac.ca/en/programs/in-committee-from-the-senate-of-canada/episodes/46657070/)

85 Ibid

86 Ibid

87 Ibid

88 Canada's Foreign Service Awards Celebrate their 30th Year, June 14 2019 (https://pafso.com/canadas-foreign-service-awards-celebrate-their-30th-year/)

89 Ibid

90 Katharine Starr, What to expect from Monday's emergency summit on Venezuela, Feb 2 2019 (https://www.cbc.ca/news/politics/what-to-expect-monday-emergency-meeting-lima-group-venezuela-1.5002225)

91 Trudeau says clause in Venezuela constitution shows Guaido is interim president, Jan 31 2019 (https://globalnews.ca/video/4913733/trudeau-says-clause-in-venezuela-constitution-shows-guaido-is-interim-president/)

92 Lucas Koerner, Venezuela: Coup d'Etat or Constitutional Transition?, Feb 6 2019 (https://venezuelanalysis.com/analysis/14304)

93 Honduran judges throw out single-term limit on presidency, Apr 24 2015 (https://www.theguardian.com/world/2015/apr/24/honduran-judges-throw-out-single-term-limit-on-presidency)

94 Tyler Shipley, Ottawa and Empire: Canada and the Military Coup in Honduras

95 Gustavo Palencia, Honduran president sworn in amid protests after election chaos, Jan 27 2018 (https://www.reuters.com/article/us-honduras-election/honduran-president-sworn-in-amid-protests-after-election-chaos-idUSKBN1FG0NL)

96 Nasralla practically assured of Honduras election win-official, Nov 27 2017 (https://www.reuters.com/article/us-honduras-election-ballots/nasralla-practically-assured-of-honduras-election-win-official-idUSKBN1DR2OQ)

97 Sarah Kinosian, Families fear no justice for victims as 31 die in Honduras post-election violence, Jan 2 2018 (https://www.theguardian.com/

world/2018/jan/02/us-silent-as-honduras-protesters-killed-in-post-election-violence)

98 Dec 22 2017 (https://twitter.com/canadafp/status/944257271353217024?ref_src=twcamp%5Eshare%7Ctwsrc%5Eios%7Ctwgr%5Ecom.apple.UIKit.activity.PostToFacebook)

99 Tyler Shipley, Dec 22 2017 (https://www.facebook.com/tyshipley/posts/10104201966807120?pnref=story)

100 Nov 9 2018 (https://twitter.com/CancilleriaHN/status/1061012038657433600) ; Dec 14 2018 (https://twitter.com/JKHillCDA/status/1073622611903635456) ; Minister Dion to travel to Mexico, Guatemala and Honduras, News Release, Oct 10 2016, Global Affairs Canada (https://www.canada.ca/en/global-affairs/news/2016/10/minister-dion-travel-mexico-guatemala-honduras.html)

101 Martin Ouellet-Diotte, Canadian Foreign Minister Chrystia Freeland greets Honduran Foreign Minister Maria Dolores Aguero (R) during the Women Foreign Ministers' Meeting in Montreal, Canada, Sept 21 2018 (https://www.gettyimages.ca/detail/news-photo/canadian-foreign-minister-chrystia-freeland-greets-honduran-news-photo/1037490600)

102 4 Feb 2019 (https://twitter.com/CancilleriaHN/status/1092555047651680257)

103 11 Dec 2018 (https://twitter.com/COPECO_HONDURAS/status/1072562044178702336) ; 20 Dec 2018 (https://twitter.com/CancilleriaHN/status/1075849382107471874)

104 19 Jun 2018 (https://twitter.com/USAmbHonduras/status/1009096559856844801)

105 Take Action: Honduran Authorities Should Not Feel Canada's Trust, Oct 2016 (https://miningwatch.ca/blog/2016/10/5/take-action-honduran-authorities-should-not-feel-canadas-trust?__cf_chl_jschl_tk__=3224b8d51a1e-24cc7b1697501103e418351f68f6-1580506020-0-ARHkqxWGF63OrE0vFNRAoDsrx_9s98iuWVsaLUR4HYqPZI8RMvJFo8-r7MrL-SYXFaVhsTtv7S_40mHSUtpIPMCdCGodODxT-WhNKbxTgj1FadNT1I0sVM8m-LMQtwJZBT8xoUdmFgCPiaMKhvuTIa-PXEOh7AXyVjBlX7tI-Yv8NsijadXQE0sE1YFKVUFKuZZ-T9GMrV6L-nhszvEGHTZuaLgk5Jv-buxhv73yDVKSLrWYIk-5KYaW0zZZEtY737NNK80VllU-9ORoHUsSRG-DYBG1t_L-zHSpm7DvV8FdGxqCXE2yu2t5t-5WwrtpOmtaDTWABicB8AEtwsiM7denOib_ROCthNQwTNymZIvU-VPu1kq)

106 Grahame Russell, Is Honduran political prisoner Edwin Espinal victim of a Canada-U.S.-Honduras backroom deal?, Rights Action, Feb 7 2019 (https://mailchi.mp/rightsaction/is-honduran-political-prisoner-edwin-espinal-victim-of-a-canada-us-honduras-backroom-deal)

107 Phil Carpenter, Montrealers protest closure of Canadian immigration office in Havana, Cuba, May 25 2019 (https://globalnews.ca/news/5316415/montrealers-protest-closure-canadian-immigration-office-havana/)

108 Karen Dubinsky, Canada closes a door on Cuban culture, May 19 2019 (https://www.thestar.com/opinion/contributors/2019/05/19/canada-closes-a-door-on-cuban-culture.html)

109 Canada cuts staff in Cuba embassy after mystery illness strikes again, Associated Press, Jan 31 2019 (https://www.theguardian.com/world/2019/jan/31/canada-cuts-staff-in-cuba-embassy-after-mystery-illness-strikes-again)

110 Dan Hurley, Was It an Invisible Attack on U.S. Diplomats, or Something Stranger?, May 15 2019 (https://www.nytimes.com/interactive/2019/05/15/magazine/diplomat-disorder.html?mtrref=www.google.com)

111 Julian Borger and Philip Jaekl, Mass hysteria may explain 'sonic attacks' in Cuba, say top neurologists, Oct 12 2017 (https://www.theguardian.com/world/2017/oct/12/cuba-mass-hysteria-sonic-attacks-neurologists) ; Ed Yong Animals Keep Creating Mysteries by Sounding Weird, Jan 8 2019 (https://www.theatlantic.com/science/archive/2019/01/sound-haunted-diplomats-cuba-crickets/579637/)

112 Prime Minister Justin Trudeau speaks with the President of Cuba, Miguel Díaz-Canel, May 3 2019 (https://pm.gc.ca/en/news/readouts/2019/05/03/prime-minister-justin-trudeau-speaks-president-cuba-miguel-diaz-canel)

113 Canada minister urges Cuba to be 'part of the solution' in Venezuela, May 7 2019 (http://www.jamaicaobserver.com/latestnews/Canada_minister_urges_Cuba_to_be_part_of_the_solution_in_Venezuela?profile=1)

114 Evan Dyer, Canada at odds with Cuban 'ally' over Maduro's fate, Mar 3 2019 (https://www.cbc.ca/news/world/venezuela-canada-cuba-1.5040857)

115 28 May 2019 (https://twitter.com/statedeptspox/status/1133406519456870402)

116 Matt Spetalnick and Sarah Marsh, In major shift, Trump to allow lawsuits against foreign firms in Cuba, Apr 16 2019 (https://www.reuters.com/article/us-usa-cuba/in-major-shift-trump-to-allow-lawsuits-against-foreign-firms-in-cuba-idUSKCN1RS1VY)

117 Alyssa Daniells, Is Cuba Safe? Debunking Travel Safety Myths, Mar 5 2018 (https://www.flightcentre.ca/blog/is-cuba-safe-debunking-travel-safety-myths/)

118 Josh Rubin, Toronto food truck caught up in Trump's battle with Cuba, Oct 2 2019 (https://www.thestar.com/business/2019/10/02/toronto-food-truck-caught-up-in-trumps-battle-with-cuba.html)

119 Alexis Abdias, Sondage de TripFoumi Enfo: 81% des participants favorables à la démission du Président Oct 7 2019 (https://www.tripfoumi.com/blog/2019/10/07/sondage-de-tripfoumi-enfo-81-des-participants-favorables-a-la-demission-du-president/?fbclid=IwAR3Oq6tgNfy9_ikY1vpe-2YzmlL-

jHky6eoVPd7Sp2XAVW_l3eIPcyjKzpxU)

120   Fabien Deglise, Le Canada appelé à lâcher le président haïtien Jovenel Moïse, Oct 4 2019 (https://www.ledevoir.com/monde/ameriques/564109/le-canada-appele-a-lacher-jovenel-moise)

121   Minister Bibeau to travel to Haiti, Global Affairs Canada, News Release, Feb16 2018, Global Affairs Canada (https://www.canada.ca/en/global-affairs/news/2018/02/minister_bibeau_totraveltohaiti.html) ; «Il faut absolument que la violence cesse», dit la ministre Bibeau, TVA Nouvelles, Feb 16 2019 (https://www.tvanouvelles.ca/2019/02/16/il-faut-absolument-que-la-violence-cesse-dit-la-ministre-bibeau)

122   Prime Minister Justin Trudeau meets with Prime Minister Jean-Henry Céant of Haiti, Dec 13 2018 (https://pm.gc.ca/en/news/readouts/2018/12/13/prime-minister-justin-trudeau-meets-prime-minister-jean-henry-ceant-haiti)

123   Prime Minister Justin Trudeau meets with Prime Minister Jean-Henry Céant of Haiti, Dec 13 2018 (https://pm.gc.ca/en/news/readouts/2018/12/13/prime-minister-justin-trudeau-meets-prime-minister-jean-henry-ceant-haiti)

124   Kathleen Harris, Helping Haiti: Bibeau begins 3-day visit focused on improving health, empowering women, Feb 18 2018 (https://www.cbc.ca/news/politics/haiti-bibeau-health-women-1.4539678)

125   Joint statement regarding announcement of definitive results of presidential election in Haiti Statement, Jan 5 2017 (https://www.canada.ca/en/global-affairs/news/2017/011/joint-statement-regarding-announcement-definitive-results-presidential-election-haiti.html)

126   Haiti 2017: From Demonstration Election to Electoral Coup Charlie Hinton (https://haitisolidarity.net/in-the-news/electoral-coup/)

127   Political crisis in Haiti could lead to president ruling single-handedly, Jan 14 2020 (https://www.france24.com/en/20200114-political-crisis-in-haiti-could-result-in-president-ruling-single-handedly)

128   July 17 2019 (https://twitter.com/moisejovenel/status/1151593928891740160)

129   Nov 23 2018 (https://twitter.com/PrimatureHT/status/1066115505361162241)

130   Oct 23 2019 (https://twitter.com/moisejovenel/status/1187040469127221249) ; Diplomacy : New Ambassador of Canada to Haiti Oct 24 2019 (https://www.haitilibre.com/en/news-29084-haiti-diplomacy-new-ambassador-of-canada-to-haiti.html)

131   26 Nov 2018 (https://twitter.com/mclaudebibeau/status/1067186885037096961)

132   «Il faut absolument que la violence cesse», dit la ministre Bibeau, TVA Nouvelles, Feb 16 2019 (https://www.tvanouvelles.ca/2019/02/16/il-faut-absolument-que-la-violence-cesse-dit-la-ministre-bibeau)

133   Communiqué de Presse du Core Group, Nov 22 2018 (https://minujusth.unmissions.org/communiqué-de-presse-du-core-group-−-22-novembre-2018)

134   5 Apr 2018 (https://twitter.com/AndreFFrenette/status/981953193205731328)

135   Yves Engler, Canada backs Haitian government, even as police force kills demonstrators, Nov 29 (https://ricochet.media/en/2439/canada-backs-haitian-government-even-as-police-force-kills-demonstrators?fbclid=IwAR1hSSAyBg-A3sWVFDeJVG0F0iUpT8yQzakwSXFm28U_0dhzPOHjReLuZaA)

136   James Doubek, Haiti's Prime Minister Resigns After Riots Over Fuel Price Hike, July 15 2018 (https://www.npr.org/2018/07/15/629198841/haitis-prime-minister-resigns-after-riots-over-fuel-price-hike)

137   Haiti: Amnesty International verifies evidence of excessive use of force against protesters, Oct 31 2019 (https://www.amnesty.org/en/latest/news/2019/10/haiti-amnesty-verifies-evidence-excessive-force-against-protesters/)

138   Samuel Maxime, Massacre in La Saline has Ties to State Officials, UN Report Finds, June 22 2019 (https://sentinel.ht/post/news/crime/10864-massacre-in-la-saline-has-ties-to-state-officials-reports-un-mission); La Saline Massacre: One Year Anniversary (https://www.ijdh.org/2019/11/projects/la-saline-massacre-one-year-anniversary/)

139   Ibid

140   Yves Engler, Canada backs Haitian government, even as police force kills demonstrators, Nov 29 2018 (https://ricochet.media/en/2439/canada-backs-haitian-government-even-as-police-force-kills-demonstrators?fbclid=IwAR1hSSAyBg-A3sWVFDeJVG0F0iUpT8yQzakwSXFm28U_0dhzPOHjReLuZaA)

141   19 Jun 2019 (https://twitter.com/AndreFFrenette/status/1141470564202274821)

142   Peace operations (http://www.rcmp-grc.gc.ca/en/peace-operations)

143   Camila Domonoske, U.N. Admits Role In Haiti Cholera Outbreak That Has Killed Thousands, Aug 18 2016 (https://www.npr.org/sections/thetwo-way/2016/08/18/490468640/u-n-admits-role-in-haiti-cholera-outbreak-that-has-killed-thousands)

144   Canada advocates a «robust» political mission to succeed Minujusth, Jun 10 2019 (https://www.haitilibre.com/en/news-27951-haiti-un-canada-advocates-a-robust-political-mission-to-succeed-minujusth.html)

145   Le Canada a présidé une réunion spéciale sur la crise d'Haïti, Oct 31, 2019 (https://rtvc.radiotelevisioncaraibes.com/national/le-canada-preside-reunion-speciale-la-crise-dhaiti.html)

146   Yves Engler, Canadian military in Haiti. Why?, Feb 22 2019 (https://yvesengler.com/2019/02/22/canadian-military-in-haiti-why/)

147   Feb 15 2019 (https://twitter.com/Haiti-

InfoProj/status/1096630200463290368?fb-clid=IwAR1a1r59Qdyyz5EAB_xREqvwGI-YRl66kQwCxJs-dHDl9vRozGgRTMfmstXs) ; Feb 15 2019 (https://twitter.com/HaitiInfoProj/status/1096629898762829824?fbclid=IwAR37Azm-bxaJX_1b0v5p2d-FDWhN2DE2M-nGGqRKSTP-0Co9phPD88zZW9fGo)

148 Five heavily armed U.S. 'mercenaries' were arrested in Haiti. Why were they allowed to fly straight home?, Feb 21 2019 (https://nationalpost.com/news/world/five-heavily-armed-u-s-mercenaries-were-captured-in-haiti-why-were-they-allowed-to-fly-straight-home)

149 Paul Szoldra, Former Navy SEAL arrested on weapons charges in Haiti says he was doing security work tied to Haiti's president, Feb 22 2019 (https://taskandpurpose.com/chris-osman-haiti-statement)

150 Richard Sanders, A Very Canadian Coup: The top 10 ways that Canada aided the 2004 coup in Haiti and helped subject Haitians to a brutal reign of terror, Apr 1 2010 (https://www.policyalternatives.ca/publications/monitor/very-canadian-coup) ; Canada feared popular uprising in Haiti after quake, Canadian Press, Mar 31 2011 (https://www.ctvnews.ca/canada-feared-popular-uprising-in-haiti-after-quake-1.625850)

151 Sandra Lemaire, Haiti Policemen Protest Demanding Better Work Conditions, Union, Oct 28 2019 (https://www.voanews.com/americas/haiti-policemen-protest-demanding-better-work-conditions-union) ; Oct 20 2019 (https://twitter.com/madanboukman/status/1186034239495725061?fbclid=IwAR3JD61Bgn-HimZVsqSQP2ZcEiWNxtrknenjKI212ifKiVSySZ-6tJvhR-VQw)

152 Jonathan Watts, Brazil minister ousted after secret tape reveals plot to topple President Rousseff, May 23 2016 (https://www.theguardian.com/world/2016/may/23/brazil-dilma-rousseff-plot-secret-phone-transcript-impeachment)

153 Canada to Continue Advancing Common Ties With Brazil Amid Impeachment, Sep 2 2016 (https://sputniknews.com/politics/201609021044874721-canada-brazil-ties-impeachment/)

154 Joint statement on the launch of negotiations toward a comprehensive free trade agreement between Canada and the Mercosur member states, Mar 9 2018 (https://www.international.gc.ca/trade-commerce/trade-agreements-accords-commerciaux/agr-acc/mercosur/joint_statement-declaration_commune.aspx?lang=eng)

155 Third Canada-Brazil Strategic Partnership Dialogue to be held in Ottawa, Global Affairs Canada, News release, Oct 22 2018 (https://www.canada.ca/en/global-affairs/news/2018/10/third-canada-brazil-strategic-partnership-dialogue-to-be-held-in-ottawa.html)

156 Oct 23 2018 (https://twitter.com/cafreeland/status/1054792365121175552?lang=ca)

157 Helder Marinho, Brazil's Lula Leaves Office With 83% Approval Rating, Folha Says, Dec 19 2010 (https://www.bloomberg.com/news/articles/2010-12-19/brazil-s-lula-leaves-office-with-83-approval-rating-folha-says)

158 Stephanie Nolen, Brazilian general sets country on edge by hinting of military intervention if courts rule in favour of former president, Apr 4 2018 (https://www.theglobeandmail.com/world/article-brazilian-general-sets-country-on-edge-by-hinting-of-military/)

159 Caroline Orr, It turns out Trudeau wasn't snubbed by Bolsonaro, July 5 2019 (https://www.nationalobserver.com/2019/07/05/analysis/it-turns-out-trudeau-wasnt-snubbed-bolsonaro)

160 Chris Arsenault, What a far-right Bolsonaro presidency in Brazil means for Canadian business, Oct 26 2018 (https://www.cbc.ca/news/world/brazil-canada-trade-bolsonaro-politics-foreign-policy-1.4878379)

161 Ibid

162 Jonathan Watts, Nicaragua president re-elected in landslide amid claims of rigged vote, Nov 7 2016 (https://www.theguardian.com/world/2016/nov/07/nicaragua-president-daniel-ortega-reelected-landslide-vote-rigging) ; Kevin Zeese and Nils McCune, Correcting The Record: What Is Really Happening In Nicaragua?, Popular Resistance, July 10 2018 (https://popularresistance.org/correcting-the-record-what-is-really-happening-in-nicaragua/)

163 Yorlis Gabriela Luna, The Other Nicaragua, Empire and Resistance, COHA, Oct 2 2019 (http://www.coha.org/the-other-nicaragua-empire-and-resistance/?eType=EmailBlastContent&eId=9e0d-5c5c-66bf-4275-8610-fe60c05c0c0b)

164 Ibid

165 Ibid

166 Nicaragua Has Lowest Murder Rate in Central America: UN, July 9 2019 (https://www.telesurenglish.net/news/Nicaragua-Has-Lowest-Murder-Rate-in-Central-America-UN-20190709-0010.html)

167 Frances Robles, Ortega vs. the Contras: Nicaragua Endures an '80s Revival, Mar 7 2016 (https://www.nytimes.com/2016/03/08/world/americas/ortega-vs-the-contras-nicaragua-endures-an-80s-revival.html) ; Jonathan Watts, Nicaragua president re-elected in landslide amid claims of rigged vote, Nov 7 2016 (https://www.theguardian.com/world/2016/nov/07/nicaragua-president-daniel-ortega-reelected-landslide-vote-rigging)

168 Ibid

169 Drazen Jorgic and Ismael Lopez, Once allies, Nicaragua's elite aim to unseat Ortega, Reuters, Nov 22 2019 (https://www.euronews.com/2019/11/22/once-allies-nicaraguas-elite-aim-to-unseat-ortega)

170 Max Blumenthal, US Gov. Meddling Machine Boasts of 'Laying the Groundwork for Insurrection' in Nicaragua, June 19 2018 (https://thegrayzone.com/2018/06/19/ned-nicaragua-protests-us-gov-

ernment/)

171 Nicaragua Honors Police Killed During US-backed Protests, June 13 2019 (https://www.telesurenglish.net/news/Nicaragua-Honors-Police-Killed-During-US-backed-Protests--20190613-0007.html)

172 Frances Robles, Ortega vs. the Contras: Nicaragua Endures an '80s Revival, Mar 7 2016 (https://www.nytimes.com/2016/03/08/world/americas/ortega-vs-the-contras-nicaragua-endures-an-80s-revival.html)

173 Canada calls for an end to the violence in Nicaragua, Global Affairs Canada, July 18 2018 (https://www.canada.ca/en/global-affairs/news/2018/07/canada-calls-for-an-end-to-the-violence-in-nicaragua.html) ; Statement by Foreign Affairs Minister on recent deaths in Nicaragua, Global Affairs Canada, Apr 23 2018 (https://www.canada.ca/en/global-affairs/news/2018/04/statement-by-foreign-affairs-minister-on-recent-deaths-in-nicaragua.html)

174 Canada imposes sanctions on Nicaraguan officials, Global Affairs Canada, News release, June 21 2019 (https://www.canada.ca/en/global-affairs/news/2019/06/canada-imposes-sanctions-on-nicaraguan-officials.html)

175 Catherine Tsalikis, For women foreign ministers and activists, a historic first in Montreal, Sept 25 2018 (https://www.opencanada.org/features/women-foreign-ministers-and-activists-historic-first-montreal/)

176 Third Canada-Brazil Strategic Partnership Dialogue to be held in Ottawa, Global Affairs Canada, News release, Oct 22 2018 (https://www.canada.ca/en/global-affairs/news/2018/10/third-canada-brazil-strategic-partnership-dialogue-to-be-held-in-ottawa.html)

177 Manuel Sandoval Cruz, After the OAS Report on Nicaragua, What's Next?, Dec 1 2019 (https://havanatimes.org/opinion/after-the-oas-report-on-nicaragua-whats-next/)

178 Juan Carlos Bow, OAS Reviews Report on Abuses by Ortega Regime in Nicaragua, Nov 29 2019 (https://confidencial.com.ni/oas-reviews-report-on-abuses-by-ortega-regime-in-nicaragua/)

179 Ibid

180 Evan Dyer, As a government crackdown in Nicaragua got bloodier, Ottawa quietly cut off aid, Apr 14 2019 (https://www.cbc.ca/news/politics/nicaragua-sandinista-protests-aid-trudeau-1.5096042)

181 Canadian sanctions amended in relation to Nicaragua Ukraine Venezuela and Yemen, Dentons, June 28 2019 (https://www.dentons.com/en/insights/alerts/2019/june/28/canadian-sanctions-amended-in-relation-to-nicaragua-ukraine-venezuela-and-yemen)

182 United States and Canada Announce Financial Sanctions to Address the Ongoing Repression in Nicaragua, Media Note, June 21 2019 (https://www.state.gov/united-states-and-canada-announce-financial-sanctions-to-address-the-ongoing-repression-in-nicaragua/)

183 Anatoly Kurmanaev and Cesar Del Castillo, How an Unknown Female Senator Came to Replace the Bolivian President Evo Morales, Nov 24 2019 (https://www.nytimes.com/2019/11/24/world/americas/how-an-unknown-female-senator-came-to-replace-the-bolivian-president-evo-morales.html)

184 Bolivia interim gov't proposes election bill as death toll mounts, Nov 21 2019 (https://www.aljazeera.com/news/2019/11/bolivia-interim-govt-proposes-election-bill-death-toll-mounts-191120222432439.html)

185 Ekaterina Blinova, Media Censorship & OAS' Participation in Election Process May Ruin Bolivia's Democracy, Jan 15 2020 (https://sputniknews.com/analysis/202001151078037535-media-censorship--oas-participation-in-election-process-may-ruin-bolivias-democracy---journo/?fbclid=IwAR3dcdvkomKGmg1vhfvC6763TfjoSePcdtpxpFhDzRq8s-JNqeDQFJ5CCWqY)

186 Canada welcomes results of OAS electoral audit mission to Bolivia, Global Affairs Canada, Nov 10 2019 (https://www.canada.ca/en/global-affairs/news/2019/11/canada-welcomes-results-of-oas-electoral-audit-mission-to-bolivia.html)

187 Evan Dyer, Canada calls for new vote after disputed Bolivian election, Oct 29 2019 (https://www.cbc.ca/news/politics/canada-bolivia-election-fraud-1.5339777)

188 Ibid

189 Prime Minister Justin Trudeau speaks with the President of Chile, Sebastián Piñera, Oct 29 2019 (https://pm.gc.ca/en/news/readouts/2019/10/29/prime-minister-justin-trudeau-speaks-president-chile-sebastian-pinera)

190 Statement of the OAS Electoral Observation Mission in Bolivia, Press Release E-085/19, Oct 21 2019 (https://www.oas.org/en/media_center/press_release.asp?sCodigo=E-085/19)

191 Karan Gill, The Bolivian Coup: Part 1, Nov 27 2019 (https://rubiconpolitics.com/master-blog/the-bolivian-coup-part-1)

192 Guillaume Long, David Rosnick, Cavan Kharrazian and Kevin Cashman, What Happened in Bolivia's 2019 Vote Count?, Nov 2019 (http://cepr.net/publications/reports/bolivia-elections-2019-11)

193 Anthony Faiola and Rachelle Krygier, Bolivia's Morales resigns amid scathing election report, rising protests, Nov 10 2019 (https://www.washingtonpost.com/world/bolivia-to-hold-new-elections-after-protests-and-international-criticism/2019/11/10/4778e842-03b2-11ea-ac12-3325d49eacaa_story.html)

194 Special Meeting of the Permanent Council, Nov 12 2019 (https://www.youtube.com/watch?v=KklG3V3PZTQ&feature=youtu.be)

195 Morales lost Bolivia after shock mutiny by police, Reuters, Nov 14 2019 (https://o.canada.com/pmn/business-pmn/morales-lost-bolivia-after-shock-mutiny-by-police/wcm/bffa67f3-15e9-

4cca-b7dd-292ea7d685e0)

196 Special Meeting of the Permanent Council, Nov 12 2019 (https://www.youtube.com/watch?v=K-klG3V3PZTQ&feature=youtu.be)

197 Canada and the US "Ministry of Colonies", PV Editorial Board, Nov 13 2019 (http://peoplesvoice.ca/2019/11/13/canada-and-the-us-ministry-of-colonies/?fbclid=IwAR0LJFjSzWopgCwLy9CjalaBF9f_UCAGCgrmElhfFwrOjpBiaAOC5t_w9r8)

198 Canada welcomes results of OAS electoral audit mission to Bolivia, Global Affairs Canada, Nov 10 2019 (https://www.canada.ca/en/global-affairs/news/2019/11/canada-welcomes-results-of-oas-electoral-audit-mission-to-bolivia.html)

199 Dave Sherwood, Support for Chile's Pinera lowest for president since Pinochet era: poll, Oct 27 2019 (https://www.reuters.com/article/us-chile-protests/support-for-chiles-pinera-lowest-for-president-since-pinochet-era-poll-idUSKBN1X60NW)

200 Chile: Amnesty International announces research mission to document grave human rights violations, Oct 24 2019 (https://www.amnesty.org/en/latest/news/2019/10/chile-investigacion-para-documentar-violaciones-derechos-humanos/)

201 Ibid ; 2019–20 Chilean protests (https://en.wikipedia.org/wiki/2019–20_Chilean_protests) ; Chile army declares curfew, president reverses fare hikes after unrest, Oct 19 2019 (https://www.reuters.com/article/us-chile-protests/chile-army-declares-curfew-president-reverses-fare-hikes-after-unrest-idUSKBN1WY0EZ)

202 Prime Minister Justin Trudeau speaks with the President of Chile, Sebastián Piñera, Oct 29 2019 (https://pm.gc.ca/en/news/readouts/2019/10/29/prime-minister-justin-trudeau-speaks-president-chile-sebastian-pinera)

203 Trudeau, Chile's Pinera speak before APEC and climate summits cancelled, Canadian Press, Oct 30 2019 (https://www.ctvnews.ca/politics/trudeau-chile-s-pinera-speak-before-apec-and-climate-summits-cancelled-1.4662892)

204 Prime Minister Justin Trudeau meets with the President of Chile Sebastián Piñera, Apr 14 2018 (https://pm.gc.ca/en/news/readouts/2018/04/14/prime-minister-justin-trudeau-meets-president-chile-sebastian-pinera)

205 Rodrigo Almonacid, le champion du retour de la droite dure en Colombie, Agence France-Presse, Le Soleil, June 17 2018 (https://www.lesoleil.com/actualite/monde/ivan-duque-le-champion-du-retour-de-la-droite-dure-en-colombie-0c14633534a-1c515a3754cc76e62cabd)

206 Canada congratulates Colombia's president-elect, Global Affairs Canada, June 18 2018 (https://www.canada.ca/en/global-affairs/news/2018/06/canada-congratulates-colombias-president-elect-following-election-victory.html)

207 Aug 7 2018 (https://twitter.com/justintrudeau/status/1027005311603953664?lang=en)

208 Sep 25 2018 (https://twitter.com/justintrudeau/status/1044720272627167232?lang=en)

209 Edith M. Lederer, UN: 2019 most violent year for ex-rebels since Colombia deal, Associated Press, Jan 2 2020 (https://www.570news.com/2020/01/02/un-2019-most-violent-year-for-ex-rebels-since-colombia-deal/)

210 Colombia: 'Staggering number' of human rights defenders killed in 2019, Jan 14 2020 (https://news.un.org/en/story/2020/01/1055272)

211 Ibid

212 Evan Dyer, Southern discomfort: How the unrest roiling Latin America is making headaches for Trudeau, Oct 31 2019 (https://www.cbc.ca/news/politics/justin-trudeau-latin-america-1.5341927)

213 Jordan Press, Trudeau touts benefits of freer trade in Argentina visit, Canadian Press, Nov 17 2016 (https://www.theglobeandmail.com/news/politics/trudeau-looks-to-gain-foothold-in-argentina-as-investment-rules-open-up/article32884355/)

214 Muhammad Ali, Pivoting from 'Merica to Mercosur, June 19 2018 (https://ipolitics.ca/2018/06/19/pivoting-from-merica-to-mersocur/)

215 Evan Dyer, Southern discomfort: How the unrest roiling Latin America is making headaches for Trudeau, Oct 31 2019 (https://www.cbc.ca/news/politics/justin-trudeau-latin-america-1.5341927)

3. Loving Monarchies, Hating Palestinians — Middle East

Is it progressive to ignore or even justify the suffering, dispossession and killing of Palestinians? Is it progressive to be a close ally of a government that proudly proclaims itself to be the state of only one religion/ethnic group and passes laws that discriminate against millions of its citizens? Is it progressive to sell billions of dollars of military equipment to anti-democratic, absolute monarchies?

***

The record is clear. Trudeau has pursued pro-Israel, US, and Gulf monarchy policies to the detriment of Palestinians, Yemenis and most ordinary people in the Middle East.

The Liberals have enabled Palestinian dispossession and subjugation. They largely ignored Israel's brutal blockade of Gaza, demolition of Palestinian homes in the West Bank and East Jerusalem and growing Jewish supremacy inside its 1948 borders. From the law of return to the nation state law, over 65 Israeli laws discriminate against non-Jews. In March 2019 Prime Minister Benjamin Netanyahu wrote, "Israel is not a state of all its citizens. According to the basic nationality law we passed, Israel is the nation state of the Jewish people – and only it."[1]

The Trudeau government has repeatedly isolated Canada from world opinion on Palestinian rights. They voted against dozens of UN resolutions, supported by most of the world, upholding the long-oppressed people's rights. In December 2017 Canada sided with the US, Israel and some tiny Pacific island states in opposing a UN resolution supporting Palestinian statehood that was backed by

176 nations.² Two years later 157 states adopted a resolution titled "Israeli settlements in the Occupied Palestinian Territory, including East Jerusalem, and the occupied Syrian Golan." Canada joined five other countries voting against it.³

The Trudeau Liberals may have had the most anti-Palestinian voting record of any recent Canadian government. In an August 2018 *Canadian Jewish News* article Montréal Liberal MP Anthony Housefather boasted about the Trudeau government's anti-Palestinian voting record at the UN. He wrote, "we have voted against 87% of the resolutions singling out Israel for condemnation at the General Assembly versus 61% for the Harper government, 19% for the Martin and Mulroney governments and 3% for the Chrétien government. We have also supported 0% of these resolutions, compared to 23% support under Harper, 52% under Mulroney, 71% under Martin and 79% under Chretien."⁴

The Liberals repeatedly expressed their fidelity to Israel. During an Israel Council on Foreign Relations gathering Freeland declared, "Canada's commitment to Israel's security is unwavering and ironclad."⁵ At the November 2018 event alongside Prime Minister Benjamin Netanyahu, Freeland added that if Canada won a non-permanent seat on the UN Security Council in 2020 it would act as an "asset for Israel."⁶

When Shimon Peres died in September 2016 Trudeau attended the "Butcher of Qana's" funeral.⁷ In 1996 Prime Minister Peres ordered the shelling of Qana, which killed 106 civilians in the Lebanese village, half of whom were children.⁸ Through his long political career, reported Patrick Martin, Peres "was deeply implicated in many of the foulest historical crimes associated with the establishment, expansion and militarization of the state of Israel."⁹ Peres' role in dispossessing Palestinians didn't stop the Trudeau government from gushing with praise after he passed away. "The whole country of Canada is supporting the whole country of Israel," Dion told the press.¹⁰

A month later Dion criticized the UN Educational, Scientific and Cultural Organization (UNESCO) for defending Palestinian rights.[11] The foreign minister also criticized the UN Human Rights Council for appointing University of Western Ontario law professor Michael Lynk as "Special Rapporteur on Palestine."[12]

The Liberals largely ignored Israeli violence against Palestinians. But, they often expressed outrage when Israelis occupying Palestinian lands were harmed. In December 2018 Freeland tweeted, "horrified by the shooting in the West Bank in which eight people — including a Canadian and his wife — were injured."[13] On another occasion Global Affairs stated, "Canada condemns the attack and murder of two citizens of Israel in the West Bank today. Our hearts go out to their families and to the injured. May their memories be a blessing. Terror and violence can never be justified."[14]

Six months later Global Affairs tweeted, "Canada condemns the barrage of rocket attacks from Gaza into Israel by Hamas and other terrorist groups, which have killed and injured civilians. This indiscriminate targeting of civilians is not acceptable. We call for an immediate end to this violence."[15] The statement was a response to an Israeli killed by rockets fired from Gaza at the same time seven Palestinians were killed in the open-air prison by the Israeli military.[16] In the year before the May 2019 statement 200 Palestinians were killed and another 5,000 injured by live fire in peaceful March of Return protests in Gaza.[17] Not a single Israeli died during these protests.[18] Where were the Global Affairs tweets condemning Israel?

In an October 2019 story titled "Is Canada's Ambassador to Israel an Anti-Palestinian Racist?" Dimitri Lascaris reported on 423 tweets and retweets issued by Trudeau appointee Deborah Lyons:

"In those tweets: Lyons has disseminated fifteen condemnations of attacks by Palestinians on Israelis, but not once has she condemned or expressed a modicum of concern about an attack by Israelis on Palestinians; On only one occasion did Lyons tweet or retweet a comment that was remotely critical of Israel; On September 19, Lyons praised Israel's former President Shimon Peres — a war criminal — as a 'great man;' Lyons tweeted or retweeted 24 tweets by or about CIJA and/or the Canadian Jewish Political Affairs Committee (CJPAC), whose core function is to promote the Israeli government's agenda in Canada; By contrast, Lyons has tweeted or retweeted only one tweet from a pro-Palestinian organization; that tweet was issued by Jewish Voice for Peace, but it related to a terrorist attack in New Zealand and had nothing to do with Israel's relentless abuse of Palestinian human rights; and Lyons retweeted a tweet praising Theodor Herzl, the founder of political Zionism, a racist ideology. Yet Lyons' one tweet that was modestly critical of Israel's government did not relate to the settlements, annexation or Israel's wanton murder and maiming of Palestinian civilians in Gaza and the West Bank. Rather, that tweet was an expression of the Canadian government's purported 'regret' that Israel had unilaterally terminated the mandate of a temporary observer force in the Palestinian city of Hebron, where Israel is brazenly committing the crime of apartheid."[19]

In January 2020 Lyons held an event at the embassy in Tel Aviv to celebrate Canadians fighting for Israel. They invited all 78 Canadians in the Israeli military to an event to demonstrate the embassy's appreciation. Referring to non-Israelis who join the IDF, Lyons told the *Jerusalem Post*, "Canadian lone soldiers are a particularly special group … This is something we want to do on a yearly basis to show our support."[20] At the event Canada's ambassador said, "we both share a love of Canada and a love of Israel. We at the embassy are very proud of what you're doing."[21]

Further enabling its illegal occupation, the Liberals "modernized" Canada's two-decade-old Free Trade Agreement (FTA) with Israel that allows products from West Bank settlements to enter Canada duty-free. International trade minister Jim Carr boasted the new accord "strengthens bilateral ties between Canada and Israel."[22] Liberal MPs on Parliament's Standing Committee on International

Trade rejected an NDP amendment to the trade accord's legislation stipulating its implementation "shall be based on respect for human rights and international law."[23] They also rejected an NDP amendment to the deal that would have required distinct labels on products originating from "Palestinian territory that has been illegally occupied since 1967."[24]

In July 2019 Palestine Liberation Organization Executive Committee member Hanan Ashrawi wrote, "the Palestinian leadership calls on the Canadian government to act in accordance with Canadian and international laws and amend, without delay, the Canada-Israel Free Trade Agreement Implementation Act (Bill C-85), which affords products originating from illegal Israeli settlements tariff free status, in flagrant violation of Canada's obligations under international law, including the Fourth Geneva Convention, and United Nations Security Council resolutions, including resolution 2334 (2016)."[25]

In July 2017 the federal government said its FTA with Israel trumped Canada's Food and Drugs Act after the Canadian Food Inspection Agency called for accurate labelling of wines produced in the occupied West Bank. After David Kattenburg repeatedly complained about inaccurate labels on two wines sold in Ontario, the CFIA notified the Liquor Control Board of Ontario (LCBO) that it "would not be acceptable and would be considered misleading" to declare wines produced in the Occupied Palestinian Territories as "products of Israel".[26] Quoting from longstanding official Canadian policy, CFIA noted that "the government of Canada does not recognize Israel's sovereignty over the territories occupied in 1967."[27] In response to pressure from the Israeli embassy, Centre for Israel and Jewish Affairs and B'nai Brith, the government announced that it was all a mistake made by a low level CFIA official and that the Canada-Israel FTA governed the labelling of such wine, not CFIA rules. "We did not fully consider the Canada-Israel Free Trade Agreement," a terse CFIA statement explained. "These wines adhere to the Agreement and therefore we can confirm that the products in question can be sold as currently labeled."[28]

In other words, the government publicly proclaimed that the FTA trumps Canada's consumer protections. But, this was little more than a pretext to avoid a conflict with B'nai B'rith, CIJA and Israeli officials, according to Canadian Centre for Policy Alternatives Trade and Investment Research Project director Scott Sinclair. "This trade-related rationale does not stand up to scrutiny," Sinclair wrote. "The Canadian government, the CFIA and the LCBO are well within their legal and trade treaty rights to insist that products from the occupied territories be clearly labeled as such. There is nothing in the CIFTA [Canada–Israel FTA] that prevents this. The decision to reverse the CFIA's ruling was political. The whole trade argument is a red herring, simply an excuse to provide cover for the CFIA to backtrack under pressure."[29]

In July 2019 the Federal Court ruled against the government's decision to allow wines produced on illegal settlements in the West Bank to be labeled as "Products of Israel". The Liberals refused to accept the court's sensible ruling that respected consumer rights and international law. Ignoring pleas from the NDP and Greens to stop wasting taxpayer money on their anti-Palestinian agenda, the government appealed the decision. Two months after the Liberals appealed the federal court's ruling the highest court in the European Union echoed the Canadian court's position in a decision that targeted one of the wineries Kattenburg complained about.[30]

The Liberals maintained and expanded various other elements of Canada's contribution to Israeli expansionism. Ottawa failed to abrogate the Conservatives' "border management and security" agreement with Israel, even though the two countries do not share a border. Canadian military officials also continued to regularly visit their Israeli counterparts.

The Liberals expanded various scientific collaborations. In September 2018 they launched the Canada-Israel Cyber Security Cooperation for the Energy Sector.[31] Funded by Natural Resources Canada and the Israel Innovation Authority, the initiative financed technology cooperation between Canadian and Israeli firms to improve the cyber resilience of Canada's energy infrastructure.[32] The initiative was an offshoot of the Canada-Israel Industrial Research and Development Foundation, which "stimulates and funds collaborative research and development between companies in both countries."[33] The multimillion dollar Canada-Israel Industrial Research and Development Foundation funded research projects (including many in the "security" field) between the two countries' corporations.[34]

The Liberals also demonized those advocating for a people under occupation. At the start of 2016 the PM and most Liberal MPs supported a Conservative Party call for the House of Commons to "reject the Boycott, Divestment and Sanctions (BDS) movement, which promotes the demonization and delegitimization of the State of Israel." The resolution also "condemned any and all attempts by Canadian organizations, groups or individuals to promote the BDS movement, both here at home and abroad."[35]

As part of its 2019 anti-racism strategy, the Liberals formally adopted the International Holocaust Remembrance Alliance's (IHRA) definition of antisemitism.[36] Seven of the 11 examples in the IHRA definition focus on discussion of Israel.[37] Even the drafter of what became the IHRA definition of antisemitism repudiated it. In 2018 US attorney Kenneth S. Stern charged that his original definition had been turned into a device to restrict debate and in December 2019 he wrote an op-ed *The Guardian* headlined "I drafted the definition of anti-Semitism. Right-wing Jews are weaponizing it."[38]

The explicit aim of the Liberal MPs pushing the IHRA's definition of antisemitism was to silence or marginalize those criticizing Palestinian dispossession and supporting the Palestinian civil society led BDS movement.[39] On CTV arch anti-Palestinian MP Anthony Housefather expressed hope that communities might consider the IHRA definition when deciding whether to let critics of Israel use their facilities while others urged universities to incorporate the odious definition in their anti-discrimination policies in the hope it would discipline faculty and students.[40] (In late 2019/early 2020 Palestine solidarity activists convinced Vancouver, Calgary and Montreal to resist efforts to adopt IHRA's definition of antisemitism.)

The PM repeatedly equated supporting Palestinian rights with hatred towards Jews. In January 2019 Trudeau declared "Jewish students still feel unwelcome and uncomfortable on some of our college and university campuses because of BDS-related intimidation."[41] When he apologized for Canada rejecting Jewish World War II refugees in November 2018, Trudeau equated BDS with hate crimes. As Michael Bueckert tweeted, "he used Canada's history of white supremacy to throw Palestinians under the bus."[42]

The PM participated in an unprecedented smear against prominent Palestinian solidarity activist Dimitri Lascaris in September 2018.[43] When Lascaris called on two Liberal MPs to denounce death threats made by B'nai B'rith supporters against a number of racialized Liberal MPs and the prime minister, Trudeau joined a number of Israel lobby groups and individuals in smearing the lawyer as anti-Jewish.

Similar to the Lascaris incident, Trudeau sided with Jewish Defence League thugs who attacked peaceful pro-Palestinian activists protesting a presentation by Israeli military reservists at York University in November 2019.[44] Pro-Israel activists knocked a pro-Palestinian supporter unconscious, attacked York Amnesty International members supporting the Palestinian cause and hurled racial taunts. In an inversion of reality, Trudeau tweeted "violence & racist chants broke out against an event organized by the Jewish community at York University. What happened that night was shocking and absolutely unacceptable. Anti-Semitism has no place in Canada. We will always denounce it & all forms of hatred."[45]

Trudeau linked fighting anti-Semitism to those opposed to Israel's state ideology: Zionism, which led to most Palestinians being ethnically cleansed from their homeland.[46] On Israel Independence Day in 2017 Trudeau delivered a speech by video to a rally in Montréal and published a statement marking the occasion. "Today, while we celebrate Israel's independence, we also reaffirm our commitment to fight anti-Semitism and anti-Zionism", declared the PM.[47]

In 2019 the government released an updated terrorist list.[48] An eighth Palestinian organization was added and the International Relief Fund for the Afflicted and Needy (IRFAN) was re-designated. The first-ever Canadian-based group designated a terrorist organization, IRFAN was listed by the Stephen Harper government for engaging in the ghastly act of supporting orphans and a hospital in the Gaza Strip through official (Hamas controlled) channels.[49]

Each year Canadian taxpayers subsidize hundreds of millions of dollars in charitable donations to Israel despite that country having a GDP per capita only slightly below Canada's. (How many Canadian charities funnel money to Sweden or Japan?) Tens of millions of dollars are also channeled to projects supporting West Bank settlements, explicitly racist institutions and Israel's powerful military, which may all contravene Canadian charitable law.[50] In response to a formal complaint submitted by four Palestine solidarity activists and Independent Jewish Voices Canada in fall 2017, the Canada Revenue Agency (CRA) began an audit of the Jewish National Fund for contravening Canadian charitable law. Despite the JNF openly supporting the Israeli military in explicit contravention of charitable law, at press time this audit has gone on for two years.[51] The CRA undoubtedly faced significant behind-the-scenes pressure to let the JNF off with little more than a slap on the wrist. In 2013 Trudeau attended a JNF gala and other Liberal cabinet ministers participated in more recent events put on by an explicitly racist organization that Liberal MP Michael Leavitt once oversaw.[52] (In a positive step, the Beth Oloth Charitable Organization, which had $60 million in revenue in 2017, had its charitable status revoked for supporting the Israeli military.[53])

The Trudeau government would deny its anti-Palestinianism. They would likely point to their aid to the United Nations Relief and Works Agency for Palestine Refugees (UNRWA) and Palestinians. While it's good they restarted UNRWA funding cut by the Harper Conservatives, their commitment to the organization was doubtful. In November 2019 they abstained on a UN resolution renewing UNRWA's mandate backed by 170 nations and the next month voted against a resolution titled "Operations of the United Nations Relief and Works Agency for Palestine Refugees in the Near East."[54] It was backed by 167 countries.[55]

A major proportion of Canada's "aid" to the Palestinians — who have one-twentieth their occupier's per capita GDP — was explicitly designed to aid Israel. It supported a security apparatus to protect the corrupt Palestinian Authority (PA) from popular disgust over its compliance in the face of Israeli settlement expansion in the West Bank. Through Operation PROTEUS, which contributed to the Office of the United States Security Coordinator, the Canadian military trains Palestinian security forces to suppress "popular protest" against the PA, the "subcontractor of the Occupation". In 2019-20 the military allocated $5 million to Operation PROTEUS.[56] About 20 troops and a handful of RCMP members were part of the long-standing Canadian effort in the West Bank. During the Liberals tenure millions of dollars in Canadian assistance supported Palestinian security forces. In 2018 they initiated the $1.25 million "Empowering the Palestinian Security Sector" and the $1.365 million "Security Sector Capacity Building in the West Bank" projects.[57] According to Global Affairs' description of the latter initiative, "these activities complement the ongoing institutional capacity-building efforts by Operation PROTEUS, Canada's contribution to the United States Security Coordinator."[58]

"There have been increasing references in the past months during high-level bilateral meetings with the Israelis about the importance and value they place on Canada's assistance to the Palestinian Authority, most notably in security/justice reform," read an internal 2012 note signed by then Canadian International Development Agency president Margaret Biggs.[59] In the heavily censored note Biggs explained that "the emergence of popular protests on the Palestinian street against the Palestinian Authority is worrying and the Israelis have been imploring the international donor community to continue to support the Palestinian Authority."[60]

Drawing on previously classified materials, Carleton Criminology Professor Jeffrey Monaghan details Canada's role in turning Palestinian security forces in the West Bank into an effective arm of Israel's occupation. In *Security Aid: Canada and the Development Regime of Security*, Monaghan describes a $1.5 million Canadian contribution to Joint Operating Centers whose "main focus ... is to integrate elements of the Palestinian Authority Security Forces into Israeli command." He writes about Canada's "many funding initiatives to the PCP [Palestinian Civilian Police]" which "has increasingly been tasked by the Israeli Defence Forces as a lead agency to deal with public order policing, most recently during IDF bombings in Gaza and during Arab Spring demonstrations."[61]

In a 2019 assessment of 80 donor reports from nine countries/institutions titled "Donor Perceptions of Palestine: Limits to Aid Effectiveness" Jeremy Wildeman concludes that Canada, the US and International Monetary Fund employed the most anti-Palestinian language. "Canada and the US," the academic writes, "were preoccupied with providing security for Israel from Palestinian violence, but not Palestinians from Israeli violence, effectively inverting the relationship of occupier and occupied."[62]

***

The Trudeau government has largely maintained the Conservatives' support for Saudi Arabia's violent, misogynistic and repressive monarchy. Unions are outlawed in the kingdom and women require a male guardian's permission to pursue a host of activities. Other religions are prohibited, and the House of Saud represses the

Shia Muslim population in the east of the country. All over the Middle East and elsewhere the Saudi royal family uses its wealth to promote a fundamentalist version of Islam and its reactionary politics.

Within six weeks of taking up his post, foreign minister Stéphane Dion met his Saudi counterpart in Ottawa. Adel Al Jubeir was the first foreign minister to make an official visit to Canada after the Liberals' election.[63] According to briefing notes for the meeting, Dion was advised to tell his Saudi counterpart, "I am impressed by the size of our trade relationship, and that it covers so many sectors ... You are our most important trading partner in the Middle East and North Africa (MENA) region."[64] In a further sign of the Liberals aligning with Riyadh, Canada's ambassador, Dennis Horak, said in April 2016 that the two countries have had "nearly similar approaches on Syria, Yemen, Iraq and the Middle East Peace Process."[65]

The Trudeau government sought to deepen ties to the Saudi-led Gulf Cooperation Council (GCC), which included the monarchies of the United Arab Emirates, Bahrain, Oman, Qatar and Kuwait. In May 2016 Dion attended the Canada-GCC Strategic Dialogue in Jeddah. The next year natural resources minister Jim Carr attended the Future Investment Initiative in Riyadh, which included a "Canada briefing" event and significant participation from Canadian financial institutions.[66]

In Spring 2016 the Trudeau government authorized the export permits required for a massive Light Armoured Vehicle (LAV) deal with the Kingdom.[67] Over a decade and a half General Dynamics Land Systems Canada was to deliver about a thousand 28 tonne vehicles equipped with machine guns and medium-or high-calibre weapons.[68] The largest arms (or any other kind) export deal in Canadian history, the $14 billion agreement included vehicle maintenance and training Saudi forces to use the LAVs.[69]

As is often the case with arms exports, the Crown-owned Canadian Commercial Corporation (CCC) brokered and signed the deal.[70] So, the agreement was effectively an Ottawa-Riyadh contract.

Highlighting the political argument employed to justify the LAV sale, the original memo to Dion for the deal characterized Saudi Arabia as "a key partner for Canada, and an important and stable ally in a region marred by instability, terrorism and conflict ... Canada appreciates Saudi Arabia's role as a regional leader promoting regional stability, as well as countering the threat posed by Iranian regional expansionism and ISIS."[71] Global Affairs added that the LAVs would help Riyadh in its efforts at "countering instability in Yemen."

The LAV contract was agreed to one year into the Saudi war against Yemen, which had left 100,000 dead by the end of 2019.[72] Millions were also left hungry and the fighting sparked a cholera epidemic that killed thousands.[73] In early 2015 the Saudis put together a coalition of mostly Gulf monarchies to intervene in Yemen as Houthi rebels from the north of the country drove president Abd-Rabbu Mansour Hadi out of the capital Sana'a. The Saudi-led coalition began to bomb, instigated a naval blockade and then deployed ground forces to Yemen.

On a number of occasions, the Liberals expressed support for Saudi-backed President Hadi. Conversely, they criticized the Houthis. A November 2018 Global Affairs release noted, "we are deeply concerned about the worsening treatment of Bahá'ís in Yemen, particularly by the Houthis in Sana'a."[74]

The Liberals mostly ignored Saudi violence in Yemen. From when they took office through November 2018 their only direct condemnation of the bombing was an October 2016 statement.[75] It noted, "the Saudi-led coalition must move forward now on its commitment to investigate this incident" after two airstrikes killed over 150 and wounded 500 during a funeral in Sana'a.[76] By contrast when the first person was killed from a rocket launched into the Saudi capital in March 2018 Freeland stated, "Canada strongly condemns the ballistic missile attacks launched by Houthi rebels on Sunday, against four towns and cities in Saudi Arabia, including Riyadh's international airport. The deliberate targeting of civilians is unacceptable."[77] In her release Canada's foreign minister also accepted the monarchy's justification for waging war. "There is a real risk of escalation if these kinds of attacks by Houthi rebels continue and if Iran keeps supplying weapons to the Houthis", noted Freeland.[78]

Ottawa also aligned with Riyadh's war aims on other occasions. With the $14 billion LAV sale to the monarchy under a court challenge in late 2016, federal government lawyers described Saudi Arabia as "a key military ally who backs efforts of the international community to fight the Islamic State in Iraq and Syria and the instability in Yemen. The acquisition of these next-generation vehicles will help in those efforts, which are compatible with Canadian defence interests."[79] In early 2020 the Canadian Embassy's website continued to claim, "the Saudi government plays an important role in promoting regional peace and stability."[80]

In an odd twist the Liberals were given a unique opportunity to turn the highest-profile stain on their 'principled, feminist, foreign policy' into a human rights image boosting campaign. In August 2018 Riyadh freaked out over an innocuous tweet from the Canadian Embassy in Riyadh, announcing the suspension of diplomatic ties, withdrawal of medical students and sale of assets in Canada.

Saudi Arabia's over-the-top response to a tweet calling for the release of civil society activists gave the Liberals a unique opportunity to distance Canada from the violent, misogynistic and repressive regime. But, they failed to seize the occasion. In fact, internal government documents uncovered by PhD researcher Anthony Fenton demonstrate that the Liberals repeatedly sought to mend relations with Riyadh. Despite the diplomatic spat, the Trudeau government mostly continued business as usual with the most powerful and repressive monarchy in the region. In December 2018 *HMCS Regina* assumed command of a 33-nation Combined Maritime Forces naval coalition patrolling the region from Saudi Arabia.[81] According to an access to information request by Fenton, Freeland phoned new Saudi foreign minister Ibrahim Abdulaziz Al-Assaf in January 2019. In briefing notes for the (unannounced) discussion Freeland was encouraged to tell her counterpart (under the headline "points to register" regarding Yemen): "Appreciate the hard work and heavy lifting by the Saudis and encourage ongoing efforts in this regard."[82] In September 2019 Freeland said publicly, "Saudi Arabia is an important partner for Canada and we continue to work with Saudi Arabia on a number of different issues at a number of different levels."[83]

After Crown Prince Mohammad bin Salman's (MBS) thugs killed and dismembered journalist Jamal Khashoggi in October 2018, Trudeau treaded carefully regarding the murder.[84] Ten days after the Canadian Press reported, "the prime minister said only that Canada has 'serious issues' with reports the Washington Post columnist was killed by Saudi Arabian operatives inside Saudi Arabia's consulate in Turkey."[85] Six weeks later the Liberals sanctioned 17 Saudi nationals over the issue but none of them were in positions of significant authority.[86]

Foreign minister Freeland looked the other way when Saudi student Mohammed Zuraibi Alzoabi fled Canada in 2019 — presumably with help from the embassy — to avoid sexual assault charges in Cape Breton. While Freeland told reporters that Global Affairs was investigating the matter, *Halifax Chronicle Herald* journalist Aaron Beswick's Access to Information request suggested they didn't even bother contacting the Saudi embassy concerning the matter.[87]

In April 2019 the Saudis beheaded 37 mostly minority Shiites. Ottawa waited 48 hours — after many other countries criticized the mass execution — to release a "muted" statement.[88] The Trudeau government stayed mum on the Saudi's effort to derail pro-democracy demonstrations in Sudan and Algeria in 2018/19 as well as Riyadh's funding for Libyan warlord Khalifa Haftar's bid to seize Tripoli by force.[89]

Throughout 2018 and 2019 large shipments of Canadian weaponry were delivered to Saudi Arabia. The year 2018 set a record for Canadian rifle and armoured vehicle sales to the Saudis.[90] Over $17 million in rifles were exported to the kingdom in 2018 and a similar amount in 2019.[91] Canada exported $2 billion worth of "tanks and other armoured fighting vehicles" to the Saudis in 2019.[92]

As Fenton documented in detail, armoured vehicles made by Canadian company Streit Group in the UAE were repeatedly videoed in Yemen.[93] Equipment from three other Canadian armoured vehicle makers — Terradyne, IAG Guardian and General Dynamics — was found with Saudi-backed forces in Yemen.[94] Fenton showed many examples of the Saudi-led coalition using Canadian-made rifles as well.

The Liberals said they found no evidence linking Canadian military exports to human rights violations committed by the Saudis.[95] A 2019 Global Affairs review found no "credible" link between arms exports to the Saudis and human rights abuses even though the April 2016 memo to Dion originally approving the LAV export permits claimed they would assist Riyadh in "countering instability in Yemen."[96]

Training and arming the monarchy's military while refusing to condemn its brutal war in Yemen should be understood for what it was: War profiteering and enabling of massive human rights abuses.

***

In fact, Trudeau diplomats and the Canadian Commercial Corporation (CCC) promoted arms sales to Saudi Arabia and other GCC monarchies bombing Yemen. In February 2018 Deputy Director of Gulf States Relations at Global Affairs, Louise Corbin, attended a Saudi arms bazaar with representatives of General Dynamics Land Systems.[97] Throughout the ongoing Liberal reign Global Affairs and CCC officials have helped firms flog their wares at the annual Abu Dhabi-based International Defence Exhibition and Conference (IDEX). In 2019, 50 Canadian arms companies received support from "15 trade commissioners and representatives from the Government of Ontario, National Defence, Global Affairs Canada, and the Canadian Commercial Corporation."[98] To help the arms companies move their products, commander of the Bahrain-based Combined Task Force 150, Commodore Darren Garnier, led the Canadian military delegation to IDEX.[99]

In January 2016 Canada's ambassador to Kuwait Martine Moreau and a CCC executive assisted CAE in its outreach to the Kuwaiti government.[100] As that country's air force bombed Yemen, the Montréal flight simulation firm provided equipment to train its pilots on KC-130J tanker aircraft.[101]

In February 2018 Parliamentary Secretary to the Minister of Innovation, Science and Economic Development, David Lametti, promoted Bombardier's delivery of surveillance planes to the UAE.[102] The Bombardier-Saab plane was used in the war on Yemen.

CAE trained UAE and Saudi Air Force pilots at a facility in Abu Dhabi.[103] The Montréal based firm also (secretly) trained Saudi pilots at a US base in Pensacola, Florida.[104] UAE and Saudi pilots also trained at NATO's Flying Training in Canada, which was run by CAE and the Canadian Forces in Alberta and Saskatchewan.[105]

Despite their contribution to the horrendous violence in Yemen, the Trudeau government deepened ties to the UAE, a federation of seven Emirates. Domestically, the UAE is a repressive monarchy that outlaws labour unions and hangs or stones individuals to death.[106] The country heavily restricts religious freedoms and women's rights. In summer 2019 the wife (one of six) of Dubai's ruler, Sheikh Mohammed bin Rashid Al Maktoum, sought asylum in the UK fearing for her life.[107]

A small number of Canadian troops are stationed in the UAE and Royal Canadian Navy vessels regularly coordinate with their Emirati counterparts.[108] Canada's ambassador in Abu Dhabi, Masud Husain, and defence minister Sajjan met UAE defence minister Mohammed bin Ahmed Al Bowardi on multiple occasions.[109] After an April 2019 meeting between Sajjan and Al Bowardi the Emirates News Agency reported that they discussed "cooperation in the military and defence sectors" and "current regional and international developments."[110] In December 2017 Sajan signed the Canada-UAE Defence Cooperation Arrangement.[111] According to Radio Canada International, the accord "will make it easier for the Canadian defence industry to access one of the world's most lucrative arms markets."[112]

In January 2020 Trudeau held a telephone call with Abu Dhabi's Crown Prince Mohammed bin Zayed to discuss regional developments and strengthening bilateral ties.[113] On July 1, 2019, officials from the two countries highlighted "the bond between Canada and the United Arab Emirates" by raising a Canadian flag-inspired display on Abu Dhabi's Burj Khalifa, the world's tallest building.[114] A week later international trade minister Jim Carr announced that Canada would participate in Expo 2020 Dubai.[115] Two weeks later they signed a memorandum of understanding regarding diplomatic and consular missions at the second session of the UAE-Canada Consular Committee.[116]

The Liberals deepened Canada's ties to a monarchy that pursued violent, anti-democratic policies in its region. The UAE propped up the Transitional Military Council in Sudan that faced massive protests calling for civilian rule. Two months after President Omar al-Bashir fell in April 2019, the oil rich country put up half of a $3 billion package with Saudi Arabia to support Sudan's military rulers. Many pro-democracy activists believed the UAE and Saudi Arabia pushed Sudan's military to destroy a major protest site that left dozens dead at the start of June 2019.[117]

Abu Dhabi feared democracy in Sudan for various reasons. One immediate concern was the likelihood that a government in Khartoum representing the popular will would withdraw the more than 10,000 Sudanese soldiers in Yemen.[118]

In Libya the UAE delivered weapons to warlord Khalifa Haftar in violation of UN sanctions.[119] Abu Dhabi financed and supported Haftar's bid to seize the Libyan capital by force.[120] The Tripoli-based Government of National Accord said a UAE F-16 fighter jet was responsible for bombing a migrant detention centre that left some 50 people dead in July 2019.[121]

From what I could find the Trudeau government stayed mum on Abu Dhabi's efforts to derail democracy in Sudan. Nor did they comment on its violation of UN sanctions in Libya and they barely made a peep about the UAE's bombing and troops in Yemen. Instead of challenging the monarchy's egregious policies, the Liberals deepened ties to the Gulf Kingdom.

The Liberals also expanded military and business relations with other less belligerent, though still repressive, Gulf monarchies. They pushed to increase military ties with the family that has ruled Kuwait for 250 years.[122] In December 2019 and again in January 2020 Harjit Sajjan traveled to Kuwait City to meet his Kuwaiti counterpart.[123] Eight months earlier Sajjan met Prime Minister and Defence Minister Sheikh Nasser Sabah Al-Ahmad Al-Sabah who oversaw a country where questioning the Amir or Islam is punishable with a significant prison sentence.[124] Sajjan's aim was "to bolster and consolidate bilateral ties."[125] Relations with Kuwait were important to the government due to the Canadian Forces base there.[126] About 200 Canadians were stationed in Kuwait to support the special forces deployed to Iraq.

The inaugural Kuwait and Canada Investment Forum took place in 2019. Finance minister Bill Morneau and Parliamentary Secretary Omar Alghabra participated.[127] At the time Alghabra wrote, "let's celebrate and continue our efforts to grow the relationship between Canada and Kuwait in investments, trade and defence."[128] In November 2019 Governor General Julie Payette sent a cable to Kuwait's Amir to wish him well after an illness and the next month Assistant Deputy Minister of Global Affairs Peter McDougall met a Kuwaiti counterpart "to strengthen bilateral relations." In August 2018 the two countries signed a memorandum of understanding on establishing regular consultations between senior officials.[129]

To the east the government negotiated a Defence Cooperation Arrangement with Bahrain, a small island nation ruled by a 220-year-old monarchy.[130] The Sunni rulers of the predominately Shia country executed pro-democracy activists, including Ahmad al-Malali and Ali Hakim al-Arab in July 2019. The UN, Amnesty International and Human Rights Watch denounced the killings, but Ottawa stayed silent.[131] Not long after the state murder, the Director-General of Middle East at Global Affairs, Sandra McCardell, met foreign minister Shaikh Khalid bin Ahmed bin Mohammed Al Khalifa. McCardell reportedly "expressed Canada's aspiration for enhancing and developing friendly [relations] with the Kingdom of Bahrain. She also appreciated the efforts exerted by the Kingdom to establish security and stability in the region."[132]

In a March 2019 interview with local media, Ambassador Stefanie McCollum boasted of growing relations between Canada and Qatar, which was ruled by a 100-year-old monarchy. She even claimed, "our values structures are very similar."[133] Five months earlier McCollum met the head of Qatar's military, Hazza bin Khalil Al Shahwani, and in December 2016 ten Canadian troops were deployed to a US base in the kingdom to operate the Unclassified Remote-Sensing Situational Awareness satellite system, which monitored maritime traffic in the Persian Gulf, Arabian Sea and Indian Ocean.[134]

At the start of 2020 Canadian General A. R. Day directed the Combined Aerospace Operations Center at the US military's Al Udeid base in Qatar.[135] Alongside two-dozen Canadian soldiers supporting US-led operations in Qatar, Bahrain and UAE, 200 Canadians were stationed in Kuwait and a Canadian frigate was nearby.[136] Approximately 500 Canadian soldiers were in Iraq. In November 2019 Governor General Julie Payette gave medals to a half dozen Canadians who recently served in military operations in the Middle East.[137]

During an April 2019 visit to Jordan, Sajjan discussed military cooperation with Jordan's King Abdullah II bin Al-Hussein.[138]

That month the Canadian and Jordanian armed forces broke ground on a road project along Jordan's border with Syria. During a ceremony for the Canadian-funded initiative, Commander of the Canadian Joint Operations Command, Lieutenant General Michael Rouleau, said: "this important road rehabilitation project is a tangible example of the close relationship between Jordan and Canada. It will help keep the people of Jordan [stay] safe by allowing the Jordanian armed forces to deter, monitor and interdict incursions along the northern border with Syria, which will help to enhance security in Jordan and in the region."[139]

Trudeau repeatedly met or spoke with Jordan's Abdullah II. In January 2020 the prime minister phoned a monarch known for prosecuting individuals for "extending one's tongue" (having a big mouth) against the King.[140] He met him seven months earlier in Paris and in November 2019 Abdullah II visited Canada "to discuss further strengthening the partnership between Canada and Jordan."[141] At the time Trudeau praised the King: "I really have to say that His Majesty has been extraordinary in being such a strong leader at a time of so much uncertainty, whether it's on refugees, or on human rights, or on economic growth and opportunities, you really have a tremendous, tremendous strong voice, and Canada is incredibly proud to be such a good friend to Jordan."[142]

To the west the Liberals barely mentioned the human rights violations by Abdel-Fattah al-Sisi's regime in Egypt. The general took charge through a bloody 2013 coup, killing and arresting thousands. In April 2018 al-Sisi won 97% of the vote for president. Eight months later Liberal MP Robert Oliphant led a Canada-Africa Parliamentary Association delegation to Egypt. The association's subsequent report whitewashed the regime's human rights violations.[143] During a May 2019 meeting with al-Sisi, Liberal Senate Speaker George Furey discussed boosting Canada-Egypt cooperation.[144] Previously Foreign Minister Dion traveled to Cairo to meet al-Sisi in May 2016.[145]

In February 2019, Oakville, Ontario's Yasser Ahmed Albaz was arbitrarily detained as he sought to fly home from Cairo. It took significant campaigning by his family before the Trudeau government raised his case publicly.[146]

In July 2019 Egypt's Emigration and Expatriate Affairs Minister Nabila Makram told a Toronto gathering in Arabic that anyone who criticized Egypt would be "sliced up".[147] Makram's comments were met with laughter from the audience, which included parliamentary secretary to the international trade minister Omar Alghabra. Afterwards Alghabra failed to denounce the Egyptian minister's comments.[148]

The Liberals' friendly relations with repressive Middle East monarchies demonstrates how little they care about democracy abroad. Their military action reveals their willingness to participate in war and disregard for a rules-based international order.

***

The Trudeau government withdrew Canadian bombers from a US-led Iraq/Syria mission that was instigated in October 2014 purportedly to counter the ISIS/Daesh/Islamic State. More precisely, they failed to renew the mission since the jets were withdrawn in February 2016, a month before the planned end of the 18-month commitment. At the same time the Liberals maintained two reconnaissance aircraft and an in-air refueling tanker to support a mission that had bombed Syria without Damascus' permission, a contravention of international law.

As they withdrew the fighter jets, the Trudeau government tripled the number of special forces on the ground in the region. A tactical helicopter detachment, intelligence officers and a combat hospital were in Iraq alongside more than 200 Canadian special forces.[149] Two hundred Canadians at a base in Kuwait supported the ground and air forces in Iraq.

Despite being labeled a "training" mission, the Canadians called in US airstrikes, provided up-to-date battle intelligence and repeatedly engaged the enemy. A Canadian even killed someone with a record-breaking 3.5-kilometre sniper shot.[150]

After February 2016 the Canadian Air Force did all air-based refueling for the US-led coalition. They also provided intelligence to US jets that led to the killing of thousands of civilians. According to a joint Amnesty International/Airwars investigation, 1,600 civilians were killed in the Syrian city of Raqqa by coalition airstrikes and artillery shelling in mid 2017.[151] Many thousands more died in Mosul. An Associated Press investigation concluded that 9,000 to 11,000 civilians were killed in the nine-month battle to free Iraq's second biggest city from ISIS control in 2017.[152] AP attributed a third of the casualties to US bombing and allied Iraqi forces, a third to Daesh and a third were unattributed.

The Canadian Forces in Iraq backed Kurdish Peshmerga forces that fought to take Mosul. The *Globe and Mail* reported, "Canadian Armed Forces members are playing a modest but vital supporting role as the operation to retake Mosul, the last major stronghold of Islamic State militants in Iraq, gets under way."[153]

Two hundred and ten highly skilled Canadian special forces soldiers helped the Peshmerga. They guided coalition airstrikes and reportedly blew up Daesh vehicles on the outskirts of Mosul.[154] A Canadian military hospital was set up on the outskirts of the city to treat Kurdish fighters and CP-140 Aurora spy planes gathered intelligence on targets to bomb. The secretive 21 Electronic Warfare Regiment also aided the fight, intercepting and deciphering enemy communications.[155]

Mosul was heavily damaged. Eighteen months after Daesh's fall, director of Amnesty International UK Kate Allen wrote: "Never before have I seen a city so completely devastated. Not just in one district area, but almost entirely. Think Dresden and you'd be close. Street after street of windowless, hollowed-out buildings. Miles of rubble. Piles of twisted metal. Utter ruin. There has been no assistance for residents desperate to rebuild, and entire families are reduced to living in bombed-out husks of buildings. Meanwhile, many children spend all day scavenging in the rubble for bits of steel and plastic they can sell so as to buy food."[156]

Few residents returned to the city. In response to the displacement and lack of reconstruction, Taylor asked "if it was not the residents of Mosul ... then who exactly were Canadian soldiers supposed to be liberating?"[157]

Beyond the wonton destruction of Mosul, the alliance with the Kurds raised other troubling questions. Kurdish forces ethnically cleansed some areas they captured and didn't want to give up territory. After the fall of Mosul "things went horribly, but predictably, wrong", noted Taylor.[158] The Kurds began fighting units loyal to the central government in Baghdad, which Ottawa purported to support. In September 2017 the Kurdish government in the north organized a regional referendum on independence that sparked an invasion of some Kurdish controlled areas by Iraq's central government.

In November 2015 Global Affairs warned Trudeau about the potential consequences of supporting the Kurds. "Should the (Daesh) threat recede," the officials wrote in an internal briefing note, "Baghdad will have to contend with a range of land disputes with the (Kurdish regional government), as well as strengthened Iraqi Kurdish forces, which have received training and equipment from coalition members, including Canada."[159]

Despite the warning, the Canadian military ramped up support for the Kurds in 2016. Concerned about the Peshmerga's growing strength, the Iraqi government blocked some Canadian weapons shipment to the Kurds and detained a Canadian military plane delivering weapons to Canadian special forces in northern Iraq.[160]

Alongside the special forces and air support operations, Canada assumed command of the NATO Mission Iraq in November 2018. A Canadian commanded 580 NATO troops, including 250 Canadians. They trained instructors at three military schools and advised Iraq's defence ministry.

In late 2019 Iraqi security forces, including military members, killed hundreds of antigovernment protesters.[161] The primary demand of the protest was an end to foreign dominance of the country's affairs whether Iranian or American. In response to questions about Canada's role in the violence, commander of the NATO mission in Iraq, Major-General Jennie Carignan, told the *Globe and Mail* "we can see there is some work to do on how [Iraqi officials] structure and organize themselves for crisis management." In a column titled "Stop propping up brutal Baghdad regime", Taylor derided Carignan's observation that there was room for improvement as out of touch.[162]

The Liberals failed to properly explain why Canada took on a second mission in Iraq. But, it was likely tied to weakening the influence of the Iranian aligned Popular Mobilization Forces, Shia militias that helped defeat ISIS. According to Taylor, "Canada agreed to take command of the NATO-led training mission in Iraq because the Liberal government knew it could not sell the Canadian public on sending troops back into the war in Afghanistan. That is where the NATO leaders wanted Canadians, which seems an incredibly ironic twist in that we originally agreed to go into Afghanistan because it was not Iraq."[163]

To date the Liberals have ploughed hundreds of millions, probably a billion, dollars into the military's efforts in Iraq.[164] In 2016 alone the armed forces spent $306 million on its operations there.[165] The 2019 federal budget committed $1.4 billion over two years to its Middle East Strategy.[166] "Between 2016 and 2021," noted the Global Affairs website, "Canada is investing up to $3.5 billion to respond to the crises in Iraq and Syria, and address their impact on Lebanon, Jordan and the region."[167]

The Trudeau government also continued the previous government's low-level support for regime change in Syria. It provided aid to groups opposed to Bashar al Assad and supported US missile strikes. Trudeau maintained sanctions on Syria and its designation as a state sponsor of terror. It also provided intelligence aircraft and air-to-air refuelling for US jets that bombed Syria.[168] The approximately 200 Canadian special forces in Iraq may have also entered Syria.

Hundreds of thousands have been killed in the tragic Syrian conflict. Millions more have been displaced in the messy, multilayered war.

Thousands of US, British, French and Turkish troops were in the country in contravention of the UN charter while Israel bombed Syria hundreds of times and continued to occupy part of its territory.[169] The CIA spent over a billion dollars backing anti-Assad groups.[170] Saudi Arabia and Qatar ploughed billions of dollars of weaponry and other forms of support to opposition insurgents. They supported extremist Sunni groups tied to Al Qaeda.[171]

On the other side, Iran, Hezbollah and Russia backed the Syrian government. Russia provided air power while Iran and Hezbollah dispatched thousands of fighters.

The Trudeau government repeatedly criticized Russia, Hezbollah and Iran's interventions, which were endorsed by Syria's internationally recognized government. The Liberals put out dozens of statements critical of the Syrian government's human rights violations. A father to son dictatorship, Bashar al-Asaad's government was undoubtedly responsible for significant rights abuses. But, Ottawa largely ignored rights violations committed by the opposition. Throughout the Liberals time in office it was clear the opposition largely consisted of sectarian extremists. The Al Qaeda-linked groups were responsible for horrendous killings of religious minorities and others.[172] There was little comment from Ottawa.

Simultaneously, they ignored the US, Saudi and Israel's role in the conflict. Instead, they deepened ties to Israel and the US and ramped up weapons sales to the Gulf monarchies that armed anti-government forces in Syria.

A December 2015 Global Affairs release praised Riyadh's efforts in Syria. Dion noted, "Canada commends Saudi Arabia's leadership in convening this broad and representative group of 116 participants from among the Syrian opposition who — despite their major differences — yesterday agreed upon the structure of the negotiating delegation that will represent them in the anticipated UN-led peace talks."[173] Five months later ambassador, Dennis Horak, told Saudi officials Ottawa and Riyadh had "nearly similar approaches on Syria."[174]

Trudeau supported US cruise missile strikes on a Syrian military base in April 2018. In a statement the prime minister said, "Canada supports the decision by the United States, the United Kingdom, and France to take action to degrade the Assad regime's ability to launch chemical weapons attacks against its own people."[175]

Ottawa also helped lay the foundation for the US-led attack. Twenty-four hours after the alleged April 7, 2018, chemical attack Freeland put out a statement claiming, "it is clear to Canada that chemical weapons were used and that they were used by the Assad regime."[176] In subsequent months Canada's envoy to the Organization to Prohibit Chemical Weapons (OPCW), Sabine Nolke, repeated this position.[177] But, Russia and Syria immediately claimed the chemical attack in Douma was staged.[178] And they offered evidence to back up their claims, including an interview with one of the purported victims.[179] On the surface of it, the Syrian government's motive to employ chemical weapons wasn't strong. With the capture of Douma imminent, the Syrian government would have gained little by employing chemical weapons. On the other hand, they risked a great deal. A chemical attack could precipitate greater US intervention, which would benefit anti-Assad forces.

The OPCW's initial report on the Douma incident suggested the Syrian government was responsible for the chemical attack. Then two whistleblowers and a stash of internal documents revealed that the OPCW management ignored or rewrote reports suggesting the April 2018 Douma incident was staged. In May 2019 a member of the OPCW Fact Finding Mission in Syria, Ian Henderson, released a document claiming the organization misled the public about the purported chemical attack in Douma. It showed that the management suppressed an assessment that contradicted the claim that a gas cylinder fell from the air.[180] In November another OPCW whistleblower added to Henderson's revelations, saying his conclusion that the incident was "a non chemical-related event" was twisted to imply the opposite.[181] Then in December 2019 WikiLeaks released a series of internal documents demonstrating that the team who wrote the OPCW's report on Douma didn't go to Syria.[182] One memo noted that 20 OPCW inspectors felt the report that was released "did not reflect the views of the team members that deployed to [Syria]."[183]

Instead of expressing concern over political manipulation of evidence, Canada's representative to the OPCW criticized the leak. In a statement after Henderson's position was made public Nolke noted, "Canada remains steadfast in its confidence in the professionalism and integrity of the FFM [Fact-Finding Mission] and its methods. However, Mr. Chair, we are unsettled with the leak of official confidential documents from the Technical Secretariat."[184]

It makes sense Ottawa was concerned about the OPCW's credibility as they pushed the organization to blame Assad for chemical attacks given that Syria joined the OPCW and had its declared chemical weapon stockpile destroyed in 2013-14.[185] So, Canadian officials ploughed tens of millions of dollars into the OPCW, including substantial contributions to its Trust Fund for Syria Missions. A June 2017 Global Affairs release boasted that "Canada and the United States are the largest national contributors to the JIM [OPCW-UN Joint Investigative Mechanism for Attributing Responsibility for Chemical Weapons Attacks in Syria]."[186] The statement also said Canada "is the largest voluntary cash contributor to the organization, having provided nearly $25 million since 2012 to help destroy chemical weapons in Libya and Syria and to support special missions and contingency operations related to chemical weapons use, investigation, verification and monitoring in Syria."

A year later Freeland announced another $7.5 million contribution to the OPCW in a statement largely focused on Syria titled "Canada welcomes OPCW actions to counter impunity for use of chemical weapons."[187] During an August 2019 "meeting focused on OPCW activities in Syria" with the organization's Director-General Fernando Arias, Governor-General Julie Payette boasted about "$23 million in voluntary funds for Syria-related activities" that Canada contributed.[188]

The White Helmets produced the probably staged video purporting to show chemical weapons use in Douma. In a release about the purported attack in Douma, Freeland expressed Canada's "admiration for ... the White Helmets", later calling them "heroes."[189] Credited with rescuing people from bombed out buildings, the White Helmets fostered opposition to Assad and promoted western intervention. They operated almost entirely in areas of Syria occupied by the Saudi–Washington backed Al Nusra/Al Qaeda insurgents and other rebels.[190] They criticized the Syrian government and disseminated images of its purported violence while largely ignoring those people targeted by the opposition. Their members were repeatedly photographed with Al Qaeda-linked Jihadists and reportedly enabled executions they carried out.[191]

The White Helmets helped establish an early warning system for airstrikes that benefited opposition insurgents. Framed as a way to save civilians, the 'Sentry' system tracked and validated information about potential airstrikes.[192]

Canada funded the Hala Systems air strike warning system, which benefited opposition fighters. It's unclear how much Canadian money was put into the initiative but in September 2018 Global Affairs boasted that "Canada is the largest contributor to the 'Sentry' project."[193] Additionally, Vancouver mining magnate Frank Giustra, a close ally of Bill Clinton, provided early financing for Hala Systems, which was set up by former Syria focused US diplomat John Jaeger.[194] In September 2019 Vanessa Beeley wrote, "Hala Systems converted the White Helmets into a paramilitary surveillance agency providing an early warning system for the armed groups dominated by Al Qaeda."[195]

The Liberals provided significant support to the White Helmets. In December 2016 they announced $4.5 million for the group and in March 2018 Global Affairs announced "$12 million for groups in Syria, such as the White Helmets, that are saving lives by providing communities with emergency response services and removing explosives."[196] The White Helmets received tens of millions of dollars from the US, British, Dutch, German and French governments.[197] They were closely associated with the Syria Campaign, which was set up by a British billionaire of Syrian descent, Ayman Asfari, actively opposed to the Assad regime.[198] The co-founder of the White Helmets, James Le Mesurier, was a former British army officer and private security contractor.

White Helmet representatives repeatedly came to Ottawa to meet government officials and Canadian officials helped members of the group escape Syria via Israel in July 2018. The effort required complicated, high-level negotiations with the Israeli government. As part of the effort, Canada committed to resettling about 150 members of the White Helmets and their families. A year after the highly publicized Israeli expedition the *Globe and Mail* revealed that 48 White Helmet members and their families who were supposed to come to Canada languished in a camp in Jordan.[199] According to the *Globe*, they "were flagged as security risks by Canadian officials" partly because of their "affiliations with the myriad groups that have fought in the civil war."[200] *Globe* reporter Mark McKinnon was not allowed to enter the secure part of camp Azraq where the White Helmets were held.

Turkey-based Canadian diplomat Robin Wettlaufer organized the complicated White Helmet evacuation effort as the Syrian army regained territory in the south-west Daraa governorate. Wettlaufer was Canada's Special Representative to the Syrian Opposition.[201] Wettlaufer told the Trek, a UBC alumni publication, "we connect in many different ways with the Opposition, the whole host of parties opposed to the Assad regime, including through social media."[202] Trek described Wettlaufer as someone who "typifies the next generation of Foreign Service Officers and a new kind of diplomacy that focuses on new partners and approaches. Wettlaufer says her role 'focuses on the grass roots [where] the progress is often incremental and long term,' saying it has involved 'bringing rebel groups together, promoting cooperation and negotiation, talking to the opposition, to youth, to religious leaders, and finding ways to strengthen the voices of democracy and moderation.'"[203]

***

The Liberals repeatedly promised to restart diplomatic relations with Iran. Before becoming PM Trudeau told the CBC, "I would hope that Canada would be able to reopen its mission [in Tehran]."[204] In March 2016 Foreign Minister Dion said, "Canada's severing of ties with Iran had no positive consequences for anyone: not for Canadians, not for the people of Iran, not for Israel, and not for global security."[205]

But this was another broken promise. The Liberals dialed down the previous government's most bombastic rhetoric against Tehran, but they did not restart diplomatic relations or remove that country from Canada's state sponsor of terrorism list. They also maintained several sanctions on Iran. With the US, Saudis and Israel generally antagonistic to Iran, Trudeau continued important components of the Harper government's 'low-level war' against Iran.

The Trudeau government criticized Iranian human rights abuses while mostly ignoring more flagrant Saudi rights violations. In January 2018 Freeland said, "Canada is deeply troubled by the recent deaths and detentions of protesters in Iran" and four months later tweeted, "our government is committed to holding Iran to account for its violations of human and democratic rights."[206] In November 2019 Global Affairs stated, "Iran must ensure that its people enjoy the rights and freedoms they deserve. Canada supports the Iranian people who are exercising these rights, including the freedom of expression and assembly."[207]

Under the Liberals Ottawa continued to present a yearly UN resolution critical of the human rights situation in Iran.[208] In response to Canada targeting it, Iran's Deputy Representative to the UN, Eshaq Al-e Habib, said in November 2019, "how can a supporter of apartheid in Palestine pose itself as a human rights defender in Iran?"[209]

Similarly, Liberal MPs participated in the annual "Iran Accountability Week" on Parliament Hill, which showcased individuals such as Foundation for the Defense of Democracies CEO Mark Dubowitz, who helped kill the Iran nuclear deal and pushed harsh sanctions against any country doing business with Iran.[210] Dubowitz was a senior research fellow at the University of Toronto's Munk School of Global Affairs.[211] In 2015 Global Affairs gave the Munk School's Digital Public Square $9 million to expand an anti-Iranian initiative, which the Trudeau government maintained.[212]

After the Trump administration withdrew from the "p5+1 nuclear deal" with Iran in May 2018 and re-imposed tough new sanctions, the Liberals increasingly echoed the warmongers in Washington and Tel Aviv. In June 2018 Liberal parliamentarians supported a Conservative MP's private member's motion that "strongly condemns the current regime in Iran for its ongoing sponsorship of terrorism around the world, including instigating violent attacks on the Gaza border."[213] In effect, the resolution made Iran responsible for Israel killing Palestinians peacefully protesting the US moving its embassy to Jerusalem, siege of Gaza and historic theft of their land. The motion also called on Canada to "immediately cease any and all negotiations or discussions with the Islamic Republic of Iran to restore diplomatic relations" and to make the highly provocative move of listing the Islamic Revolutionary Guard Corps as a terrorist entity.

While they ostensibly backed the Iran nuclear deal, the Liberals' promoted a one-sided view of the 2015 Joint Comprehensive

Plan of Action (JCPOA) between Iran and the US, France, Germany, Russia and China. Canada put up more than $10 million for the International Atomic Energy Agency (IAEA) to monitor and verify Iran's implementation of its commitments under the JCPOA. Iran was consistently in compliance with JCPOA's strict rules regarding its uranium enrichment. Nonetheless, the Donald Trump administration withdrew from the JCPOA in May 2018 and imposed sanctions on other countries' companies doing business with Iran.

For their part, the Western European signatories to the agreement largely failed to stand up to US pressure by creating the space for their companies to do business with Iran and in January 2020 the UK, Germany and France delivered a further blow to an agreement on life support. In a release titled "Canada supports diplomatic efforts established for Iran to return to full implementation of Joint Comprehensive Plan of Action", Global Affairs expressed "support" for the UK, Germany and France "activating the Dispute Resolution Mechanism" under the JCPOA and "urged Iran to immediately restore its full commitments to the JCPOA."[214] But, this position amounted to calling on Iran to be the only party to abide by the deal while its economy was crippled by sanctions.

The Liberals also legitimated the illegal US sanctions on Iran when they arrested Huawei's chief financial officer, Meng Wanzhou, at the Vancouver airport in December 2018. The US claimed Meng's company defied its illegal sanctions against Iran. But, between when the US judicial system sought her detention and the Trump administration requested Ottawa detain her, Meng traveled to six countries with US extradition treaties.[215] Only Canada arrested her.

At the military level Ottawa also aligned with the US-Saudi-Israeli axis stoking conflict with Iran. One aim of the Canada-Gulf Cooperation Council Strategic Dialogue was to isolate Iran. A communiqué after the May 2016 Canada-GCC ministerial meeting expressed "serious concerns over Iran's support for terrorism and its destabilizing activities in the region."[216] Similarly, an April 2016 Global

Affairs memo authorizing Light Armoured Vehicle export permits to the House of Saud noted, "Canada appreciates Saudi Arabia's role as a regional leader promoting regional stability, as well as countering the threat posed by Iranian regional expansionism."[217] At the November 2019 Dubai International Air Chiefs Conference the Commander of the Royal Canadian Air Force, Al Meinzinger, participated in a panel titled "Watch out Iran!"[218] A year earlier Chief of the Defence Staff Jonathan Vance told a parliamentary committee that Iran was "an interested party and, in some cases, a malign agent in Iraq."[219]

Five hundred Canadian troops were in Iraq partly to counter Iranian influence. Specifically, the Canadian-led NATO Mission Iraq was designed to weaken the influence of the Iranian aligned Popular Mobilization Forces.

In the fall of 2019 Canada seized and sold $28 million worth of Iranian properties in Ottawa and Toronto to compensate individuals in the US who had family members killed in a 2002 Hamas bombing in Israel and others who were held hostage by Hezbollah in 1986 and 1991.[220] The Supreme Court of Canada and federal government sanctioned the seizure under the 2012 Justice for Victims of Terrorism Act, which lifts immunity for countries labeled "state sponsors of terrorism" to allow individuals to claim their non-diplomatic assets.

Iranian Foreign Ministry Spokesman Seyyed Abbas Mousavi called the seizure "illegal" and in "direct contradiction with international law" while a spokesperson for Iran's Guardian Council, Abbasali Kadkhodaei, accused Canada of "economic terrorism".[221] A senior member of Iran's parliament said the country's military should confiscate Canadian shipments crossing the Strait of Hormuz.[222]

In a right side up world, the Iranian asset sale would lead to various more legitimate seizures. Relatives of the Lebanese-Canadian el-Akhras family Israel wiped out, including four children aged one to eight, in 2006 were certainly at least as worthy of Canadian government-backed compensation.[223] Ditto for Paeta Hess-Von Kruedener, a Canadian soldier part of a UN mission, killed by an Israeli fighter jet in Lebanon in 2006.[224] Or Palestinian-Canadian Ismail Zayid, who was driven from a West Bank village demolished to make way for the Jewish National Fund's Canada Park.[225]

In Haiti there were hundreds, maybe thousands, of individuals whose family members were killed at peaceful protests by a police force paid, trained and politically supported by Canada after US, French and Canadian troops overthrew the country's elected president in 2004.[226] Ten months after the coup I met a young man in Port-au-Prince who fled the country after armed thugs searching for him came to his house and killed his aunt. Before the coup Jeremy had been a journalist with the state television, which was identified with the ousted government. Should US or Canadian assets be seized to compensate him?

There are hundreds of Canadians and countless individuals elsewhere who have been victimized by Israeli, Canadian and US-backed terror more deserving of compensation than the Americans paid with Iranian assets for what Hamas and Hezbollah purportedly did decades ago. Should Israeli, US and Canadian government assets be seized to pay them?

The Trudeau government failed to speak against the asset seizure. It could have undercut this obscenity by delisting Iran as a "state sponsor of terror" or repealing Harper's Justice for Victims of Terrorism Act. But, it didn't even keep its promise to restart diplomatic relations with Iran. As such, the Liberals have empowered US-Israeli hawks hurtling towards a major conflict.

While there is much to dislike about the government in Tehran, supporting the arbitrary withdrawal from agreements, stealing foreign governments' assets and engaging in threats of war make a mockery of a rules-based international order.

But this hypocrisy of claiming to support certain principles while doing the opposite is matched by the duplicity of the Liberals' rhetoric and policies towards Russia, which is the subject of the next chapter.

Chapter 3 Notes

1 Benjamin Netanyahu says Israel is 'not a state of all its citizens', AFP, Mar 10 2019 (https://www.theguardian.com/world/2019/mar/10/benjamin-netanyahu-says-israel-is-not-a-state-of-all-its-citizens)

2 Tovah Lazaroff, 176 nations at UN call for Palestinian statehood, Dec 20 2017 (https://www.jpost.com/Arab-Israeli-Conflict/176-nations-at-UN-call-for-Palestinian-statehood-518535)

3 Israeli settlements in the Occupied Palestinian Territory, including East Jerusalem, and the occupied Syrian Golan : resolution/adopted by the General Assembly 2019 (https://digitallibrary.un.org/record/3839967?ln=en) ; General Assembly Adopts 8 Resolutions on Middle East, including Text Urging States Not to Recognize Changes on Status of Jerusalem, Pre-1967 Borders (https://www.un.org/press/en/2019/ga12220.doc.htm) ; UN General Assembly Votes in Favor of 8 Resolutions on Palestine Nov 17 2018 (http://imemc.org/article/un-general-assembly-votes-in-favor-of-8-pro-palestine-resolutions/)

4 Anthony Housefather, Liberal MP defends his party's record on Israel and Jewish community, Aug 28 2018 (http://www.cjnews.com/perspectives/opinions/liberal-mp-defends-his-partys-record-on-israel-and-jewish-community)

5 Mike Blanchfield, Israel has Canada's 'unwavering and ironclad' support, Freeland says in speech, Canadian Press Nov 1 2018 (https://nationalpost.com/news/world/israel-middle-east/freeland-affirms-ironclad-support-of-israel-following-pittsburgh-murders)

6 Jennifer Tzivia MacLeod, Canada's support for Israel is 'ironclad,' Foreign Minister says, Nov 2 2018 (https://www.cjnews.com/news/canada/canadas-support-for-israel-is-ironclad-foreign-minister-says?fbclid=IwAR3R5HM5O3Et24Iq6iwVwFDrr-4zuB2l5Zg25SiCOQJHbu_TvFd-O2kdXgi0)

7 Robert Fisk, The Butcher of Qana: Shimon Peres Was No Peacemaker, Sept 29 2016 (https://www.counterpunch.org/2016/09/29/the-butcher-of-qana-shimon-peres-was-no-peacemaker/)

8 Ibid

9 Patrick Martin, Shimon Peres (1923-2016), Oct 1 2016 (https://www.wsws.org/en/articles/2016/10/01/obit-o01.html)

10 Trudeau leads Canadian delegation to Peres funeral in Israel, Canadian Press, Sept 29 2016 (https://www.thestar.com/news/canada/2016/09/29/trudeau-leaves-ottawa-for-peres-funeral-in-israel.html)

11 Janice Arnold, Stephane Dion slams latest UNESCO resolution on Jerusalem, Oct 27 2016 (https://www.cjnews.com/news/canada/dion-slams-latest-unesco-resolution-jerusalem)

12 Dion questions appointment of Canadian as UN human rights advisor, Canadian Press, Mar 26 2016 (https://www.macleans.ca/news/canada/dion-questions-canadian-appointment-as-un-human-rights-advisor/)

13 Janice Arnold, Montreal family mourns infant victim of West Bank terrorism, Dec 13 2018 (https://www.cjnews.com/news/canada/montreal-family-mourns-infant-victim-of-west-bank-terrorism)

14 Deborah Lyons, Oct 7 2018 (https://twitter.com/lyonsinisrael/status/1048899851734458368)

15 May 5 2019 (https://twitter.com/canadafp/status/1125058624060104705)

16 Almog Ben Zikri, Jack Khoury, Yaniv Kubovich and Noa Landau, Over 400 Gaza Rockets Fired at Israel; One Israeli Killed, Seven Palestinians, May 5 2019 (https://www.haaretz.com/israel-news/over-400-gaza-rockets-fired-at-israel-one-israeli-killed-seven-palestinians-said-killed-1.7196935)

17 Israeli forces kill Amal a-Taramsi, 44, and 'Abd a-Ra'uf Salahah, 13, in March of Return protests on 11 Jan. 2019, Feb 7 2019 (https://www.btselem.org/firearms/20190207_killing_of_amal_a_taramsi_and_abd_a_rauf_salahah_in_gaza_demonstrations)

18 Gaza protest deaths: Israel may have committed war crimes – UN, Feb 28 2019 (https://www.bbc.com/news/world-middle-east-47399541)

19 Dimitri Lascaris, Is Canada's Ambassador to Israel an Anti-Palestinian Racist?, Oct 14 2019 (https://dimitrilascaris.org/2019/10/14/is-canadas-ambassador-to-israel-an-anti-palestinian-racist/)

20 Anna Ahronheim, Bringing the True North to Canadian lone soldiers in the IDF, Jan 16 2020 (https://www.jpost.com/Israel-News/Bringing-the-True-North-to-Canadian-lone-soldiers-in-the-IDF-614348)

21 Jennifer Tzivia MacLeod, Ambassador welcomes Canadian IDF Lone Soldiers, Jan 20 2020 (https://www.cjnews.com/news/israel/ambassador-welcomes-canadian-idf-lone-soldiers)

22 Minister Carr strengthens bilateral ties between Canada and Israel, News release, Global Affairs Canada, June 24 2019 (https://www.canada.ca/en/global-affairs/news/2019/06/minister-carr-strengthens-bilateral-ties-between-canada-and-israel.html)

23 David Kattenburg, Canada, Israel and the "Rule of Law", Canada Talks Israel/Palestine, Feb 13 2019 (https://canadatalksisraelpalestine.ca/2019/02/13/canada-israel-and-the-rule-of-law/)

24 Ron Csillag, Liberals pass new Israel free trade deal, despite NDP objections, Feb 12 2019 (https://

www.cjnews.com/news/canada/liberals-pass-new-israel-free-trade-deal-despite-ndp-objections)

25   Elad Benari, PLO official welcomes Canadian ruling on Judea and Samaria wine, July 31 2019 (http://www.israelnationalnews.com/News/News.aspx/266727)

26   Brennan Doherty, LCBO asks vendors to stop selling West Bank wines mislabeled as 'Product of Israel', Canadian Press, July 13 2017 (https://www.thestar.com/business/2017/07/13/lcbo-asks-vendors-to-stop-selling-west-bank-wines-mislabelled-as-product-of-israel.html)

27   Paul Lungen, Activist threatens court action over 'Product of Israel' wine labelling, Aug 11 2017 (https://www.cjnews.com/news/canada/activist-threatens-court-action-product-israel-wines)

28   "Product of Israel" Wine Labelling, July 13 2017 (https://www.inspection.gc.ca/food-label-requirements/labelling/product-of-israel-wine-labelling/eng/1499970240524/1499970592331)

29   Scott Sinclair, Politics, not trade, behind Canada's reversal on Israeli wine labelling decision, July 25 2017 (http://behindthenumbers.ca/2017/07/25/politics-not-trade-behind-canadas-reversal-israeli-wine-labelling-decision/)

30   Paul Lungen, EU court deals blow to Psagot's West Bank winery, Nov 14 2019 (https://www.cjnews.com/news/israel/eu-court-deals-blow-to-psagots-west-bank-winery)

31   Launch of Canada-Israel cybersecurity program for energy sector, Global Affairs Canada, News release, Sept 6 2018 (https://www.canada.ca/en/global-affairs/news/2018/09/launch-of-canada-israel-cybersecurity-program-for-energy-sector.html)

32   New Call for Proposals: Canada-Israel Cyber Security Cooperation for the Energy Sector (https://ciirdf.ca/ciirdf-launches-new-call-for-canada-israel-rd-projects-2-2/)

33   (https://ciirdf.ca)

34   Kole Kilibarda, Canadian and Israeli Defense-Industrial and Homeland Security Ties: An Analysis, Nov 2008 (https://www.sscqueens.org/sites/sscqueens.org/files/Canadian%20and%20Israeli%20Defense%20Industrial%20and%20Homeland%20Security%20Ties.pdf)

35   Patrick Martin, Parliament votes to reject Israel boycott campaign, Feb 23 2016 (https://www.theglobeandmail.com/news/world/parliament-votes-to-reject-campaign-to-boycott-israel/article28863810/)

36   Nora Barrows-Friedman, Canada adopts Israel lobby's contested definition of anti-Semitism, June 28 2019 (https://electronicintifada.net/blogs/nora-barrows-friedman/canada-adopts-israel-lobbys-contested-definition-anti-semitism)

37   Ash Sarkar, The IHRA definition of antisemitism is a threat to free expression, Sep 3 2018 (https://www.theguardian.com/commentisfree/2018/sep/03/ihra-antisemitism-labour-palestine)

38   George Wilmers, Why the man who drafted the IHRA definition condemns its use, Aug 1 2018 (https://www.jewishvoiceforlabour.org.uk/article/why-the-man-who-drafted-the-ihra-definition-condemns-its-use/)

39   Anthony Housefather and Michael Levitt, Why Canada's adopting the IHRA definition of Anti-Semitism, June 25 2019 (https://www.cjnews.com/perspectives/opinions/housefather-levitt-why-canadas-adopting-the-ihra-definition-of-anti-semitism)

40   Jeffrey Sachs, Canada's new definition of anti-Semitism is a threat to campus free speech, Sep 10 2019 (https://www.universityaffairs.ca/opinion/in-my-opinion/canadas-new-definition-of-anti-semitism-is-a-threat-to-campus-free-speech/)

41   Patrick Martin, Parliament votes to reject Israel boycott campaign, Feb 23 2016 (https://www.theglobeandmail.com/news/world/parliament-votes-to-reject-campaign-to-boycott-israel/article28863810/) ; TOI STAFF, Trudeau blasts BDS movement as anti-Semitic, Jan 17 2019 (https://www.timesofisrael.com/trudeau-blasts-bds-movement-as-anti-semitic/)

42   Nov 7 2018 (https://twitter.com/mbueckert/status/1060277153835745283?lang=en)

43   Yves Engler, Canadian Zionists' Unprecedented Smear Campaign against Dimitri Lascaris, Sept 10 2018 (http://www.palestinechronicle.com/canadian-zionists-unprecedented-smear-campaign-against-dimitri-lascaris/)

44   Nora Barrows-Friedman, JDL Canada thugs attack York students then cry "anti-Semitism", Nov 26 2019 (https://electronicintifada.net/blogs/nora-barrows-friedman/jdl-canada-thugs-attack-york-students-then-cry-anti-semitism)

45   Ibid

46   Ilan Pappé, The Ethnic Cleansing of Palestine

47   Statement by the Prime Minister of Canada on Israel Independence Day, May 2 2017 (https://pm.gc.ca/en/news/statements/2017/05/02/statement-prime-minister-canada-israel-independence-day)

48   Currently listed entities (https://www.publicsafety.gc.ca/cnt/ntnl-scrt/cntr-trrrsm/lstd-ntts/crrnt-lstd-ntts-en.aspx#42)

49   Yves Engler, Canada's double standard, Jan 1 2013 (https://yvesengler.com/2013/01/01/canadas-double-standard/)

50   Ibid

51   Evan Dyer, Canadian charity used donations to fund projects linked to Israeli military, Jan 4 2019 (https://www.cbc.ca/news/politics/jnf-charity-donations-1.4949072)

52   Sep 18 2013 (https://twitter.com/justintrudeau/status/380384547130449921)

53   Stewart Bell, Government revokes charity status of Canadian Jewish group that supported 'foreign armed forces', Jan 28 2019 (https://globalnews.ca/news/4893430/canada-charity-jewish-group-for-

eig-armed-forces/)

54   Omri Nahmias, Khaled Abu Toameh, Tovah Lazaroff, UN extends UNRWA's mandate for three more years, Nov 16 2019 (https://www.jpost.com/Israel-News/UN-fourth-committee-votes-to-extend-UNRWAs-mandate-607983)

55   (https://www.haaretz.com/middle-east-news/palestinians/despite-israel-u-s-pressure-and-ongoing-probe-un-renews-unrwa-mandate-1.8131376

56   Yves Engler, Canada's Effort to suppress "Popular Protests" against Israeli Occupation, May 5 2017 (https://dissidentvoice.org/2017/05/canadas-effort-to-suppress-popular-protests-against-israeli-occupation/) ; Planned Costs for Major Canadian Armed Forces Operations (https://www.canada.ca/en/department-national-defence/corporate/reports-publications/departmental-plans/departmental-plan-2019-20-index/supporting-documents-index/planned-costs-major-caf-operations.html)

57   Project profile — Empowering the Palestinian Security Sector (https://w05.international.gc.ca/projectbrowser-banqueprojets/project-projet/details/p005189001) ; Project profile — Security Sector Capacity Building in the West Bank (https://w05.international.gc.ca/projectbrowser-banqueprojets/project-projet/details/P005283001)

58   Ibid

59   Israel urged Canadian government not to cut aid to Palestinians over UN vote: documents, July 9 2013 (https://nationalpost.com/news/politics/israel-urged-canadian-government-not-to-cut-aid-to-palestinians-over-un-vote-documents)

60   Ibid

61   Jeffrey Monaghan, In Security Aid: Canada and the Development Regime of Security

62   Jeremy Wildeman, Donor Perceptions of Palestine: Limits to Aid Effectiveness, June 19 2019 (https://al-shabaka.org/commentaries/donor-perceptions-of-palestine-limits-to-aid-effectiveness/)

63   Martin Lukacs, The Trudeau Formula: seduction and betrayal in an age of discontent, 195

64   Vassy Kapelos, Saudi Arabia Canada's 'most important' trading partner in the Middle East: government documents, Mar 30 2016 (https://globalnews.ca/news/2608640/saudi-arabia-canadas-most-important-trading-partner-in-the-middle-east-government-documents/)

65   Ghazanfar Ali Khan, Saudi-Canada relations set to scale new heights, Apr 18 2016 (https://www.arabnews.com/saudi-arabia/news/912026)

66   Oct 10 2018 (https://twitter.com/anthonyfenton/status/1050149030683140096) ; Oct 10 2018 (https://twitter.com/anthonyfenton/status/1050143248608612353) ; Oct 10 2018 (https://twitter.com/anthonyfenton/status/1050143244749819904)

67   Steven Chase, Dion quietly approved arms sale to Saudi Arabia in April: documents, Apr 12 2016 (https://www.theglobeandmail.com/news/politics/liberals-quietly-approved-arms-sale-to-saudis-in-april-documents/article29612233/)

68   Martin Lukacs, The Trudeau Formula: seduction and betrayal in an age of discontent, 196

69   Ibid, 192

70   Ibid, 197

71   Editorial, The Trudeau government's Saudi hypocrisy, Apr 14 2016 (https://www.theglobeandmail.com/opinion/editorials/the-trudeau-governments-saudi-hypocrisy/article29636734/)

72   Hollie McKay, Nearly 100,000 have been killed in ongoing Yemen war, report finds, June 19 2019 (https://www.foxnews.com/world/100000-civilians-killed-yemen-war)

73   2016–19 Yemen cholera outbreak (https://en.wikipedia.org/wiki/2016–19_Yemen_cholera_outbreak)

74   Joint Statement on Bahá'ís in Yemen, Global Affairs Canada, Nov 8 2018 (https://www.canada.ca/en/global-affairs/news/2018/11/joint-statement-on-bahais-in-yemen.html)

75   Oct 16 2018 (https://twitter.com/anthonyfenton/status/1052340922904539137)

76   Canada condemns attack in Yemen and urges rapid investigation, News Release, Global Affairs Canada, Oct 9 2016 (https://www.canada.ca/en/global-affairs/news/2016/10/canada-condemns-attack-yemen-urges-rapid-investigation.html) ; Oct 16 2018 (https://twitter.com/anthonyfenton/status/1052340922904539137) ; 2016 Sanaa funeral airstrike (https://en.wikipedia.org/wiki/2016_Sanaa_funeral_airstrike)

77   Canada condemns attack in Yemen and urges rapid investigation, News Release, Global Affairs Canada, Oct 9 2016 (https://www.canada.ca/en/global-affairs/news/2016/10/canada-condemns-attack-yemen-urges-rapid-investigation.html)

78   Statement by Foreign Affairs Minister on missile attack in Saudi Arabia, Global Affairs Canada, Global Affairs Canada, Mar 27 2018 (https://www.canada.ca/en/global-affairs/news/2018/03/statement-by-foreign-affairs-minister-on-missile-attack-in-saudi-arabia.html)

79   Justin Ling, Canada admits the weapons it sells to Saudi Arabia could be used in Yemen's civil war, Dec 20 2016 (https://www.vice.com/en_ca/article/mb9mvp/canada-admits-the-weapons-it-sells-to-saudi-arabia-could-be-used-in-yemen-civil-war)

80   Embassy of Canada to Saudi Arabia (https://www.canadainternational.gc.ca/saudi_arabia-arabie_saoudite/index.aspx?lang=eng)

81   Todd Coyne, Esquimalt-based HMCS Regina seizes 2.5 tonnes of hash, Apr 10 2019 (https://vancouverisland.ctvnews.ca/esquimalt-based-hmcs-regina-seizes-2-5-tonnes-of-hash-1.4374170?cache=yes%3FclipId%3D375756%3FclipId%3D104062%3FclipId%3D89563)

82   Apr 23 2019 (https://twitter.com/anthonyfen-

ton/status/1120753644171698176)

83 Sep 9 2019 (https://twitter.com/anthonyfenton/status/1171118907295297537)

84 James McCarten, Trudeau treads warily over Khashoggi mystery, Canadian Press, Oct 12 2018 (https://www.thespec.com/news-story/8962870-trudeau-treads-warily-over-khashoggi-mystery-defends-canada-s-criticism-of-saudis/)

85 James McCarten, Trudeau treads warily over Khashoggi mystery, Canadian Press, Oct 12 2018 (https://www.therecord.com/news-story/8962870-trudeau-treads-warily-over-khashoggi-mystery-defends-canada-s-criticism-of-saudis/)

86 Elise von Scheel, Turkey passed up Canada's offer of help with Khashoggi investigation, documents show, Dec 22 2019 (https://www.cbc.ca/news/politics/turkey-canada-khashoggi-investigation-1.5397162)

87 Steve Bartlett, Journalist's work uncovers systemic gaps, Apr 22 (https://www.cbncompass.ca/news/journalists-work-uncovers-systemic-gaps-303973/)

88 Levon Sevunts, Canada issues muted criticism of Saudi mass beheading, Apr 25 2019 (https://www.rcinet.ca/en/2019/04/25/canada-issues-muted-criticism-of-saudi-mass-beheading/)

89 The Sudanese military: A pawn of the Saudis?, Apr 22 2019 (https://www.dw.com/en/the-sudanese-military-a-pawn-of-the-saudis/a-48433645) ; Algeria activist: Saudi, UAE want us to abort popular movement, Mar 12 2019 (https://www.middleeastmonitor.com/20190312-algeria-activist-saudi-uae-want-us-to-abort-popular-movement/) ; Tripoli Jared Malsin and Summer Said, Saudi Arabia Promised Support to Libyan Warlord in Push to Seize, Apr 12 2019 (https://www.wsj.com/articles/saudi-arabia-promised-support-to-libyan-warlord-in-push-to-seize-tripoli-11555077600)

90 20 Feb 2019 (https://twitter.com/anthonyfenton/status/1098458319377690624)

91 6 Mar 2019 (https://twitter.com/anthonyfenton/status/1103365937825144832)

92 Canadian International Merchandise Trade Database, Table 980-0087 87. Domestic exports - Vehicles other than railway or tramway rolling-stock, and parts and accessories thereof (https://www5.statcan.gc.ca/cimt-cicm/topNCountryCommodities-marchandises?country=Saudi+Arabia&lang=eng&chapterId=87&sectionId=0&sectionLabel=XVII+-+Vehicles%2C+aircraft%2C+vessels+and+associated+transport+equipment&refMonth=4&refYr=2019&freq=12&countryId=369&usaState=0&provId=1&dataTransformation=0&arrayId=9800087&commodityId=871000&commodityName=Tanks+and+other+armoured+fighting+vehicles%2C+motorised%2C+and+parts&topNDefault=10&tradeType=1&monthStr=April)

93 14 Oct 2018 (https://twitter.com/anthonyfenton/status/1051538953076015104)

94 15 Oct 2018 (https://twitter.com/anthonyfenton/status/1052005635871539200)

95 Andrew Russell Global News Global Affairs finds no 'credible evidence' linking Saudi arms sales to human rights abuses, Nov 22 2019 (https://globalnews.ca/news/6204472/global-affairs-no-credible-evidence-saudi-arms-sales-human-rights-abuses/)

96 Steven Chase, Dion quietly approved arms sale to Saudi Arabia in April: documents, Apr 12 2016 (https://www.theglobeandmail.com/news/politics/liberals-quietly-approved-arms-sale-to-saudis-in-april-documents/article29612233/)

97 Oct 5 2018 (https://twitter.com/anthonyfenton/status/1048386647996346368)

98 Brett Boudreau, Representing Canada in the UAE IDEX 2019 FrontLine (Vol 16, No 1) (https://defence.frontline.online/article/2019/1/11186-Representing-Canada-in-the-UAE)

99 Feb 19 2019 (https://twitter.com/anthonyfenton/status/1097994150123692032)

100 Steven Chase, Ottawa pushes military deals with Kuwait despite UN concerns, Jan 31 2016 (https://www.theglobeandmail.com/news/politics/ottawa-pushes-military-deals-with-kuwait-despite-un-concerns/article28475526/)

101 Ibid

102 Hugo Joncas, Lametti vantait des avions destinés aux forces émiraties, Jan 18 2019 (https://www.journaldemontreal.com/2019/01/18/lametti-vantait-des-avions-destines-aux-forces-emiraties)

103 Jon Lake, Simulators for the Gulf [IDX15D3], Feb 25 2015 (https://www.janes.com/article/49390/simulators-for-the-gulf-idx15d3) ; CAE awarded contract to provide comprehensive RPA training solution to UAE Air Force & Air Defence, May 8 2017 (https://www.cae.com/news-events/press-releases/cae-awarded-contract-to-provide-comprehensive-rpa-training-solution-to-uae-/)

104 Nicholas Bogel-Burroughs, Pensacola Attack Probed for Terrorism Link. Saudi Suspect Clashed With Instructor, Dec 8 2019 (https://www.nytimes.com/2019/12/08/us/pensacola-gunman.html)

105 David Pugliese, training for the Future RCAF, Volume 24-10, Jan 2 2018 (http://espritdecorps.ca/feature/training-for-the-future-rcaf)

106 Capital punishment in the United Arab Emirates (https://en.wikipedia.org/wiki/Capital_punishment_in_the_United_Arab_Emirates)

107 Julia Webster, Princess Haya, Wife of Dubai's Ruler Sheikh Mohammed Al Maktoum, Is Reportedly Seeking Protection in London, July 3 2019 (https://time.com/5619647/princess-haya-dubai-sheikh-mohammed-al-maktoum-protection-london/) ; Employers Associations and Trade Unions in United Arab Emirates, Dec 16 2013 (https://knowledge.leglobal.org/employers-associations-and-trade-unions-in-united-arab-emirates/)

108 Apr 24 2019 (https://twitter.com/anthonyfenton/status/1121097243837124608)

109 UAE, Canada discuss boosting bilateral ties, WAM Emirates News Agency, July 1 2019 (http://

wam.ae/en/details/1395302771367)

110 Al Bowardi explores cooperation with Canadian counterpart, WAM Emirates News Agency, Apr 21 2019 (http://www.wam.ae/en/details/1395302756967)

111 Government of Canada Signs Defence Cooperation Arrangement with the UAE, National Defence, News Release, Dec 18 2017 (https://www.canada.ca/en/department-national-defence/news/2017/12/government_of_canadasignsdefencecooperationarrangementwiththeuae.html)

112 Levon Sevunts, Canada and UAE sign defence cooperation agreement Dec 18 2017 (https://www.rcinet.ca/en/2017/12/18/canada-and-uae-sign-defence-cooperation-agreement/)

113 Abu Dhabi crown prince speaks with Canada's Trudeau, Germany's Merkel on regional issues, Jan 15 2020 (https://www.arabnews.com/node/1613791/middle-east)

114 Ashfaq Ahmed, National Flag of Canada to light up the Burj Khalifa on July 1 to mark Canada Day, June 27 2019 (https://gulfnews.com/uae/national-flag-of-canada-to-light-up-the-burj-khalifa-on-july-1-to-mark-canada-day-1.1561641402888)

115 Minister Carr announces award of contract for Canada Pavilion at Expo 2020 Dubai, Global Affairs Canada, News release, July 8 2019 (https://www.canada.ca/en/global-affairs/news/2019/07/minister-carr-announces-award-of-contract-for-canada-pavilion-at-expo-2020-dubai.html)

116 UAE-Canada Consular Committee held in Ottawa, WAM Emirates News Agency, July 21 2019 (http://wam.ae/en/details/1395302775513)

117 After bloody attack, Sudan army scraps agreements with protesters, Jun 4 2019 (https://www.aljazeera.com/news/2019/06/bloody-attack-sudan-army-scraps-agreements-protesters-190604005733226.html)

118 Sudan withdraws 10,000 Sudanese soldiers from Yemen, Oct 31 2019 (https://www.middleeastmonitor.com/20191031-sudan-withdraws-10000-sudanese-soldiers-from-yemen/)

119 Daniel Larison, The UAE Is Giving Haftar American Weapons June 29 2019 (https://www.theamericanconservative.com/larison/the-uae-is-giving-haftar-american-weapons/)

120 UN investigation into UAE military role in Libya conflict, May 8 2019 (https://www.middleeastmonitor.com/20190508-un-investigation-into-uae-military-role-in-libyan-conflict/)

121 Ghazi Balkiz, Libya claims UAE bombed migrant center with US-made jet, July 5 2019 (https://www.cnn.com/2019/07/05/africa/libya-uae-migrant-center-intl/index.html)

122 Apr 9 2019 (https://twitter.com/anthonyfenton/status/1115717205444816896)

123 Dec 19 2019 (https://twitter.com/anthonyfenton/status/1207751838256074753)

124 Kuwait at risk of sliding into deeper repression amid growing clampdown on critics, Dec 14 2015 (https://www.amnesty.org/en/latest/news/2015/12/kuwait-at-risk-of-sliding-into-deeper-repression-amid-growing-clampdown-on-critics/)

125 Kuwait- Acting PM meets Canada DM, Kuwait News Agency, Apr 23 (https://menafn.com/1098429099/Kuwait-Acting-PM-meets-Canada-DM)

126 Levon Sevunts, GG visits Canadian troops in Iraq and Kuwait, Jan 21 2019 (https://www.rcinet.ca/en/2019/01/21/gg-visits-canadian-troops-in-iraq-and-kuwait/)

127 Apr 9 2019 (https://twitter.com/anthonyfenton/status/1115717201158213632)

128 Apr 9 2019 (https://twitter.com/anthonyfenton/status/1115717205444816896)

129 Kuwait, Canada in official talks, Kuwait News Agency, Dec 12 2019 (https://menafn.com/1099412922/Kuwait-Canada-in-official-talks)

130 Jul 27 2019 (https://twitter.com/anthonyfenton/status/1155171693121290240)

131 Sondos Asem, Two Bahraini prisoners may be executed within hours, rights groups warn, July 26 2019 (https://www.middleeasteye.net/news/two-bahraini-dissidents-risk-imminent-execution-warns-rights-group)

132 Foreign Minister receives Canadian official, Bahrain News Agency, Nov 23 2019 (https://www.bna.bh/en/news?cms=q8FmFJgiscL2fwIzON1%2BDvWnT6PcH6NI0toh%2FmUGEMA%3D)

133 Canada Keen on Increasing Trade Volume With Qatar, Mar 10 2019 (https://www.albawaba.com/business/canada-keen-increasing-trade-volume-qatar-1263020)

134 Amiri Guard Commander meets Ambassador of Canada, Nov 8 2018 (https://www.thepeninsulaqatar.com/article/08/11/2018/Amiri-Guard-Commander-meets-Ambassador-of-Canada) ; Joshua Karsten, Canadian troops in Bahrain bust drug runners on the 'hash highway', Stars and Stripes, Jan 28 (https://www.stripes.com/news/canadian-troops-in-bahrain-bust-drug-runners-on-the-hash-highway-1.566363)

135 Promotions and senior appointments 2019 - General and Flag Officers, National Defence, Backgrounder CANFORGEN 020/19 CMP 010/19 111413Z, Feb 19 2019 (https://www.canada.ca/en/department-national-defence/news/2019/02/promotions-and-senior-appointments-2019---general-and-flag-officers.html)

136 Joshua Karsten, Canadian troops in Bahrain bust drug runners on the 'hash highway', Stars and Stripes, Jan 28 2019 (https://www.stripes.com/news/canadian-troops-in-bahrain-bust-drug-runners-on-the-hash-highway-1.566363) ; Apr 24 2019 (https://twitter.com/anthonyfenton/status/1121097243837124608) ; Operation FOUNDATION (https://www.canada.ca/en/department-national-defence/services/operations/military-operations/current-operations/opera-

tion-foundation.html)

137   Governor General to Honour Remarkable Canadians at Rideau Hall, Media Advisory, Governor General of Canada, Nov 8 2019 (https://www.newswire.ca/news-releases/media-advisory-governor-general-to-honour-remarkable-canadians-at-rideau-hall-865498945.html)

138   Jordanian King Receives Canada's National Defense Minister, WAM, Apr 23 2019 (https://www.defaiya.com/news/Regional%20News/Jordan/2019/04/24/jordanian-king-receives-canada-s-national-defense-minister)

139   Freihat, Canadian officials break ground on military road project along border, Apr 9 2019 (http://www.jordantimes.com/news/local/freihat-canadian-officials-break-ground-military-road-project-along-border)

140   Prime Minister Justin Trudeau speaks with King Abdullah of Jordan, Mar 27 2019 (https://pm.gc.ca/en/news/readouts/2019/03/27/prime-minister-justin-trudeau-speaks-king-abdullah-jordan) ; Jordanian regime responsibility and the assassination of Nahid Hattarin Amman--under the watchful eyes of the Jordanian mukhabarat, Sept 25 2016 (http://angryarab.blogspot.com/2016/09/jordanian-regime-responsibility-and.html)

141   Prime Minister Justin Trudeau meets with His Majesty King Abdullah II bin Al-Hussein of Jordan, May 15 2019 (https://pm.gc.ca/en/news/readouts/2019/05/15/prime-minister-justin-trudeau-meets-his-majesty-king-abdullah-ii-bin-al)

142   King holds talks with Canadian PM in Ottawa, Nov 19 2019 (https://www.jordantimes.com/news/local/king-holds-talks-canadian-pm-ottawa)

143   Ahmed Abdelkader Elpannann, Why is Canada ignoring the horrendous human-rights violations in Egypt?, July 3 2018 (https://nationalpost.com/opinion/why-is-canada-ignoring-the-horrendous-human-rights-violations-in-egypt)

144   Egypt, Canada discuss boosting ties, May 5 2019 (http://www.xinhuanet.com/english/2019-05/20/c_138072468.htm)

145   Minister Dion heading to North Africa and the Gulf, News Release, Global Affairs Canada, May 19 2016 (https://www.canada.ca/en/global-affairs/news/2016/05/minister-dion-heading-to-north-africa-and-the-gulf.html)

146   Mohamed Omar, Yasser Ahmed Albaz's Detention In Notorious Egyptian Prison Renewed Yet Again, Apr 25 2019 (https://www.huffingtonpost.ca/entry/yasser-ahmed-albaz-egypt_ca_5cd5958ae4b-07bc72979737b)

147   Michelle Carbert, 2019 Canada urged to condemn Egyptian minister's remarks saying critics will be 'sliced up', July 25 (https://www.theglobeandmail.com/politics/article-canada-urged-to-condemn-egyptian-ministers-remarks-saying-critics/)

148   Ibid

149   Canadian military resumes some operations in Iraq following Iran scare, Canadian Press, Jan 16 2020 (https://www.cbc.ca/news/politics/canadian-military-resumes-iraq-operations-1.5428965)

150   Gareth Corfield, Canadian sniper makes kill shot at distance of 3.5 KILOMETRES, Jun 22 2017 (https://www.theregister.co.uk/2017/06/22/canadian_sniper_3450m_shot_iraq/)

151   Syria: Unprecedented investigation reveals US-led Coalition killed more than 1,600 civilians in Raqqa 'death trap', Apr 25 2019 (https://www.amnesty.org/en/latest/news/2019/04/syria-unprecedented-investigation-reveals-us-led-coalition-killed-more-than-1600-civilians-in-raqqa-death-trap/)

152   Susannah George, Mosul is a graveyard: Final IS battle kills 9,000 civilians, Dec 20 2017 (https://apnews.com/bbea7094fb954838a2fdc11278d65460/Mosul-is-a-graveyard:-Final-IS-battle-kills-9,000-civilians)

153   Steven Chase, Canadian forces providing crucial support in battle to recapture Mosul, Oct 17 2016 (https://www.theglobeandmail.com/news/politics/canadian-forces-providing-crucial-support-in-battle-to-recapture-mosul/article32403507/)

154   Scott Taylor, Canada In Iraq: What's The Plan?, Feb 12 2018 (http://espritdecorps.ca/on-target-4/on-target-canada-in-iraq-whats-the-plan)

155   Steven Chase, Canadian forces providing crucial support in battle to recapture Mosul, Oct 17 2016 (https://www.theglobeandmail.com/news/politics/canadian-forces-providing-crucial-support-in-battle-to-recapture-mosul/article32403507/)

156   Kate Allen, Raqqa is in ruins like a modern Dresden. This is not 'precision bombing', May 23 2019 (https://www.theguardian.com/commentisfree/2019/may/23/raqqa-ruins-bombing)

157   Scott Taylor, Sajjan must explain what's next for Canada in Iraq, Feb 14 2018 (https://www.hilltimes.com/2018/02/14/sajjan-must-explain-whats-next-canada-iraq/134124)

158   Ibid

159   Lee Berthiaume, Support of Kurds could put Canada in awkward spot when Daesh is defeated in Mosul, Canadian Press, Mar 4 2017 (https://www.thestar.com/news/canada/2017/03/04/support-of-kurds-could-put-canada-in-awkward-spot-when-daesh-is-defeated-in-mosul.html)

160   Canadian military plane detained in Iraq for several days: Defence, Canadian Press, Nov 10 2015 (https://www.thestar.com/news/canada/2015/11/10/canadian-military-plane-detained-in-iraq-for-several-days-defence.html)

161   Iraqi protests (2019–present) (https://en.wikipedia.org/wiki/Iraqi_protests_(2019–present))

162   Scott Taylor, Stop propping up brutal Baghdad regime, Dec 13 2019 (https://www.thechronicleherald.ca/opinion/national-perspectives/on-target-stop-propping-up-brutal-baghdad-regime-387974/)

163   Scott Taylor, Amid U.S.-Iran brinksmanship, Canadian troops ought to leave Iraq, May 22 2019

(https://www.hilltimes.com/2019/05/22/amid-us-iran-brinksmanship-canadian-troops-ought-to-leave-iraq/200911)

164   David Pugliese, Cost of Canada's military mission in Iraq expected to exceed $1 billion, Jan 9 2020 (https://ottawacitizen.com/news/national/defence-watch/cost-of-canadas-military-mission-in-iraq-expected-to-exceed-1-billion)

165   Murray Brewster, Canadian troops spending more time at front lines in Iraq as future of mission is unclear, Oct 6 2016 (https://www.cbc.ca/news/politics/iraq-canada-troops-1.3794722)

166   Chapter 4: Delivering Real Change (https://www.budget.gc.ca/2019/docs/plan/chap-04-en.html)

167   Canada's Middle East engagement strategy, Aug 22 2019 (https://www.international.gc.ca/world-monde/international_relations-relations_internationales/mena-moan/strategy-strategie.aspx?lang=eng)

168   Contract awarded for in-service support of CC-150 Polaris fleet, National Defence, News release, Dec 6 2018 (https://www.canada.ca/en/department-national-defence/news/2018/12/contract-awarded-for-in-service-support-of-cc-150-polaris-fleet.html)

169   Alissa J. Rubin and Ronen Bergman, Israeli Airstrike Hits Weapons Depot in Iraq, Aug 22 2019 (https://www.nytimes.com/2019/08/22/world/middleeast/israel-iraq-iran-airstrike.html)

170   Mark Mazzetti, Adam Goldman and Michael S. Schmidt, Behind the Sudden Death of a $1 Billion Secret C.I.A. War in Syria, Aug 2 2017 (https://www.nytimes.com/2017/08/02/world/middleeast/cia-syria-rebel-arm-train-trump.html)

171   Ivan Angelovski, Miranda Patrucic and Lawrence Marzouk, Revealed: the £1bn of weapons flowing from Europe to Middle East, July 27 2016 (https://www.theguardian.com/world/2016/jul/27/weapons-flowing-eastern-europe-middle-east-revealed-arms-trade-syria)

172   Jiyar Gol, Syria conflict: The 'war crimes' caught in brutal phone footage, BBC Persian, Nov 3 2019 (https://www.bbc.com/news/world-middle-east-50250330)

173   Canada welcomes outcome of Syrian opposition conference Statement, Global Affairs Canada, Dec 11 2015 (https://www.canada.ca/en/global-affairs/news/2015/12/canada-welcomes-outcome-of-syrian-opposition-conference.html)

174   Ghazanfar Ali Khan, Saudi-Canada relations set to scale new heights, Apr 18 2016 (https://www.arabnews.com/saudi-arabia/news/912026)

175   Statement by the Prime Minister on airstrikes in Syria, Apr 13 2018 (https://pm.gc.ca/eng/news/2018/04/13/statement-prime-minister-airstrikes-syria)

176   Lee Berthiaume, Trudeau supports U.S.-led military airstrikes against Assad after alleged Syrian chemical attack, Canadian Press, Apr 14 2018 (https://nationalpost.com/news/syrian-government-to-blame-for-chemical-weapons-attack-free-land-says)

177   Mike Corder, Chemical weapons watchdog members voice concerns over Syria, July 9 2019 (https://apnews.com/82e448f70bdf4cd-6876947b350a31326) ; Nov 27 2019 (https://twitter.com/CanadaOPCW/status/1199630298331398144)

178   Russia 'proves' Syria attack was staged, Apr 26 2018 (https://news.sky.com/story/live-russia-proves-syria-attack-was-staged-11347363)

179   Russian top brass reports it has proof of UK's involvement in Douma chemical incident, Apr 13 2018 (https://tass.com/defense/999641)

180   Robert Fisk, The evidence we were never meant to see about the Douma 'gas' attack, May 23 2019 (https://www.independent.co.uk/voices/douma-syria-opcw-chemical-weapons-chlorine-gas-video-conspiracy-theory-russia-a8927116.html)

181   Jonathan Steele, The OPCW and Douma: Chemical Weapons Watchdog Accused of Evidence-Tampering by Its Own Inspectors, Nov 15 2019 (https://www.counterpunch.org/2019/11/15/the-opcw-and-douma-chemical-weapons-watchdog-accused-of-evidence-tampering-by-its-own-inspectors/)

182   Caitlin Johnstone, OPCW: Deluge of new leaks further shreds the establishment Syria narrative, Dec 18 2019 (https://www.newcoldwar.org/deluge-of-new-leaks-further-shreds-the-establishment-syria-narrative/)

183   Ibid

184   STATEMENT OF CANADA TO THE 91st SESSION OF THE OPCW EXECUTIVE COUNCIL DELIVERED BY H.E. SABINE NOLKE, PERMANENT REPRESENTATIVE, July 9 2019 (https://www.opcw.org/sites/default/files/documents/2019/07/EC-91%20Statement%20-%20final%20-%20EN.pdf)

185   Destruction of Syria's chemical weapons (https://en.wikipedia.org/wiki/Destruction_of_Syria%27s_chemical_weapons)

186   Canada announces additional support for prohibition of chemical weapons in Syria, Global Affairs Canada, June 29 2017 (https://www.canada.ca/en/global-affairs/news/2017/06/canada_announcesadditionalsupportforprohibitionofchemicalweapons.htm)

187   Canada welcomes OPCW actions to counter impunity for use of chemical weapons, Global Affairs Canada, June 27 2018 (https://www.canada.ca/en/global-affairs/news/2018/06/canada-welcomes-opcw-actions-to-counter-impunity-for-use-of-chemical-weapons.html)

188   Governor General of Canada Visits OPCW, Aug 30 2019 (https://www.opcw.org/media-centre/news/2019/08/governor-general-canada-visits-opcw)

189   Canada condemns reported chemical attack in eastern Ghouta, Global Affairs Canada, Apr 8 2018 (https://www.canada.ca/en/global-affairs/news/2018/04/canada-condemns-reported-chemical-attack-in-eastern-ghouta.html)

190 'They don't care about us': Syrians on White Helmets' true agenda, RT, Sep 2 2017 (https://www.youtube.com/watch?v=Jq4LEIO740A)

191 Ben Norton and Max Blumenthal, Yet Another Video Shows U.S.-Funded White Helmets Assisting Public Executions in Rebel-Held Syria, AlterNet, May 23 2017 (https://www.alternet.org/grayzone-project/white-helmets-assisting-public-executions-rebel-held-syria)

192 Danny Gold, Saving Lives With Tech Amid Syria's Endless Civil War, Aug 16 2018 (https://www.wired.com/story/syria-civil-war-hala-sentry/)

193 Sep 18 2018 (https://twitter.com/CanadaSyria/status/1042087518072713219)

194 Danny Gold, Saving Lives With Tech Amid Syria's Endless Civil War, Aug 16 2018 (https://www.wired.com/story/syria-civil-war-hala-sentry/)

195 Vanessa Beeley, The White Helmets, Hala Systems and the Grotesque Militarization of "Humanitarianism" in Syria, Sept 30 2019 (https://www.mintpressnews.com/white-helmets-hala-systems-militarization-humanitarianism-syria/262115/)

196 Statement by Foreign Affairs Minister on Seven Years of Conflict in Syria, Global Affairs Canada, Mar 26 2018 (https://www.canada.ca/en/global-affairs/news/2018/03/statement-by-foreign-affairs-minister-on-seven-years-of-conflict-in-syria.html)

197 Syria's volunteer rescue workers (http://syriacivildefense.org/our-partners)

198 Max Blumenthal, Inside the Shadowy PR Firm That's Lobbying for Regime Change in Syria Written, AlterNet, Sept 30 2016 (https://www.alternet.org/world/inside-shadowy-pr-firm-thats-driving-western-opinion-towards-regime-change-syria)

199 Mark McKinnon, Ottawa promised to bring 10 members of Syria's White Helmets to Canada. One year later, they languish in a Jordanian camp, June 18 2019 (https://www.theglobeandmail.com/world/article-we-can-never-go-out-a-year-later-white-helmets-bound-for-canada/)

200 Ibid

201 Eva Bartlett, Decision to bring White Helmets to Canada dangerous and criminal, Aug 10 2018 (https://www.rt.com/op-ed/435670-white-helmets-canada-syria/?fbclid=IwAR0Jvq-AjZVhkMrMXwsc5988GDpVBlUCDU4O1A0R-5Jp-LOh9SsTQHFgdEJ0)

202 Jillian Stirk, UBC Alumni Diplomats, Feb 2015 (https://trekmagazine.alumni.ubc.ca/2015/february-2015/extras/ubc-alumni-diplomats/)

203 Ibid

204 John Paul Tasker, Justin Trudeau: I'll end ISIS combat mission, restore relations with Iran, Jun 23 2015 (https://www.cbc.ca/news/politics/justin-trudeau-i-ll-end-isis-combat-mission-restore-relations-with-iran-1.3124949)

205 Stéphane Dion, On 'responsible conviction' and Liberal foreign policy, Mar 29 2016 (https://www.macleans.ca/politics/ottawa/stephane-dion-how-ethics-inspires-liberal-foreign-policy/)

206 May 8 2018 (https://twitter.com/cafreeland/status/994003237811490816?lang=en) ; Statement by Foreign Affairs Minister on protests in Iran, Global Affairs Canada, Jan 3 2018 (https://www.canada.ca/en/global-affairs/news/2018/01/statement_by_foreignaffairsministeronprotestsiniran.html)

207 Ibid

208 Canada welcomes international community's clear support for Iranian people and for human rights reforms in Iran, Global Affairs Canada, News Release, Nov 14 2017 (https://www.canada.ca/en/global-affairs/news/2017/11/canada_welcomes_internationalcommunitysclearsupportforiranianpeo.htm)

209 Iran's envoy condemns UNGA's anti Iran resolution, Iran Press, Nov 15 2019 (https://en.abna24.com/news//irans-envoy-condemns-ungas-anti-iran-resolution_987984.html)

210 James Carden, This Think Tank Is Pushing Regime Change in Iran—and the White House is Listening, July 12 2018 (https://www.thenation.com/article/think-tank-pushing-regime-change-iran-white-house-listening/)

211 Munk School's Mark Dubowitz wins Intelligence Squared debate, May 28 2015 (https://munkschool.utoronto.ca/munk-schools-mark-dubowitz-wins-intelligence-squared-debate/)

212 Yves Engler, The Munk School of Global Affairs and University Propaganda, Oct 30 2016 (https://dissidentvoice.org/2016/10/the-munk-school-of-global-affairs-and-university-propaganda/)

213 U.S. applauds Canadian lawmakers' rebuke of Iran over terrorism, 15 June 2018 (https://ir.usembassy.gov/usapplaudscanadianlawmakers/)

214 Canada supports diplomatic efforts established for Iran to return to full implementation of Joint Comprehensive Plan of Action, Global Affairs Canada, Jan 14 2020 (https://www.canada.ca/en/global-affairs/news/2020/01/canada-supports-diplomatic-efforts-established-for-iran-to-return-to-full-implementation-of-joint-comprehensive-plan-of-action.html)

215 Robert Fife and Steven Chase, Inside the final hours that led to the arrest of Huawei executive Meng Wanzhou, Nov 30 2019 (https://www.theglobeandmail.com/politics/article-inside-the-final-hours-that-led-to-the-arrest-of-huawei-executive-meng/)

216 Canada–Gulf Cooperation Council (GCC) Strategic Dialogue, Joint Communique: Second Joint Ministerial Meeting on Strategic Dialogue between the Gulf Cooperation Council and Canada Jeddah, Saudi Arabia May 23 2016 (https://www.international.gc.ca/world-monde/international_relations-relations_internationales/mena-moan/gcc-canada-ccg.aspx?lang=eng)

217 Editorial, The Trudeau government's Saudi hypocrisy, Apr 14 2016 (https://www.theglobeand-

mail.com/opinion/editorials/the-trudeau-governments-saudi-hypocrisy/article29636734/)

218   Nov 17 2019 (https://twitter.com/anthonyfenton/status/1196238929302712321)

219   Standing Committee on National Defence, Dec 6 2018 (https://www.ourcommons.ca/DocumentViewer/en/42-1/NDDN/meeting-122/evidence)

220   Dominic Dudley, Iran Takes Aim At Canada Over Property Seizures In Toronto And Ottawa, Sep 17 2019 (https://www.forbes.com/sites/dominicdudley/2019/09/17/iran-canada-property-seizures/#4ac234391910)

221   Iran to retaliate if Canada refuses to release seized assets, Mehr News Agency, Sept 16 2019 (https://en.mehrnews.com/news/150122/Iran-to-retaliate-if-Canada-refuses-to-release-seized-assets) ; Stewart Bell, Iranian legislator urges military to seize Canadian ships, Sept 16 2019 (https://globalnews.ca/news/5907562/iran-legislator-urges-military-seize-canadian-ships/?utm_expid=.kz0UD5JkQOCo6yMqxGqECg.0&utm_referrer=https%3A%2F%2Fwww.google.com%2F)

222   Ibid

223   Relatives of Montrealers killed in Lebanon condemn 'massacres', July 17 2006 (https://www.cbc.ca/news/canada/montreal/relatives-of-montrealers-killed-in-lebanon-condemn-massacres-1.581517)

224   Adam Day, One Martyr Down: The Untold Story Of A Canadian Peacekeeper Killed At War, Jan 2 2013 (https://legionmagazine.com/en/2013/01/one-martyr-down-the-untold-story-of-a-canadian-peacekeeper-killed-at-war/)

225   Mersiha Gadzo, Canada Park, a popular picnicking spot for Israelis, created upon the rubble of Palestinian homes, Mondoweiss, June 19 2017 (https://mondoweiss.net/2017/06/picnicking-israelis-palestinian/)

226   Richard Sanders, A Very Canadian Coup: The top 10 ways that Canada aided the 2004 coup in Haiti and helped subject Haitians to a brutal reign of terror, Apr 1 2010 (https://www.policyalternatives.ca/publications/monitor/very-canadian-coup)

4. Commies No More, But ... — Russian Bogeyman

The Liberals have promoted Russophobia. Complicated conflicts in Ukraine and Syria, as well as nuclear proliferation, are reduced to 'blame Russia'. Aping Hillary Clinton, cold warriors and other segments of the US establishment, the Liberals have pushed the idea of Russian electoral interference. In April 2019 Freeland said she was "very concerned that Russia is meddling" in Canada's election and claimed there had "already been efforts by malign actors to disrupt our democracy."[1] For his part, Trudeau opined that "countries like Russia are behind a lot of the divisive campaigns ... that have turned our politics even more divisive and more anger-filled than they have been in the past."[2] Ten months before the 2019 federal election the government established a special task force to monitor potential threats to Canada's democracy that included representatives of CSIS, RCMP, Communications Security Establishment and Global Affairs' intelligence branch.[3]

It was all for naught. Two days after the 2019 election the Privy Council Office quietly announced no foreign actor attempted to interfere.[4]

Alongside claims of electoral interference, Liberal officials claimed Russia was a strategic rival. In a major June 2017 foreign policy speech Freeland called, "Russian military adventurism and expansionism ... clear strategic threats to the liberal democratic world, including Canada."[5]

The Liberals repeatedly criticized Russian policy as a threat to "the rules-based international order" Canada purportedly upheld.[6] The Liberals also rejected calls by Donald Trump to let Russia return to the G7.[7]

The Liberals maintained the previous government's sanctions on Russia and called on other nations to do the same. In November 2016 Foreign Minister Dion told a news conference, "Canada is insisting that all countries must be very firm about these sanctions."[8] The Liberals added multiple rounds of sanctions on Russia. In March 2016 they added 19 entities and individuals to a blacklist and expanded its scope.[9] Subsequently they added dozens more individuals to a list of those subjected to an asset freeze and dealings prohibition under the Special Economic Measures (Ukraine) Regulations.

In Fall 2017 the government adopted sanctions legislation, modeled after the 2012 US Magnitsky Act, that further strained relations with Moscow. The Justice for Victims of Corrupt Foreign Officials Act was designed to demonize Russia and Ottawa immediately targeted Russian officials under legislation that allowed the government to freeze individuals' assets/visas and prohibit Canadian companies from dealing with sanctioned individuals.

The legislation was named after Sergei Magnitsky who proponents claim was tortured to death for exposing Russian state corruption. The source of the claim was William Browder, an American who got rich amidst the fire sale of Russian state assets in the 1990s. With billionaire banker Edmond J. Safra, Browder co-founded Hermitage Capital Management, which became the largest hedge fund in Russia. Hermitage Capital earned a staggering 2,697% return between 1996 and 2007.[10] Those who question the western-backed story line say Magnitsky was an accountant who helped Browder claim illicit tax breaks. According to this version of the story, Browder exploited Magnitsky's death — caused by inhumane jail conditions — to avoid being extradited to Russia on tax fraud charges.

(While it's hard to be confident about the truth, it's difficult to believe that a US capitalist who got rich in Russia in the 1990s would simply turn into a human rights activist. On the other hand, the idea that a wealthy and powerful individual meshed self-preservation with growing Russophobia seems plausible. A November 2019

Der Spiegel expose titled "The Case of Sergei Magnitsky: Questions Cloud Story Behind U.S. Sanctions" gave credence to this view.[11])

The Liberals blamed Russia for the nuclear arms control impasse. They claimed Moscow was responsible for the demise of the Intermediate-Range Nuclear Forces (INF) Treaty, which banned an entire class of nuclear weapons. Freeland said, "Russia has failed to comply with this important treaty, and Canada is disappointed that Russia's actions have led to" the US pulling out of the INF in 2019.[12] But, as mentioned above, it was not clear Russia violated the INF.[13] The Trump administration, on the other hand, began to develop new ground-launched intermediate-range missiles prohibited under the pact long before it formally withdrew from the INF. US military planners wanted to deploy intermediate-range missiles against China, which was not party to the INF.

In a dangerous game of brinksmanship, the Trudeau government expanded Canada's military presence on Russia's doorstep. In 2017 the number of Canadian troops in Eastern Europe was more than doubled from approximately 300 in the Ukraine and Poland to 800 in the Ukraine, Romania and Latvia. Alongside these forces, Canada had a naval frigate and a half dozen CF-18 fighter jets in Eastern Europe. Freeland and Sajjan made it clear that Russia was the target of Canada's military buildup. In 2017 they wrote, "we send a strong message of deterrence to Russia by continuing our military training in Ukraine, through our air policing in Romania, our frigate in the Black Sea, and our recently-announced Canadian-led NATO battlegroup in Latvia."[14]

A Canadian frigate regularly patrolled the Black Sea, which borders Russia, Bulgaria, Turkey, Romania, Georgia and Ukraine. In July 2019 *HMCS Toronto* led a four ship Standing NATO Maritime Group exercise in the Black Sea.[15] Soon after, it participated with two-dozen other ships in a NATO exercise that included training in maritime interdiction, air defence, amphibious warfare and anti-submarine warfare.[16]

During most of their first three years in power the Liberals maintained a contingent of troops in Poland.[17] In August 2016, 100 soldiers from Edmonton were deployed to Poland as part of NATO's Operation Reassurance.[18]

Royal Canadian Air Force members were regularly dispatched to Romania.[19] In the Fall of 2019, for instance, a 135-person air task force was sent on a four month mission to train and exercise with their Romanian counterparts.[20] Canada's air controllers were stationed in Bucharest to aid the Air Force's Control and Reporting Centre. The CF-18s in Romania also trained with US F-15s and NATO airborne early warning and control aircraft (AWACS).[21] In October 2018 Canadian fighter jets stationed in Romania were scrambled by NATO's Combined Air Operations Centre in Spain to intercept Russian aircraft over the Black Sea, which is 8,000 kilometers from Canadian territory.

In the most significant deployment, Canada led a thousand strong NATO battle group in Latvia. About 450 Canadian soldiers were deployed to the small nation bordering Russia in 2017. Concurrently, the US, Britain and Germany lead thousand member NATO groups in Poland, Lithuania and Estonia. Increased to 550 soldiers a year later, Canadian troops are to remain in Latvia until at least 2023.[22] In December 2019 the Secretary General of NATO, Jens Stoltenberg, suggested they could stay longer, saying "this is a presence which doesn't have a specific time limit."[23]

The Canadians, so far away from home, trained their Latvian counterparts. The Royal Canadian Artillery School, for instance, helped Latvian forces use M109 self-propelled howitzers.[24] The Canadian-led NATO battlegroup was integrated with the Latvian Land Forces Infantry Brigade. In the Fall of 2019 they were part of the largest wargame in Latvia since the fall of the Soviet Union. At one point 44 NATO tanks were engaged, which Captain Kendell Jacobson said was "the largest gathering of different tanks on the planet at that time."[25] The troops in Latvia were a "tripwire" force.

Insufficient to stop Russia from invading, they were considered a large enough force that their capture or killing would compel NATO to respond. That scenario would probably unleash a full-scale war between countries with the bulk of the world's nuclear weapons.

Massing NATO troops on Russia's border was highly belligerent. It also violated a US, German and French promise to Soviet/Russian leader Mikhail Gorbachev regarding the reunification of Germany, an important Cold War divide. In 1990 Gorbachev agreed not to obstruct German reunification, to withdraw tens of thousands of troops from the east and for the new Germany to be part of NATO in return for assurances that the alliance wouldn't expand "one inch eastward".[26] Now, the alliance includes countries on Russia's border and North American troops are stationed there.

Canada's military build-up in Eastern Europe was the outgrowth of a coup in Kiev. In 2014 the right-wing nationalist EuroMaidan movement ousted president Viktor Yanukovych who was oscillating between the European Union and Russia. The US-backed coup divided the Ukraine politically, geographically and linguistically (Russian is the mother tongue of 30% of Ukrainians and as much as 75% of those in eastern cities).[27] After Yanukovych's ouster Russia reinforced its military presence — or "seized" — the southern area of Crimea and then organized a referendum on secession. Home to Moscow's major Baltic naval base, Crimea had long been part of Russia and the bulk of the population preferred Moscow's rule to the post-coup right wing nationalist government in Kiev.[28]

The largely Russian-speaking east protested the ouster of Yanukovych who was from the region. After a referendum and fighting the Donetsk and Luhansk People's Republics were proclaimed in the Donbas region bordering Russia. Moscow aided the movement but showed little interest in absorbing the newly proclaimed republics into Russia as many in the Donbas would have liked.

While we heard about Russia's nefarious influence in the Ukraine, little attention was given to Canada or the US's role in stoking tensions there. In July 2015 the Canadian Press reported that opposition protesters were camped in the Canadian Embassy for a week during the February 2014 rebellion against Yanukovych. "Canada's embassy in Kyiv was used as a haven for several days by anti-government protesters during the uprising that toppled the regime of former president Viktor Yanukovych," the story noted.[29] Since the mid-2000s Ottawa has provided significant support to right wing, nationalist opponents of Russia in the Ukraine.[30]

In March 2017 the Liberals renewed Canada's military training mission in the Ukraine and expanded its mandate. During parliamentary debate that month Sajjan said, "through Operation UNIFIER, we sent a clear signal of deterrence to Russia."[31]

As part of Operation UNIFIER, 200 Canadian troops — rotated every six months — worked with Ukrainian soldiers on military engineering, explosive-device disposal, sniper training, etc. When extending the mission, the Liberals also eased restrictions that required the Canadians to stay in the western half of Ukraine, away from the fighting in the east that left over 10,000 dead.[32] (In July 2018 International Development Minister Marie-Claude Bibeau was the first G7 minister to travel to the line of contact between the warring factions.[33]) Alongside US and UK troops, UNIFIER reinforced Ukrainian military forces fighting in the east.[34]

Another aim of Operation UNIFIER was to help "modernize the Ukrainian Armed Forces", noted Sajjan, so the country could join NATO.[35] While some in the Ukraine aspired to join the alliance, the move would antagonize Moscow. To support Ukraine's possible accession to the alliance, Canada supported the NATO-Ukraine Joint Working Group on Defence Reform and Canada shared the role of NATO Contact Point Embassy in Kiev.[36] The Liberals also equipped the Ukrainian military, donating tens of millions of dollars worth of helmets, vehicles, clothing and bulletproof vests.[37]

In December 2017 the Liberals added Ukraine to Canada's Automatic Firearms Country Control List, which allowed companies to export weapons to that country with little restriction.[38] In 2019 Winnipeg based PGW Defence Technologies delivered $1 million worth of heavy caliber sniper rifles to the Ukrainian military.[39]

To strengthen military ties the two countries signed a Defence Cooperation Agreement in April 2017.[40] Three months earlier the Liberals appointed former assistant deputy minister at national defence, Jill Sinclair, to Ukraine's Defence Reform Advisory Board. "This representative provides strategic advice on defence reform to Ukraine's Minister of Defence and senior officials", noted Global Affairs.[41]

In July 2016 Trudeau traveled to Kiev to sign a free-trade agreement. During the visit the prime minister said Canadian troops were preparing Ukrainian soldiers to "liberate" its "territory".[42] At that time Ukrainian troops were actively fighting secessionist forces in the east of the country. The Liberals denied the legitimate grievances of the predominantly Russian-speaking population in eastern Ukraine who revolted against the ultra-nationalist government in Kiev that took power after the overthrow of Yanukovych. In response to a March 2017 question about whether Canada saw the conflict in eastern Ukraine as a separatist movement or Russian aggression, Sinclair told a Ukrainian press outlet, "I think Canada has been clear since the outset of Russian aggression against Ukraine that it's Russian aggression against Ukraine, in Crimea and in the East."[43]

For her part, Freeland framed the conflict in eastern Ukraine as a global battle between good and evil. In November 2019 she declared that Ukraine was at the "forefront of the struggle between democracy and authoritarianism" and that "modern Ukraine is the country where the struggle is ongoing and the future of the rules-based international order and genuine democracy in the world will be determined."[44]

Ottawa's words and actions emboldened far-right militarists responsible for hundreds of deaths in eastern Ukraine. Far right militia members were part of the force fighting Russian-aligned groups in eastern Ukraine and Canadians troops trained a force that included the best-organized neo-Nazis in the world.[45] In June 2018 Canada's military attaché in Kiev, Colonel Brian Irwin, met privately with officers from the Azov battalion, who used the Nazi "Wolfsangel" symbol and praised officials who helped slaughter Jews and Poles during World War II.[46] According to Azov, Canadian military officials concluded the briefing by expressing "their hopes for further fruitful cooperation."[47]

Sympathy for the far right in Ukraine was displayed by the Canadian Forces on other occasions. In February 2016, for instance, "nearly 200 officer cadets and professors of Canada's Royal Military College" attended a screening of The Ukrainians: God's Volunteer Battalion, which praised far right militias fighting in the east of the country.[48]

Alongside the US, Canada funded, equipped and trained the neo-Nazi infiltrated National Police of Ukraine (NPU), which was founded after Yanukovych was overthrown. A former deputy commander of the Azov Battalion, Vadim Troyan had a series of senior positions in the NPU, including acting chief.[49] When a policeman was videoed in early 2019 disparaging a far right protester as a supporter of Stepan Bandera, the National Police chief, National Police spokesman, Interior Minister and other officers repudiated the constable by publicly professing their admiration for Bandera.[50] During World War II Bandera aligned with the Nazi occupation, carrying out murderous campaigns against Poles and Jews.[51]

Soon after it was set up, Foreign Minister Dion announced $8.1 million for the NPU, which replaced the former regime's police.[52] Canada provided the force with thousands of uniforms and cameras and helped establish the country's first national police academy.[53] Beginning in June 2016 up to 20 Canadian police were in the Ukraine to support and advise the NPU. In July 2019 that number was increased to 45 and the deployment was extended until at least 2021.[54]

While they talked about the danger of the far right, the Liberals refused to back a number of UN resolutions opposed to glorifying Nazism, neo-Nazism and racial discrimination.[55] On November 19, 2015, they voted against a UN General assembly resolution critical of the aforementioned subject supported by 126 states.[56] The US, Palau and Ukraine were the only other countries to vote against the resolution titled "Combating glorification of Nazism, neo-Nazism and other practices that contribute to fuelling contemporary forms of racism, racial discrimination, xenophobia and related intolerance."[57] In subsequent years the Liberals abstained on a similar resolution.[58]

The post Maiden Ukrainian government included a number of neo-Nazis. During his 2016 trip to Ukraine Trudeau was photographed with Andriy Parubiy, Ukrainian Parliament speaker, who had a background with the far right and was accused of praising Hitler.[59] Liberal and other party politicians in Canada also spoke alongside and marched with members of Ukraine's Right Sector, which said it was "defending the values of white, Christian Europe against the loss of the nation and deregionalisation."[60]

In early 2017 it came to light that Chrystia Freeland's Ukrainian grandfather, Michael Chomiak, was a Nazi propagandist during World War II. Canada's foreign minister deflected questions regarding the matter by saying Moscow was seeking to "destabilize" Canadian democracy.[61] But, Chomiak did in fact edit a Ukrainian language newspaper that published speeches by Hitler and Goebbels, as well as the Nazi's anti-Jewish/Soviet screeds. While obviously not responsible for her grandpa's misdeeds, Freeland publicly praised him. Moreover, she deflected questions on the matter by stoking Russophobia.

To a large extent Ottawa and Washington used the Ukraine as a proxy to weaken Russia. Despite the fact the Cold War ended decades ago, the Russian bogeyman remains an effective tool that supporters of the US Empire are eager to employ.

But the Liberals were not only willing to stoke anti-Russian sentiment, they also tinkered with old racist tropes about Asians as a tool in their efforts to toe the US geopolitical line. The next chapter discusses the dangerous words and actions taken by Trudeau's government to appease those who view China's economic power as a challenge to the US-led world order.

Chapter 4 Notes

1 Scott Taylor, We are our own worst enemy, Oct 28 2019 (https://www.thechronicleherald.ca/opinion/national-perspectives/scott-taylor-we-are-our-own-worst-enemy-368806/)

2 John Irish, Canada expects foreign meddling in October election: foreign minister, Apr 5 2019 (https://ca.reuters.com/article/topNews/idCAKCN-1RH16Y-OCATP)

3 Rachel Aiello, Feds unveil plan to tackle fake news, interference in 2019 election, Jan 30 2019 (https://www.ctvnews.ca/politics/feds-unveil-plan-to-tackle-fake-news-interference-in-2019-election-1.4274273)

4 Scott Taylor, We are our own worst enemy, Oct 28 2019 (https://www.thechronicleherald.ca/opinion/national-perspectives/scott-taylor-we-are-our-own-worst-enemy-368806/)

5 Address by Minister Freeland on Canada's foreign policy priorities, Global Affairs Canada, June 6 2017 (https://www.canada.ca/en/global-affairs/news/2017/06/address_by_ministerfreelandoncanadasforeignpolicypriorities.html)

6 Trudeau cites propaganda against Freeland as Russian interference in Canada, Canadian Press, Apr 4 2018 (https://ipolitics.ca/2018/04/04/trudeau-cites-propaganda-against-freeland-as-russian-interference-in-canada/)

7 Kathleen Harris, Canada rejects Trump's call to let Russia back into G7, Jun 8 2018 (https://www.cbc.ca/news/politics/trump-russia-g7-canada-1.4697655)

8 Canada says Russian sanctions must be upheld by all countries, Nov 11 2016 (https://ca.reuters.com/article/worldNews/idUSKBN136292)

9 Additional sanctions on individuals and entities for activities related to Russia and Ukraine, News Release, Global Affairs Canada, Mar 18 2016 (https://www.canada.ca/en/global-affairs/news/2016/03/additional-sanctions-on-individuals-and-entities-for-activities-related-to-russia-and-ukraine.html)

10 William Browder (Bill Browder) Feb 8 2010 (http://www.opalesque.tv/youtube/William_Browder_Bill_Browder/1)

11 Von Benjamin Bidder, The Case of Sergei Magnitsky Questions Cloud Story Behind U.S. Sanctions, Nov 26 2019 (https://www.spiegel.de/international/world/the-case-of-sergei-magnitsky-anti-corruption-champion-or-corrupt-anti-hero-a-1297796.html)

12 James McCarten, Canada echoes NATO, pins blame on Russia for U.S. pullout from nuclear treaty, Canadian Press, Feb 1 2019 (https://www.ctvnews.ca/politics/canada-echoes-nato-pins-blame-on-russia-for-u-s-pullout-from-nuclear-treaty-1.4279370)

13 Farewell to the INF-Treaty (III) (https://www.german-foreign-policy.com/en/news/detail/7998/)

14 Chrystia Freeland and Harjit S. Sajjan, Canada Steps up Military Support for Ukraine, But Several Important Issues Remain, New Pathway, Mar 27 2017 (https://www.newpathway.ca/canada-military-support-ukraine-issues/)

15 HMCS Toronto joins SNMG2 in Black Sea, July 4 2019 (https://navaltoday.com/2019/07/04/hmcs-toronto-joins-snmg2-in-black-sea/) ; Max Channon, Royal Navy joins huge Black Sea exercise that angers Russia, July 4 2019 (https://www.cornwalllive.com/news/uk-world-news/royal-navy-joins-huge-black-3053768) ; Roger Jordan, Canada's Liberal government hosts anti-Russia conference on Ukraine, World Socialist Web Site, July 13 2019 (https://www.wsws.org/en/articles/2019/07/13/ukra-j13.html)

16 US and Ukraine conclude maritime exercise Sea Breeze 2019, July 6 2019 (https://www.naval-technology.com/news/us-and-ukraine-conclude-maritime-exercise-sea-breeze-2019/)

17 J.R. McKay, Deliverology and Canadian military commitments in Europe circa 2017, Canadian Foreign Policy Journal, Vol 24, Issue 1, 2018

18 Edmonton troops join NATO mission in Poland, Aug 22 2016 (https://www.cbc.ca/news/canada/edmonton/edmonton-troops-join-nato-mission-in-poland-1.3731267)

19 Marie-France Poulin, RCAF Air Task Force Romania completes bilateral training DND, Royal Canadian Air Force, Apr 8 2016 (http://cafdispatch.blogspot.com/2016/04/rcaf-air-task-force-romania-completes.html)

20 Chris Thatcher, RCAF Hornets intercept Russian Su-27 Flanker, Oct 26 2018 (https://www.

skiesmag.com/news/rcaf-hornets-intercept-russian-su-27-flanker/)

21 Chris Thatcher, Su-27 intercept a highlight as CF-188 Hornets conclude NATO air policing mission, Dec 19 2018 (https://www.skiesmag.com/news/su-27-intercept-a-highlight-as-cf-188-hornets-conclude-nato-air-policing-mission/)

22 Teresa Wright, Justin Trudeau adding more Canadian troops in Latvia, extending mission, Associated Press, July 10 2018 (https://globalnews.ca/news/4322396/justin-trudeau-canadian-troops-latvia-extending-mission/)

23 Lee Berthiaume, NATO chief says Canadian missions in Latvia, Iraq helping strengthen alliance, Canadian Press, Dec 4 2019 (https://www.ctvnews.ca/politics/nato-chief-says-canadian-missions-in-latvia-iraq-helping-strengthen-alliance-1.4714363)

24 Jerome Lessard, Canadian Army gunners train Latvians on newly acquired M109A50 self-propelled howitzer, Jan 18 2019 (http://espritdecorps.ca/army-articles/canadian-army-gunners-train-latvians-on-newly-acquired-m109a50-self-propelled-howitzers)

25 Philippe Teisceira-Lessard, La Presse en Lettonie: Noël face aux Russes, Dec 23 2019 (https://www.lapresse.ca/actualites/201912/22/01-5254745-la-presse-en-lettonie-noel-face-aux-russes.php)

26 Dave Majumdar, Newly Declassified Documents: Gorbachev Told NATO Wouldn't Move Past East German Border, Dec 12 2017 (https://nationalinterest.org/blog/the-buzz/newly-declassified-documents-gorbachev-told-nato-wouldnt-23629)

27 Russian language in Ukraine (https://en.wikipedia.org/wiki/Russian_language_in_Ukraine)

28 Kenneth Rapoza, One Year After Russia Annexed Crimea, Locals Prefer Moscow To Kiev, Mar 20 2015 (https://www.forbes.com/sites/kenrapoza/2015/03/20/one-year-after-russia-annexed-crimea-locals-prefer-moscow-to-kiev/#71d40191510d)

29 Murray Brewster, Canadian embassy used as safe haven during Ukraine uprising, investigation finds, Canadian Press, Jul 12 2015 (https://www.cbc.ca/news/politics/canadian-embassy-used-as-safe-haven-during-ukraine-uprising-investigation-finds-1.3148719)

30 Yves Engler, Canada & Eastern Europe, April 13 2009 (https://zcomm.org/zcommentary/canada-and-eastern-europe-by-yves-engler/)

31 Norman Hillmer and Philippe Lagassé, Justin Trudeau and Canadian Foreign Policy, 294

32 An end to the war in eastern Ukraine looks as far away as ever, Oct 11 2018 (https://www.economist.com/europe/2018/10/11/an-end-to-the-war-in-eastern-ukraine-looks-as-far-away-as-ever)

33 Executive Committee, Alexandra Chyczij, President (https://ucc.ca/about-ucc/leadership-1/executive-committee/)

34 Ben Watson, In Ukraine, the US Trains an Army in the West to Fight in the East, Oct 5 2017 (https://www.defenseone.com/threats/2017/10/ukraine-us-trains-army-west-fight-east/141577/)

35 Christopher Guly, Canadian government non-committal on arming Ukraine as tensions escalate between Kyiv and Moscow, Ukrainian Weekly, Dec 7 2018 (http://www.ukrweekly.com/uwwp/canadian-government-non-committal-on-arming-ukraine-as-tensions-escalate-between-kyiv-and-moscow/)

36 Canada's engagement in Ukraine, Dec 27 2019 (https://www.international.gc.ca/world-monde/country-pays/ukraine/relations.aspx?lang=eng)

37 Lee Berthiaume, Ottawa quietly eases restrictions on Canadian military mission in Ukraine, Canadian Press, June 14 2017 (https://www.theglobeandmail.com/news/politics/ottawa-quietly-eases-restrictions-on-canadian-military-mission-in-ukraine/article35308910/) ; 56 new police vehicles for the Ukrainian Military Police, The Maple Leaf, Defence Stories, Mar 25 2019 (https://ml-fd.caf-fac.ca/en/2019/03/26082)

38 Canada adds Ukraine to Automatic Firearms Country Control List, Global Affairs Canada, News Release, Dec 13 2017 (https://www.canada.ca/en/global-affairs/news/2017/12/canada_adds_ukrainetoautomaticfirearmscountrycontrollist0.html)

39 David Pugliese, Ukraine buys Canadian sniper rifles – delivery expected soon, Nov 7 2019 (https://ottawacitizen.com/news/national/defence-watch/ukraine-buys-canadian-sniper-rifles-delivery-expected-soon) ; Ukrainian snipers are about to get this powerful new upgrade courtesy of Canada Ian D'Costa (https://www.militarytimes.com/off-duty/gearscout/irons/2019/01/07/ukrainian-snipers-are-about-to-get-this-powerful-new-upgrade-courtesy-of-canada/)

40 Government of Canada Signs Defence Cooperation Arrangement With Ukraine, National Defence, News Release, Apr 3 2017 (https://www.canada.ca/en/department-national-defence/news/2017/04/government_of_canadasignsdefencecooperationarrangementwithukrain.html)

41 Canada's engagement in Ukraine (https://www.international.gc.ca/world-monde/country-pays/ukraine/relations.aspx?lang=eng)

42 Roger Jordan, Canada extends military missions in Ukraine and Mideast, allies with Trump in refugee crackdown, Mar 23 2019 (https://www.wsws.org/en/articles/2019/03/23/ukca-m23.html)

43 Canada Steps up Military Support for Ukraine, But Several Important Issues Remain, New Pathway, Mar 27 2017 (https://www.newpathway.ca/canada-military-support-ukraine-issues/)

44 It's not about diaspora: Freeland explains why Canada supports Ukraine, Nov 2 2019 (https://www.ukrinform.net/rubric-polytics/2810721-its-not-about-diaspora-freeland-explains-why-canada-supports-ukraine.html)

45 Christopher Miller, In Ukraine, Ultranation-

alist Militia Strikes Fear In Some Quarters, Radio Free Europe, Jan 30 2018 (https://www.rferl.org/a/ukraine-azov-right-wing-militia-to-patrol-kyiv/29008036.html) ; Ukraine: On patrol with the far-right National Militia, BBC Newsnight, Apr 3 2018 (https://www.youtube.com/watch?v=hE6b4ao8gAQ)

46 Asa Winstanley, Israel is arming neo-Nazis in Ukraine, Electronic Intifada, July 4 2018 (https://electronicintifada.net/content/israel-arming-neo-nazis-ukraine/24876)

47 Ibid

48 "The Ukrainians: God's Volunteer Battalion" is screened at Canada's Royal Military College, Mar 4 2016 (http://www.ukrweekly.com/uwwp/the-ukrainians-gods-volunteer-battalion-is-screened-at-canadas-royal-military-college/) ; Tony Seed, Canada's Unacceptable Mission in Ukraine, Communist Party of Canada (Marxist-Leninist), No. 23 Supplement, June 24 2017 (http://cpcml.ca/Tmlw2017/PDF/W47023S.pdf)

49 Oleksiy Kuzmenko, "Defend the White Race": American Extremists Being Co-Opted by Ukraine's Far-Right, Feb 15 2019 (https://www.bellingcat.com/news/uk-and-europe/2019/02/15/defend-the-white-race-american-extremists-being-co-opted-by-ukraines-far-right/)

50 Christopher Miller, 'Banderite' Rebrand: Ukrainian Police Declare Admiration For Nazi Collaborators To Make A Point, Feb 11 2019 (https://www.rferl.org/a/banderite-rebrand-ukrainian-police-declare-admiration-for-nazi-collaborators-to-make-a-point/29764110.html)

51 Lev Golinkin, Neo-Nazis and the Far Right Are On the March in Ukraine, Feb 22 2019 (https://www.thenation.com/article/neo-nazis-far-right-ukraine/)

52 Ukrainian law enforcement sector needs $6.5 mln for National Police, 112.International, Sept 14 2015 (https://112.international/society/ukrainian-law-enforcement-sector-needs-65-mln-for-national-police-780.html) ; Levon Sevunts, Canada donates $8.1 for Ukrainian police reform, Oct 3 2016 (https://www.rcinet.ca/en/2016/10/03/canada-donates-8-1-for-ukrainian-police-reform/)

53 Murray Brewster, More Canadian police trainers wanted in Ukraine, Canadian Press, Dec 17 2015 (https://www.ctvnews.ca/ctv-news-channel/more-canadian-police-trainers-wanted-in-ukraine-1.2704448) ; Canada's engagement in Ukraine (https://www.international.gc.ca/world-monde/country-pays/ukraine/relations.aspx?lang=eng)

54 Royal Canadian Mounted Police, Current operations (http://www.rcmp-grc.gc.ca/en/current-operations#a5)

55 Roger Annis, Canada votes no on UN resolution condemning racism and neo-Nazism. Again. Nov 23 2015 (http://rabble.ca/blogs/bloggers/roger-annis/2015/11/canada-votes-no-on-un-resolution-condemning-racism-and-neo-nazism)

56 Ibid

57 Seventieth session Third Committee Agenda item 70 (a) Elimination of racism, racial discrimination, xenophobia and related intolerance A/C.3/70/L.59/Rev.1, Nov 13 2015 (https://undocs.org/A/C.3/70/L.59/Rev.1)

58 Loulla-Mae Eleftheriou-Smith, US one of only three countries to vote against UN resolution condemning glorification of Nazism, Nov 21 2017 (https://www.independent.co.uk/news/world/americas/us-un-nazi-glorification-resolution-vote-against-free-speech-far-right-white-supremacist-neo-alt-a8066761.html)

59 Jon Hellevig, Meet Andriy Parubiy, the Neo-Nazi Leader Turned Speaker of Ukraine's Parliament, Mondialisation.ca, Apr 17 2016 (https://www.mondialisation.ca/meet-andriy-parubiy-the-former-neo-nazi-leader-turned-speaker-of-ukraines-parliament/5520502)

60 Michael Laxer, What is far-right organization Right Sector doing marching in Toronto's Ukrainian Festival Parade?, Sept 19 2016 (http://theleftchapter.blogspot.com/2016/09/what-is-far-right-organisation-right.html) ; Ultra Nationalist Group 'Right Sector' Fundraises at Toronto Ukrainian Event, Aug 25 2014 (https://www.youtube.com/watch?v=8y6P4nCjcws) ; Emmanuel Dreyfus, Ukraine beyond politics, Le Monde diplomatique, March 2014 (https://mondediplo.com/2014/03/02ukraine)

61 Justin Ling, Canada's foreign minister warns of Russian destabilization efforts — and she might be a target, Mar 6 2017 (https://www.vice.com/en_ca/article/8xmyna/canadas-foreign-minister-warns-of-russian-destabilization-efforts-and-she-might-be-a-target) ; David Pugliese, Chrystia Freeland's granddad was indeed a Nazi collaborator – so much for Russian disinformation, Mar 8 2017 (https://ottawacitizen.com/news/national/defence-watch/chrystia-freelands-granddad-was-indeed-a-nazi-collaborator-so-much-for-russian-disinformation)

5. The Asian Contradiction
— China and North Korea

Pity the Canadian government. Relations with China were certainly difficult for the Liberals. Trudeau was squeezed between corporate interests that saw a large market and Washington's drive to stall China's ascendance.

Trudeau participated in a number of significant fundraisers organized by Chinese-Canadian capitalists with interests there.[1] The Liberals had deeper ties to Power Corporation, Bank of Montreal, Manulife and other big firms operating in China. Through the Canada China Business Council these firms pushed for better relations with China. For their part, Bell and Telus resisted a push to subvert their partnership with Chinese telecommunications giant Huawei.

On the other hand, Washington has taken an increasingly belligerent line towards Beijing. With China dislodging US–Japanese economic hegemony over the region, the Barrack Obama administration "pivoted" militarily towards China. Donald Trump's administration ratcheted up the pressure. At its most extreme, the anti-Chinese campaign reflected a worldview that longed for a divided and imperially dominated country like before 1949 and reflected a longstanding anti-Asian racism.

Early on, the Liberals explored a free trade agreement with China and, contrary to Washington's wishes, joined the Asia Infrastructure Investment Bank.[2] But, over time the Liberals have increasingly aligned with the US-led campaign against China, which Beijing legitimated by repressing Uyghurs, Hong Kong and various dissidents. In a sign of the Liberals' reversal, they agreed to an article (32.10) in the US-Mexico-Canada trade accord that granted

Washington influence over any possible Canadian trade deal with China.

Canada's arrest of Huawei Chief Financial officer Meng Wanzhou spurred the downward spiral in relations with Beijing. At Washington's request, Canadian officials detained Meng during a stopover at the Vancouver airport on December 1, 2018. The US claimed Meng's company defied its illegal sanctions against Iran. But, between when the US judicial system sought her detention and the Trump administration requested Ottawa detain her, Meng traveled to six countries with US extradition treaties.[3] Apprehended on her way to Mexico, officials from that country told the *Globe and Mail* they would not have adhered to a US request to arrest Meng.[4] China responded by detaining two Canadians and undercutting some Canadian exports.

Trump openly said the US would use Meng as a bargaining chip in its trade war with China.[5] The extradition request for Meng was part of a broader effort to weaken the "Crown Jewel of China Inc." The US effectively banned the world's largest 5G network provider from building its cutting-edge broadband and pressed others to follow suit. A *Wall Street Journal* story titled "Spy chiefs agreed to contain Huawei" detailed a July 2018 Five Eyes meeting in Ottawa where the intelligence officials agreed to contain the company's global growth.[6] Washington claimed that country's first global technological powerhouse posed a security risk. But, driving the campaign was a bid to halt China's ascendance in this critical industrial sector.

Of course the US, Australia, New Zealand, UK and Canada intelligence agencies also worried about a firm less willing to follow their directives. In fact the Five Eyes sought what they accused Huawei/China of. In September 2018 the intelligence alliance requested communication providers build "back doors" in their systems, allowing the Five Eyes espionage agencies access to communications. The Australian government actually published a statement, which was later removed, stating that "technical, legislative, coercive or other measures" should be considered to implement these "back doors".[7] The campaign to paint Huawei as a privacy violator was the racist pot calling the kettle black.

In May 2019 Ottawa joined the US, Japan and Australia in creating a competitor to China's Belts and Road Initiative (BEI).[8] As part of the BEI, Beijing invested a few hundred billion dollars in ports, trains, highways, etc. in Asia, Africa and Europe. Among the largest infrastructure and investment projects in history, the stated aim of the 'New Silk Road' was "to construct a unified large market and make full use of both international and domestic markets, through cultural exchange and integration, to enhance mutual understanding and trust of member nations, ending up in an innovative pattern with capital inflows, talent pool, and technology database."[9]

As part of the US-led response, Export Development Canada put up an initial $300 million to fund projects.[10] They worked with the US Overseas Private Investment Corporation, Australia's Department of Foreign Affairs and Trade and Japan's Bank for International Cooperation "to promote high-quality, trusted standards for global infrastructure development in an open and inclusive framework."[11]

To lessen Chinese dominance over electric vehicle batteries, smart phones and other 'green technologies' Canada joined a US-led initiative to help discover and develop reserves of lithium, cobalt, copper and rare earth elements. Nine countries are part of the Energy Resource Governance Initiative (ERGI) established in 2019. According to the US State Department's description of ERGI, "80 percent of the global supply chain of, important minerals for electric vehicles and wind turbine components, is controlled by one country."[12] Ottawa and Washington signed a number of bilateral agreements to increase US access to "minerals used in products like solar cells, permanent magnets and rechargeable batteries."[13]

To counter China's growing influence in Asia, Washington sought to stoke longstanding territorial and maritime boundary disputes in the South China Sea between China and the Philippines, Malaysia, Vietnam and other nations. As part of efforts to rally regional opposition to China, the US Navy engaged in regular "freedom of navigation" operations, which saw warships travel through or near disputed waters. From 2017 through 2019 Canada regularly deployed warships through waters that Beijing claimed in the South China Sea, Strait of Taiwan and East China Sea.[14]

HMCS Ottawa and *HMCS Winnipeg's* six-month tour of Asia in 2017 included "freedom of navigation" operations and exercises alongside US, Japanese, Australian and other countries' warships. When the two Canadian gunboats traveled through the South China Sea with their allies, Chinese vessels came within three nautical miles and "shadowed" them for 36 hours.[15] On another occasion a Chinese intelligence vessel monitored the two vessels while they exercised with a South Korean ship.[16]

In October 2017 the first ever Victoria-class submarine was deployed to the Asia-Pacific. *HMCS Chicoutimi* spent nearly 200 days at sea in the Asia-Pacific region, the longest-ever deployment for a Victoria-class sub.[17] It probably monitored Chinese vessels. After visiting *HMCS Ottawa* and *HMCS Winnipeg* in Singapore in July 2017 Chief of Defence Staff Jonathan Vance declared, "if one wants to have any respect or gravitas you have to be in that region."[18]

***

But it wasn't just geopolitical competition with China that Canada engaged in to please the US government. The Liberals also sought to bolster the US campaign to isolate North Korea. With a liberal, pro-reunification, minded president taking office in South Korea in mid-2017 Trudeau's government undercut efforts to reduce tension on the Korean Peninsula.

Canada opposed inter-Korean rapprochement, preferring the 70-year old war footing (only an armistice agreement was signed to end the 1950–53 Korean War). The Liberals openly allied with those who feared peace might break out on the Korean peninsula.

In a February 2019 *Ottawa Citizen* op-ed headlined "Canada should re-activate relations with North Korea", Senator Lois Wilson, who led Canada's first parliamentary delegation to North Korea in 2000, wrote, "Canada continues to give full and vocal support to the American approach of 'maximum pressure' and international sanctions against North Korea — the well-known and failed tactic of all sticks and no carrots."[19]

Canadian officials described North Korea as a threat. In a major June 2017 speech Freeland claimed, "the dictatorship in North Korea ... pose clear strategic threats to the liberal democratic world, including Canada."[20]

Ottawa and Washington organized an international summit in January 2018 to promote sanctions on North Korea.[21] In a highly belligerent move, the countries invited to the conference in Vancouver were those that fought against North Korea and China in the early 1950s conflict. The US pressed the 16 countries that deployed soldiers with it during the Korean War to increase their contributions to the United Nations Command (UNC) in South Korea.

"We went over there and fought the war and eventually burned down every town in North Korea," General Curtis LeMay, head of US air command during the fighting, explained three decades later. "Over a period of three years or so, we killed off ... twenty percent of the population of Korea as direct casualties of war, or from starvation and exposure."[22] As many as four million died during the war and it was the US–led UN force that was primarily responsible for massively expanding what was essentially a civil war.[23] Nonetheless, seven decades later a military website continued to claim, "more than 26,000 Canadians served in the cause of peace and freedom during the Korean War."[24]

The Liberals also promoted sanctions on North Korea. A 2016 Global Affairs release noted, "Canada co-sponsors UNSC resolution imposing tough sanctions against North Korea."[25] In addition Freeland pushed an aggressive diplomatic posture. In March

2018 she agreed with her Japanese counterpart to send a "strong message" to Pyongyang at the Group of Seven meetings.[26] During a subsequent get together, Freeland and Japanese officials pledged to maintain "maximum pressure" on North Korea while in March 2018 she applauded "South Korea's critical role in maintaining diplomatic and economic pressure on North Korea."[27]

As part of reducing tensions, ridding the peninsula of nuclear weapons and possibly reunifying their country, the two Korean governments sought a formal end to the Korean War. As an initial step the Korean leaders signed an agreement in April 2018. They asked the UN to circulate a peace declaration calling for an official end to hostilities. But, Canada's foreign minister responded gingerly to these efforts. In response to Seoul and Pyongyang's joint announcement to seek a formal end to the Korean War, Freeland said, "we all need to be careful and not assume anything."[28]

Two Global Affairs statements released later in 2018 on the "North Korea nuclear crisis" studiously ignored the Koreas' push for an official end to hostilities. Instead they called for "sanctions that exert pressure on North Korea to abandon its weapons of mass destruction and ballistic missile programs completely, verifiably and irreversibly."[29] The second statement said UN Security Council sanctions "must ... remain in place until Pyongyang takes concrete actions in respect of its international obligations."[30] Global Affairs' position flew in the face of South Korea, Russia, China and other nations that brought up easing UN sanctions on North Korea.[31] Washington, on the other hand, sought to tighten sanctions.

While Kim Jong-un's nuclear weapons testing and assassinations were condemnable, the sanctions harmed the rural population, not the elite in Pyongyang.[32] An October 2019 study on "The Human Costs and Gendered Impact of Sanctions on North Korea" noted: "There is increasing evidence that the sanctions regime on the DPRK [North Korea] is having adverse humanitarian consequences, even as the relevant UN resolutions explicitly state this is not the intention. The UN Panel of Experts has determined that the '[UN] sectoral sanctions are affecting the delivery of humanitarian-sensitive items' and that their implementation has 'had an impact on the activities of international humanitarian agencies working to address chronic humanitarian needs in the country.'"[33]

A Canadian Lieutenant General also attempted to undercut inter-Korean rapprochement. In October 2018 Wayne Eyre told a Washington audience that the North Koreans were "experts at separating allies" and that a bid for a formal end to the Korean war represented a "slippery slope" for the 28,500 US troops there. "So what could an end-of-war declaration mean? Even if there is no legal basis for it, emotionally people would start to question the presence and the continued existence of the United Nations Command," said Eyre at the Carnegie Institute for International Peace. "And it's a slippery slope then to question the presence of U.S. forces on the peninsula."[34] The first non-US general to hold the post since the command was created to fight the Korean War in 1950, Eyre became deputy commander of the UNC in mid 2018.[35] He joined 14 other Canadian officers with UNC.[36]

Responsible for overseeing the 1953 armistice agreement, the UNC itself undercut Korean rapprochement. In October 2018 the *Financial Times* reported, "the US-spearheaded United Nations Command has in recent weeks sparked controversy in host nation South Korea with a series of moves that have highlighted the chasm between Seoul's pro-engagement attitude to Pyongyang and Washington's hard line."[37] The UN force, for instance, blocked a train carrying South Korean officials from crossing the Demilitarized Zone separating the North and South as part of an initiative to improve relations by modernizing cross-border railways.

As it prepared to concede operational control over its forces to Seoul by 2023, Washington pushed to "revitalize" UNC, which was led by a US General who simultaneously commanded US troops in Korea. According to the *Financial Times*, the UN force "serves to bolster and enhance the US's position in north-east Asia at a time when China is rising."[38] As discussed above, to "revitalize" UNC the US pressed the 16 countries that deployed soldiers during the Korean War to increase their contributions at a January 2018 gathering in Vancouver to promote sanctions against the North.[39]

In other words, Washington and Ottawa preferred the existing state of affairs in Korea because it offered an excuse for keeping tens of thousands of troops near China.

Partly to bolster the campaign to isolate North Korea the Liberals deployed numerous vessels to patrol the region. A CP-140 Aurora surveillance aircraft and 40 military personnel were sent to a US base in Japan from which British, Australian and US forces monitored the North's efforts to evade UN sanctions.[40] Through 2019 the Royal Canadian Navy participated in a US-led coalition of seven countries maintaining surveillance on North Korea and engaging in sanctions enforcement in the Yellow Sea and East China Sea.[41]

A September 2018 Global Affairs statement titled "Canada renews deployment in support of multinational initiative to enforce UN Security Council sanctions on North Korea" noted: "A Canadian Armed Forces maritime patrol aircraft will return to the region to help counter North Korea's maritime smuggling, in particular its use of ship-to-ship transfers of refined petroleum products. In addition, Her Majesty's Canadian Ship (HMCS) Calgary, on operations in the area as part of Canada's continued presence in the region, was named to contribute to this effort."[42]

It was a thin line between enforcing UN sanctions on North Korea and targeting China. In October 2018 Canada's CP-140 Aurora was targeted 18 times by Chinese military aircraft in what Jonathan Vance described as "inappropriate" interactions. The Chief of Defence Staff told the *Toronto Star*, "this is flexing your muscles. You don't do that between friends. You don't do that between good trading partners."[43] But, Chinese military planners surely must have viewed Canadian aircraft and vessels on their doorstep as a sign of "flexing your muscles".

A "progressive" government would surely understand how we would see foreign military patrols near our coasts. A "progressive" government would do to others what we wished others to do to us.

Chapter 5 Notes

1 Robert Fife and Steven Chase, Trudeau attended cash-for-access fundraiser with Chinese billionaires, Nov 22 2016 (https://www.theglobeandmail.com/news/politics/trudeau-attended-cash-for-access-fundraiser-with-chinese-billionaires/article32971362/)

2 Josh Dehaas, Canada launches consultations on free trade with China, Mar 3 2017 (https://www.ctvnews.ca/politics/canada-launches-consultations-on-free-trade-with-china-1.3310129)

3 Robert Fife and Steven Chase, Inside the final hours that led to the arrest of Huawei executive Meng Wanzhou, Nov 30 2019 (https://www.theglobeandmail.com/politics/article-inside-the-final-hours-that-led-to-the-arrest-of-huawei-executive-meng/)

4 Ibid

5 Arjun Kharpal, Pompeo says the US message on Huawei is clear. Trump's words say otherwise, Aug 22 2019 (https://www.cnbc.com/2019/08/23/huawei-mike-pompeo-appears-to-be-contradicting-president-donald-trump-on-the-chinese-firm.html)

6 Rob Taylor and Sara Germano, At Gathering of Spy Chiefs, U.S., Allies Agreed to Contain Huawei Concerns are shared by top intelligence leaders from "Five Eyes" intelligence-sharing, Dec 14 2018 (https://www.wsj.com/articles/at-gathering-of-spy-chiefs-u-s-allies-agreed-to-contain-huawei-11544825652)

7 Five Eyes (https://www.german-foreign-policy.com/en/detail/7841/)

8 Robert Fife and Steven Chase, Canada strikes alliance with U.S. to counterweight to China's Belt and Road Initiative, May 14 2019 (https://www.theglobeandmail.com/politics/article-canada-strikes-alliance-with-us-counterweight-to-chinas-belt-and/)

9 What is the One Belt One Road Initiative? (https://tsangsgroup.co/areas-of-expertise/what-is-one-belt-one-road-initiative/)

10 Robert Fife and Steven Chase, Canada strikes alliance with U.S. to counterweight to China's Belt and Road Initiative, May 14 2019 (https://www.theglobeandmail.com/politics/article-canada-strikes-alliance-with-us-counterweight-to-chinas-belt-and/)

11 Peter Koenig, China: The Belt and Road Initiative The Bridge that Spans the World, Nov 24 2019 (https://dissidentvoice.org/2019/11/china-the-belt-and-road-initiative/#more-99006)

12 Energy Resource Governance Initiative (ERGI) (https://www.state.gov/wp-content/uploads/2019/06/Energy-Resource-Governance-Initiative-ERGI-Fact-Sheet.pdf)

13 Trudeau government doing spadework on minerals crucial to economy, Canadian Press, Dec 3 2019 (https://nationalpost.com/pmn/news-pmn/canada-news-pmn/trudeau-government-doing-spadework-on-minerals-crucial-to-economy)

14 Steven Chase, For second time in three months, Canadian warship transits Taiwan Strait, Sept 10 2019 (https://www.theglobeandmail.com/politics/article-for-second-time-in-three-months-canadian-warship-transits-taiwan/) ; Canada joins effort to counter China with Asian warship drills, Nov 7 2018 (https://www.reuters.com/article/us-japan-canada-defence/canada-joins-effort-to-counter-china-with-asian-warship-drills-idUSKCN1ND0DL)

15 Matthew Fisher, Canadian warships shadowed by Chinese navy in South China Sea, July 14 2017 (https://nationalpost.com/news/canada/matthew-fisher-canadian-warships-shadowed-by-chinese-navy-in-south-china-sea)

16 Ibid

17 HMCS Chicoutimi arrives home after six-month Asia-Pacific deployment, News release, National Defence, Mar 21 2018 (https://www.canada.ca/en/department-national-defence/news/2018/03/hmcs-chicoutimi-arrives-home-after-six-month-asia-pacific-deployment.html)

18 Matthew Fisher, Canadian warships shadowed by Chinese navy in South China Sea, July 14 2017 (https://nationalpost.com/news/canada/matthew-fisher-canadian-warships-shadowed-by-chinese-navy-in-south-china-sea)

19 Lois Wilson, Canada should re-activate relations with North Korea, Feb 21 2019 (https://ottawacitizen.com/opinion/columnists/sen-lois-wilson-canada-should-re-activate-relations-with-north-korea)

20 Address by Minister Freeland on Canada's foreign policy priorities, Global Affairs Canada, June

6 2017 (https://www.canada.ca/en/global-affairs/news/2017/06/address_by_ministerfreelandoncanadasforeignpolicypriorities.html)

21 Murray Brewster, North Korea summit in Vancouver to focus on enforcing sanctions ahead of diplomacy, Jan 15 2018 (https://www.cbc.ca/news/politics/north-korea-meeting-1.4485445)

22 Blaine Harden, The US war crime North Korea won't forget, Mar 24 2015 (https://www.washingtonpost.com/opinions/the-us-war-crime-north-korea-wont-forget/2015/03/20/fb525694-ce80-11e4-8c54-ffb5ba6f2f69_story.html)

23 Yves Engler, The Korean War Gangnam Style, May 12 2013 (https://yvesengler.com/2013/05/12/the-korean-war-gangnam-style/)

24 Canada Remembers Hill 355 (https://www.veterans.gc.ca/eng/remembrance/history/korean-war/hill355_sheet)

25 Canada co-sponsors UNSC resolution imposing tough sanctions against North Korea, Global Affairs Canada, Mar 2 2016 (https://www.canada.ca/en/global-affairs/news/2016/03/canada-co-sponsors-unsc-resolution-imposing-tough-sanctions-against-north-korea.html)

26 Japanese and Canadian foreign ministers agree to put North Korea on G-7 agenda, Mar 27 2018 (https://www.japantimes.co.jp/news/2018/03/27/national/politics-diplomacy/japanese-canadian-foreign-ministers-agree-put-north-korea-g-7-agenda/#.WwJIeC8ZPUo)

27 Japan and Canada vow to maintain pressure on North Korea, KYODO, APR 22 2018 (https://www.japantimes.co.jp/news/2018/04/22/national/politics-diplomacy/japan-canada-vow-maintain-pressure-north-korea/#.XjH0hy0ZPBI) ; Read Out: Minister Freeland speaks with foreign affairs minister of South Korea, Global Affairs Canada, Mar 29 2018 (https://www.international.gc.ca/gac-amc/news-nouvelles/read-out-south_korea-freeland-coree_sud.aspx?lang=eng)

28 Terry Pedwell, World must 'not assume anything' when it comes Korea peace deal, Freeland says, Canadian Press, Apr 27 2018 (https://globalnews.ca/news/4173572/canada-north-korea-summit/)

29 Canada encouraged by ongoing dialogue between North Korea and South Korea, Global Affairs Canada, Sept 20 2018 (https://www.canada.ca/en/global-affairs/news/2018/09/canada-encouraged-by-ongoing-dialogue-between-north-korea-and-south-korea.html)

30 Ibid

31 Julian Borger, China and Russia call on UN to ease North Korea sanctions, Sep 27 2018 (https://www.theguardian.com/world/2018/sep/27/un-security-council-north-korea-sanctions-china-russia-pompeo)

32 Joseph Essertier, Cutting Off the Lifelines of North Koreans? That's Called a Siege, Not "Sanctions", Jan 9 2020 (https://www.counterpunch.org/2020/01/09/cutting-off-the-lifelines-of-north-koreans-thats-called-a-siege-not-sanctions/)

33 Korea Peace Now, The Human Costs and Gendered Impact of Sanctions on North Korea, Oct 2019 (https://koreapeacenow.org/wp-content/uploads/2019/10/human-costs-and-gendered-impact-of-sanctions-on-north-korea.pdf)

34 David Brunnstrom, War-end declaration 'slippery slope' for U.S. Korea presence: U.N. Command general Oct 5 2018 (https://www.reuters.com/article/us-northkorea-usa-military/war-end-declaration-slippery-slope-for-u-s-korea-presence-u-n-command-general-idUSKCN1MF2FS)

35 Canadian takes key role with UN forces on Korean Peninsula, Canadian Press, May 14 2018 (https://globalnews.ca/news/4206939/canadian-military-wayne-eyre-un-korea/)

36 Song Sang-ho, Canadian three-star general takes office as deputy UNC chief, July 30 2018 (https://en.yna.co.kr/view/AEN20180730008500315)

37 S Korea peace drive complicated by 'revitalisation' of UN Command, Oct 2 2018 (https://www.ft.com/content/68a16b60-c520-11e8-8670-c5353379f7c2)

38 Ibid

39 Murray Brewster, North Korea summit in Vancouver to focus on enforcing sanctions ahead of diplomacy, Jan 15 2018 (https://www.cbc.ca/news/politics/north-korea-meeting-1.4485445)

40 Canada, Australia to send military aircraft to monitor North Korean ships, Apr 28 2018 (https://www.cbc.ca/news/world/north-korea-un-sanctions-surveillance-1.4640082)

41 Christy Somos, 'We're always ready': Life aboard Canada's HMCS Ottawa enforcing sanctions against North Korea, Nov 18 2019 (https://www.ctvnews.ca/canada/we-re-always-ready-life-aboard-canada-s-hmcs-ottawa-enforcing-sanctions-against-north-korea-1.4690565)

42 Canada renews deployment in support of multinational initiative to enforce UN Security Council sanctions on North Korea, Global Affairs Canada, Sept 21 2018 (https://www.canada.ca/en/global-affairs/news/2018/09/canada-renews-deployment-in-support-of-multinational-initiative-to-enforce-un-security-council-sanctions-on-north-korea.html)

43 Bruce Campion-Smith, Canadian air force aircraft harassed by Chinese during patrols off North Korea, Dec 20 2018 (https://www.thestar.com/politics/federal/2018/12/20/canadian-air-force-aircraft-harassed-by-chinese-during-patrols-off-north-korea.html)

6. Buddies With Africa's Most Ruthless Dictator — Curious Case of Kagame

The Trudeau government has supported Africa's most ruthless dictator, which is certainly not "progressive".

After amending the constitution to be able to run indefinitely Paul Kagame won 98.63% of votes in Rwanda's 2017 presidential election.[1] In response, Canada's High Commissioner Sara Hradecky tweeted, "congratulations to Rwandans for voting in peaceful presidential election" and "Canada congratulates Paul Kagame on his inauguration today as President of Rwanda." The latter tweet was picked up by the state propaganda organ *New Times* in a story titled "Heads of State, diplomats laud Kagame's 'visionary leadership'."[2]

If garnering 99% of the vote wasn't a clue that Kagame is a dictator, the High Commissioner could have taken a look at Canada's 'paper of record,' whose Africa bureau chief had recently shined a critical light on Rwanda. At the start of 2016 the *Globe and Mail* reported on two new books describing the totalitarian nature of the regime.

"Village informers," wrote South Africa-based Geoffrey York. "Re-education camps. Networks of spies on the streets. Routine surveillance of the entire population. The crushing of the independent media and all political opposition. A ruler who changes the constitution to extend his power after ruling for two decades. It sounds like North Korea, or the totalitarian days of China under Mao. But this is the African nation of Rwanda — a long-time favourite of Western governments and a major beneficiary of millions of dollars in Canadian government support."[3]

In 2014 York wrote a story headlined "Inside the plots to kill Rwanda's dissidents," which provided compelling evidence that the regime had extended its assassination program outside of east Africa, killing (or attempting to) a number of its former top officials who were living in South Africa.[4] After the initial investigation York reported on Rwandan dissidents who had to flee Belgium for their safety, while the *Toronto Star* revealed five individuals in Canada who were fearful of the regime's killers.[5]

On top of international assassinations and domestic repression, Kagame unleashed mayhem in the Congo. In 1996 Rwandan forces marched 1,500 km to topple the regime in Kinshasa and then re-invaded after the Congolese government it installed expelled Rwandan troops.[6] This led to an eight-country war between 1998 and 2003, which left millions dead. Rwandan proxies repeatedly re-invaded the mineral rich eastern Congo. In 2012 the *Globe and Mail* described how "Rwandan sponsored" M23 rebels "hold power by terror and violence" there.[7]

Despite the regime's violence, Governor General Julie Payette traveled to Kigali to meet Kagame in August 2019. She lauded "the long-standing partnership between Canada and Rwanda."[8]

On at least four occasions in 2018 and 2019 Trudeau was photographed with Kagame during one-on-one meetings on the sidelines of different international summits.[9] At one of those meetings the PM announced he planned to attend the 2020 Commonwealth summit in Kigali and "affirmed the importance of strong and growing bilateral relations" between Canada and Rwanda.[10]

Canadian-based Rwandan dissident David Himbara criticized the PM's embrace of Kagame. In April 2018 he wrote, "the romance between Canada's Prime Minister Justin Trudeau and Rwanda's strongman Paul Kagame is difficult to fathom. For the past several months, the romance between the two and among their respective ministers has blossomed beyond belief."[11]

In November 2017 Rwanda's environment minister visited Ottawa to meet her Canadian counterpart, Catherine McKenna, who lauded "our close friendship."[12] Later that year Defence Minister

Harjit Sajjan hosted his Rwandan counterpart General James Kabarebe.[13] In 2015 Kabarebe was arrested in London under a Spanish indictment for war crimes committed between 1990 and 2002 in Rwanda, including the murder of two Quebec priests.[14] Previously, Kabarebe had been the subject of an arrest warrant by a French judge for his role in shooting down President Juvénal Habyarimana's plane, which unleashed the genocidal violence in Spring 1994. A 2012 UN report claimed Kabarebe organized and armed deadly M23 rebels in eastern Congo, labeling Kabarebe "a central player in recruiting on behalf of M23" and noted that "he has often been in direct contact with M23 members on the ground to coordinate military activities."[15] After former Rwandan spy chief, turned Kagame critic Patrick Karegeya, was strangled to death in a South African hotel in January 2014 Kabarebe said, "when you choose to be a dog, you die like a dog, and the cleaners will wipe away the trash."[16]

The Rwandan government's domestic repression, international assassinations and violence in the Congo was well documented. Yet I couldn't find any criticism of Kagame by the Trudeau government. Instead, Ottawa provides about $25 million annually in assistance to Rwanda.[17]

How to explain pandering to a dictatorial regime half-way across the planet? Part of the answer is geopolitical. Kagame, who trained at the United States Army Command and General Staff College in Kansas, moved his country away from the French orbit towards the US so "interests" south of the border are happy to see Ottawa cozy up to him. Second, his regime is viewed as foreign investor friendly, which pleases the Liberals corporate sponsors. Third, the Liberal Party has long "talked left" but governed from the right, which generally means kowtowing to power. Kagame is one of the most powerful leaders in his corner of Africa.

What becomes clear after studying Canadian foreign policy for two decades is that despite the humanitarian justifications, noble sounding words like "democracy promotion" and "aid", the bottom line of what determines how this country acts towards people across the planet is the bottom line. And not the bottom line of ordinary people, but that of the wealthiest Canadians, whose interests are intertwined with those of US, European and other capitalists. Whatever is perceived as good for their business holds great sway over, if not determines, policy. So long as dictatorship, corruption, human rights abuses, political assassinations, and extreme economic inequality do not get in the way of making a profit they are acceptable.

Nowhere is this primacy of profit over people and principle clearer than in the supposedly progressive Trudeau government's policy regarding the planet-wide climate changing effects of spewing "Canadian" carbon into the international atmosphere. This is the subject of the next chapter.

Chapter 6 Notes

1 Rwanda's Kagame won election with 98.63 percent of vote: electoral board, Aug 5 2017 (https://www.reuters.com/article/us-rwanda-elections-tally-idUSKBN1AL0HX)

2 Athan Tashobya, Heads of State, diplomats laud Kagame's 'visionary leadership', Aug 20 2017 (https://www.newtimes.co.rw/section/read/218359/)

3 Geoffrey York, As Rwanda's totalitarian regime is revealed, sponsors reconsider support, Jan 8 2016 (https://www.theglobeandmail.com/news/world/world-insider/as-rwandas-totalitarian-regime-is-revealed-sponsors-reconsider-support/article28068199/)

4 Geoffrey York and Judi Rever, Assassination in Africa: Inside the plots to kill Rwanda's dissidents, May 2 2014 (https://www.theglobeandmail.com/news/world/secret-recording-says-former-rwandan-army-major-proves-government-hires-assassins-to-kill-critics-abroad/article18396349/)

5 Geoffrey York and Judi Rever, Rwandan dissident in Belgium warned of suspected targeted attack, May 14, 2014 (https://www.theglobeandmail.com/news/world/rwandan-dissident-in-belgium-a-suspected-target/article18653424/) ; Robert Cribb and Debra Black, Four other Canadians believe they're being targeted by Rwanda, Apr 11 2015 (https://www.thestar.com/news/world/2015/04/11/four-other-canadians-believe-theyre-being-targeted-by-rwanda.html)

6 John Pomfret, Rwandans Led Revolt In Congo, July 9 1997 (https://www.washingtonpost.com/wp-srv/inatl/longterm/congo/stories/070997.htm)

7 Geoffrey York, Potemkin village in Congo hides M23 rebels' violent rule, Dec 3 2012 (https://www.theglobeandmail.com/news/world/potemkin-village-in-congo-hides-m23-rebels-violent-rule/article5945653/)

8 Highlights of the Governor General's Visit to the Republic of Rwanda, Apr 8 2019 (https://www.gg.ca/en/media/news/2019/highlights-governor-generals-visit-republic-rwanda)

9 Prime Minister concludes successful week at the United Nations General Assembly, Prime Minister's Office, Sep 26 2018 (https://www.newswire.ca/news-releases/prime-minister-concludes-successful-week-at-the-united-nations-general-assembly-694383471.html

10 Paul Kagame, Prime Minister Justin Trudeau meets with the President of Rwanda, Aug 25 2019 (https://pm.gc.ca/en/news/readouts/2019/08/25/prime-minister-justin-trudeau-meets-president-rwanda-paul-kagame)

11 David Himbara, Kagame Has A New Friend—Justin Trudeau, Apr 20 2018 (https://medium.com/@david.himbara_27884/kagame-has-a-new-friend-justine-trudeau-c0393b7743c6)

12 Canada and Rwanda agree to cooperate on environmental protection and climate change, News Release, Nov 20 2017 (https://www.canada.ca/en/environment-climate-change/news/2017/11/canada_and_rwandaagreetocooperateonenvironmentalprotectionandcli.html)

13 David Himbara, Kagame Has A New Friend—Justin Trudeau, Apr 20 2018 (https://me-

dium.com/@david.himbara_27884/kagame-has-a-new-friend-justine-trudeau-c0393b7743c6)

14 Rwanda's Intelligence Chief Arrested in London, Wanted for War Crimes in Spain, Jun 23 2015 (https://news.vice.com/en_us/article/a39z7a/rwandas-intelligence-chief-arrested-in-london-wanted-for-war-crimes-in-spain)

15 Joe Lauria, Under Fire, U.N. Adds Rwanda to Council, Oct 18 2012 (https://www.wsj.com/articles/SB10000872396390444592704578064901437269178)

16 Geoffrey York, South Africa calls inquest into murder of Rwandan dissident, Nov 1 2018 (https://www.theglobeandmail.com/world/article-south-africa-calls-inquest-into-murder-of-rwandan-dissident/)

17 Canada - Rwanda Relations (https://www.canadainternational.gc.ca/kenya/bilateral_relations_bilaterales/canada_rwanda.aspx?lang=eng)

7. Climate Criminal — Spewing Carbon Dioxide

The situation is dire. Temperatures are increasing steadily and so too the frequency/intensity of "natural" disasters. In 2019 there were 15 natural disasters linked to climate change that caused more than a billion dollars in damage. Seven of them destroyed more than $10 billion.[1] Hundreds of thousands have already died as a result of anthropocentric climate disturbances and the numbers will grow exponentially.[2] A December 2019 *Globe and Mail* headline noted, "extreme weather leaves 45 million in southern Africa facing severe food shortages."[3] In a profound injustice, most of those worst hit by climate disturbances have emitted relatively little greenhouse gases (GHG).

Trudeau's failure to declare, legislate and fund a massive justice-based transition off fossil fuels is disgraceful. The decisions he made that will increase fossil fuel production and consumption for decades to come should be considered criminal.

The Liberals eliminated the planned toll on a new $4.4 billion Champlain Bridge to the South Shore of Montréal. The move told suburbanites the federal government would subsidize the most costly, unhealthy and ecologically destructive form of land transport for every metre of their 20, 40 or 80 kilometre daily drive (alone) into the city.

The Liberals spent tens of billions of dollars on heavy carbon emitting fighter jets and naval vessels. In the best-case scenario, these weapons will only emit GHG during training. In the worst-case scenario, they will spew significant GHG while destroying lives and ecosystems.

The Liberals broke their pre-election promise to eliminate fossil fuel subsidies.[4] Ottawa continues to offer billions of dollars (as much as $46 billion, according to one IMF working paper) a year in assistance to oil, gas and other fossil fuel firms.[5] While Finance Minister Bill Morneau's 2015 mandate letter from the PM said he should "work with the Minister of Environment and Climate Change to fulfil our G20 commitment and phase out subsidies for the fossil fuel industry over the medium-term", there was no mention of this objective in either Morneau's or Environment and Climate Change Minister Jonathan Wilkinson's 2019 mandate letters.[6]

The Liberals spent $4.5 billion on the Trans Mountain pipeline and related infrastructure. The move was designed to expand extraction of heavy carbon emitting tar sands oil in Alberta. It takes significantly more energy to extract bitumen than conventional crude. The tremendous amount of energy required to bring the oily sand to the surface and separate out a useful product emits huge amounts of carbon dioxide.

In March 2017 Trudeau told oil executives in Houston, "no country would find 173 billion barrels of oil in the ground and just leave them there."[7] With these words the PM made it clear his government chose business (and profits) as usual over the survival of human civilization.

Found in a wealthy, heavy emitting country, the tar sands are a 'carbon bomb' that needs to be defused. Extracting Canada's "173 billion barrels of oil" would drive ever-greater numbers of the planet's most vulnerable over the edge. The narrow ecological argument for phasing out tar sands production is powerful. It is bolstered by international equity considerations. Canada's large current and accumulated carbon footprint is another reason to keep this country's oil in the soil.

Per capita emissions in many African countries amount to one or two per cent of Canada's rate.[8] Even more startling is the historical imbalance among nations in global greenhouse gas emissions. According to a 2009 *Guardian* comparison, Canada released 23,669 million tonnes of carbon dioxide between 1900 and 2004 while Afghanistan released 77 million tonnes, Chad seven million tonnes, Morocco 812 million tonnes and Egypt 3,079 million tonnes.[9] Canada's contribution to global warming over this period was more than the combined total of every sub-Saharan African country.

A sense of 'carbon equity' demands a rapid cut in Canadian GHG emissions. So does economic justice. The richest countries should be the first to leave fossil fuel wealth in the ground. Only a sociopath would suggest the Congo, Haiti or Bangladesh stop extracting fossil fuels before Canada. Additionally, Canada has far greater means to transition off fossil fuels than many other places. Most of the world's fossil fuels need to be left untouched to have any chance of avoiding catastrophic climate change and Canadian oil ought to be in front of the 'keep it in the ground' line for a combination of ecological and equity reasons.

Expansion of the tar sands guarantees that Canada will flout its international commitments to reduce GHG emissions. At the 2015 Paris climate negotiation the Trudeau government committed Canada to reducing GHG emissions 30 percent below 2005 levels by 2030 (a major step backwards from Canada's commitment under the Kyoto Protocol and 2009 Copenhagen Accord). But, a slew of different reports suggest this target is unlikely to be achieved.[10] In December 2019 Environment Minister Jonathan Wilkinson, said Canada was expected to emit 603 million tonnes of GHG in 2030, far above the 511 million tonnes agreed to in Paris (to meet the recommendations of the Intergovernmental Panel on Climate Change, Canada would need to reduce its GHG emissions to 381 million tonnes by 2030).[11] Between 2017 and 2018 Canadian GHG emissions actually increased from 716 million to 723 million tonnes.[12]

A November 2019 Nature Communications study seeking to reconcile the 2015 Paris Agreement's goal of limiting global temperature increases to 1.5-to-2 C concluded that if the rest of the world flouted its commitments in a similar way to Canada temperatures would increase between 3 C and 4 C by the end of the century.[13] A Climate Transparency report card found that Canada's plan to meet its GHG targets was among the worst (along with Australia and South Korea) in the G20.[14] The November 2019 study found that the emissions intensity of Canada's buildings, transportation and agriculture were all above the G20 average and that Canadians produced nearly three times more GHG per capita than the G20 average.

At the COP25 climate summit in December 2019 Canada "won a few Fossils of the Day" from environmentalists for undermining negotiations, noted Elizabeth May in a post conference email. "I asked Justin Trudeau to come in person", the Green Party leader added. But, the PM declined to attend the summit.

Trudeau sought to avoid conflict with Donald Trump over his administration's shocking climate criminality. Spiegel Online reported that Trudeau rejected a proposal by Chancellor Angela Merkel to support a German initiative at the 2017 G20 summit to pressure Trump on climate change.[15] At the time of publication the Liberals hadn't committed Canada to improved automobile fuel mileage standards the Barack Obama administration negotiated with the auto industry. Trump announced the US would freeze planned fuel-economy targets at 2020 levels, which prompted a bitter battle with California and a number of other US states. With Canada, the collection of dissident states represented 40 per cent of the North American auto market, enough to push the (divided) auto industry to follow the previously agreed fuel mileage standards.[16] But, the Liberals failed to publicly commit to push forward with steadily improved fuel mileage standards.

Despite claiming to take the climate crisis seriously, the Trudeau government has failed to put the country on track to meet even dangerously insufficient targets for reducing GHG emissions. This is largely because of the oil industry's power. The profits from oil and natural gas flow to their producers and distributers, as well as the banks that finance them, and other investors whose portfolios include these stocks. These are the people who, under the current economic system, mostly determine government policy.

More on this in the next chapter.

Chapter 7 Notes

1 Climat: 15 catastrophes à plus d'un milliard de dollars en 2019, Dec 26 2019 (https://www.lapresse.ca/actualites/environnement/201912/26/01-5255013-climat-15-catastrophes-a-plus-dun-milliard-de-dollars-en-2019.php)

2 Climate Vulnerability Monitor (https://en.wikipedia.org/wiki/Climate_Vulnerability_Monitor)

3 Geoffrey York, Extreme weather leaves 45 million in southern Africa facing severe food shortages, Dec 16 2019 (https://www.theglobeandmail.com/world/article-extreme-weather-leaves-45-million-in-southern-africa-facing-severe/)

4 Trinh Theresa, Justin Trudeau's environment plan: End fossil fuel subsidies, invest in clean tech, Jun 29 2015 (https://www.cbc.ca/news/politics/justin-trudeau-s-environment-plan-end-fossil-fuel-subsidies-invest-in-clean-tech-1.3131607)

5 Bob Weber, 'Intimidating:' Alberta's energy war room singles out climate campaigner, Canadian Press, Dec 21 2019 (https://nationalpost.com/news/canada/intimidating-albertas-energy-war-room-singles-out-climate-campaigner) Mia Rabson, Fossil-fuel subsidies on Scheer's list of possible corporate cuts, Canadian Press, Sept 20 2019 (https://nationalpost.com/pmn/news-pmn/canada-news-pmn/conservatives-promise-to-spend-1-5-billion-to-buy-new-medical-imaging-equipment)

6 Jolson Lim, Morneau asked to wrap up fossil fuel subsidy review, as advocates worry phase-out plan is stalling, Dec 18 2019 (https://ipolitics.ca/2019/12/18/morneau-asked-to-wrap-up-fossil-fuel-subsidy-review-as-advocates-worry-that-phase-out-plans-are-stalling/)

7 Jeremy Berke, 'No country would find 173 billion barrels of oil in the ground and just leave them': Justin Trudeau gets a standing ovation at an energy conference in Texas, Mar 10 2017 (http://www.businessinsider.com/trudeau-gets-a-standing-ovation-at-energy-industry-conference-oil-gas-2017-3)

8 (https://docs.google.com/spreadsheets/d/1Fz-TF_G0qNN9TC1RiVrvMr_hRSfuY5W2uXDTyCt3HBqE/edit#gid=0)

9 A history of CO2 emissions (https://www.theguardian.com/environment/datablog/2009/sep/02/co2-emissions-historical)

10 Perspectives on Climate Change Action in Canada—A Collaborative Report from Auditors General, Mar 2018 (http://www.oag-bvg.gc.ca/internet/English/parl_otp_201803_e_42883.html)

11 Alexandre Shields, Le Canada sur la voie de l'échec climatique, Jan 2020 (https://www.ledevoir.com/societe/environnement/570178/climat-le-gouvernement-federal-est-loin-du-compte) Les prévisions d'émissions de GES du Canada revues à la baisse, Presse Canadienne, Dec 20 2019 (https://www.lapresse.ca/actualites/environnement/201912/20/01-5254500-les-previsions-demissions-de-ges-du-canada-revues-a-la-baisse.php)

12 Quinn Patrick, Trudeau government hides emissions stats, Jan 8 2020 (https://www.thepostmillennial.com/trudeau-government-hides-emissions-stats/)

13 Jonathon Gatehouse, Canada among worst offenders as world falls short of climate-change targets, Nov 16 2018 (https://www.cbc.ca/news/thenational/national-today-newsletter-climate-change-twitter-1.4902717)

14 Mia Rabson, Canada among G20 countries least likely to hit emissions targets, Canadian Press, Nov 11 2019 (https://www.cbc.ca/news/technology/canada-climate-action-1.5355517)

15 Von Christiane Hoffmann , Peter Müller und Gerald Traufetter, Merkel's G-20 Climate Alliance Is Crumbling, June 9 2017 (http://www.spiegel.de/international/germany/angela-merkel-s-anti-trump-alliance-crumbling-ahead-of-g-20-a-1151439.html)

16 Editorial, Fuel efficiency, Donald Trump and Canada's battle against climate change, Jan 7 2020 (https://www.theglobeandmail.com/opinion/editorials/article-fuel-efficiency-donald-trump-and-canadas-battle-against-climate/)

8. Same Old, Same Old — Business Above All Else

Those who "own" the economy wield substantial power over any government's domestic policy and overwhelming control over foreign policy where there are few democratic checks and balances. Based on accumulated evidence there is little difference in this regard between Liberal and Conservative governments. Certainly, the Trudeau regime pushed corporate interests through various forums. They signed investor accords and expanded the Trade Commissioner Service (TCS) while demonstrating little interest in reining in corporate abuses and Export Development Canada. Trudeau empowered international investors by negotiating and signing <u>Foreign Investment Promotion and Protection Agreements</u>. FIPAs give corporations the right to sue governments — in private, investor-friendly tribunals — for pursuing policies that interfere with their profit making. As such, they undermine governments' ability to democratically determine economic and ecological policy.

The Liberals signed FIPAs with Nigeria, Moldova and negotiated them with a half dozen more states.[1] Following his participation in the November 2018 Africa Investment Forum, Parliamentary Secretary to the Minister of International Trade Omar Alghabra wrote: "To further help Canadian companies compete and succeed in this thriving region, the Canadian government has negotiated foreign investment promotion and protection agreements (FIPAs) with Benin, Burkina Faso, Cameroon, Ivory Coast, Guinea, Mali, Senegal and Tanzania. These agreements encourage increased bilateral investments between our countries by helping to reduce risk and by increasing investor confidence in our respective markets. We continue to advance FIPA negotiations with a number of other African countries."[2]

The "free trade" agreement the Liberals signed with the Ukraine included a FIPA style Investor State Dispute Settlement (ISDS) mechanism.[3] Against the wishes of New Delhi, the Liberals pushed for an ISDS provision in the "free trade" accord it negotiated with India.[4] A similar dynamic played out with the US-Mexico-Canada Accord. Donald Trump insisted on removing ISDS from NAFTA (Chapter 11) while the Liberals pushed for a "progressive" ISDS mechanism in the updated accord.[5] The 2018 Comprehensive and Progressive Agreement for Trans-Pacific Partnership included an ISDS provision.[6] The Liberals' main addition to the accord with Australia, Brunei, Chile, Japan, Malaysia, Mexico, New Zealand, Peru, Singapore and Vietnam was to add the word "progressive" to its name.[7]

The Liberals finalized the Comprehensive Economic and Trade Agreement (CETA) with the European Union, which included a "progressive" ISDS provision. Freeland claimed CETA was the "most progressive free trade agreement in history" that would "advance environmental protections, transparent investment rules, workers rights and world-class public services."[8] Notwithstanding the over-the-top rhetoric, barely any of the 1,600 pages of text the previous Conservative government negotiated with the EU were altered in the final CETA accord. The agreement gives multinational corporations unprecedented rights to bid on public contracts to the detriment of provincial and municipal agencies' ability to buy local and pursue other environmental and socially minded policies. It also extended patents, driving up pharmaceutical drug costs. Finally, environmental and labour provisions in the accord were not binding.

The Liberals' bid to strengthen the World Trade Organization (WTO) reinforced international inequities. In October 2018 international trade minister Jim Carr created a coalition of 13 WTO members (EU, Japan, Australia, Brazil, Chile, Kenya, Mexico, Singapore, New Zealand, South Korea, Norway and Switzerland).[9] The group met in Ottawa amidst trade tensions between the US and China and while the US president was criticizing the WTO. The aim of the initiative was to find an agreement on WTO reform that could later be brought to the institution's broader membership. The spokesperson for the African Group, South Africa's envoy to the WTO, Xavier Carim, criticized the Canadian-led scheme. "When we look at these proposals, we see them as making the imbalance that we have even worse," said Carim. "They should make it difficult for developing countries to advance."[10] Carim said the African Group wanted greater policy space to industrialise and reforms to agricultural trade distortions.

Through the WTO the Liberals challenged EU restrictions on gene-edited crops. In July 2018 the European Court of Justice ruled that agricultural gene editing should be regulated under the EU's genetically modified organisms (GMO) protocols. In response Canada, the US and 11 other countries criticized EU farm product regulations at the WTO.[11] They claimed that exports with a low-level presence of gene-edited crops should not be restricted even if the product was unapproved in the recipient nation. Changing food at the molecular level, gene-editing is used to modify the flavour or texture of fruits. Big agricultural firms such as Monsanto/Bayer promote gene editing partly to tighten their grip over the food supply.[12] But, there were unresolved questions about the long-term effects of gene-edited organisms on human health and the environment.

The Liberals took up big agriculture's challenge to other European health and environmental legislation as well.[13] A July 2019 *Le Devoir* story detailed Canadian efforts to weaken various EU regulations on pesticides and GMOs. The Liberals, for instance, pushed the EU to allow the herbicide 2,4-D, which was used on Canadian soybeans but classified as a probable carcinogen by the International Agency for Research on Cancer.[14] Framing their effort as defending free trade, the Liberals effectively undercut environmental protections and the precautionary principle.

The Liberals have also been nonchalant about companies dumping Canadian trash abroad. In 2013 and 2014 more than 100 containers of household garbage were shipped from Canada to the Philippines. Officially labeled as plastics for recycling, the containers were actually filled with diapers, food waste, discarded electronics, etc. A Filipino court ordered Canada to take back the garbage and during trips to the Philippines in 2015 and 2017 Trudeau promised to deal with the trash.[15] The government stalled until civil society campaigning and threats by Filipino President Rodrigo Duterte forced their hand in Spring 2019. Still, the Liberals refused to ban the export of waste to developing countries.[16] They failed to ratify the Basel Ban Amendment, which prohibited rich countries from exporting waste to poor countries.[17] The amendment became binding in late 2019 after it was ratified by 97 countries.

  The Liberals also did little to weaken corporate tax avoidance. Often called "transfer pricing" or "trade misinvoicing", multinational corporations artificially adjust the price of goods sold between their subsidiaries or partner companies in order for profits to end up in low (or no) tax jurisdictions while costs appear in high tax countries where they're deducted from a company's tax bill. Resource starved African governments lose tens of billions of dollars annually from "transfer pricing". Canadian mining companies often have subsidiaries in a multitude of locations, including well-known tax havens. In 2017, for instance, Toronto-based Barrick Gold had some 80 interlinked, but distinct, corporate entities sprinkled across the globe, including in the Bahamas and Cayman Islands. The aim was partly to lessen tax payments.[18]

  The Liberals have remained largely passive regarding reforms to the international corporate tax system.[19] They don't, for instance, appear to have engaged with the OECD's Inclusive Framework "new practice notes" for countries dealing with tax avoidance/evasion in the mining industry.[20]

  But the Liberals did aid Canadian firms operating abroad by boosting the Trade Commissioner Service (TCS). In November 2018 they increased the Global Affairs run TCS' budget by $184 million over five years.[21] TCS had over 1,000 officials at Canadian embassies, high commissions and consulates in 160 cities.[22]

'Our business is helping Canadian business' has long been the ethos driving TCS. From working with European colonial administrators in Africa a century ago to selling arms to Gulf monarchies bombing Yemen in 2019, TCS has been little troubled by ethical considerations. Barrick Gold, SNC Lavalin and other controversial Canadian firms have benefited from TCS services in recent years. TCS also aided the Canadian Association of Defence and Security Industries and Canadian weapons sellers.[23]

TCS has promoted privatization in Africa. In September 2019 the CEO of the Canadian Council for Public-Private Partnerships, Mark Romoff, lauded TCS in a story describing how its representatives brought CPCS Ventures together with Zambia's publicly owned power utility during the 2019 Africa Energy Forum in London. As a result, the Ottawa-based consulting firm — an aggressive proponent of Public-Private Partnerships in Africa — was awarded a $9.4 million contract by ZESCO to advise it on developing a 750-megawatt hydro power plant. Having TCS help set up the initial meeting with ZESCO "brought a lot of additional weight," explained CPCS Ventures CEO Arif Mohiuddin. "If a trade commissioner who represents the Canadian government says, 'I know this company, I know the work it does,' it helps."[24]

Export Development Canada (EDC) is another pillar of Canada's corporate empowering foreign policy apparatus that the Liberals have failed to rein in. The crown corporation offers trade financing, insurance, bonding services and foreign market expertise. With 1,500 employees at dozens of Canadian and international offices, EDC is one of the largest government export credit agencies in the world.[25] As this book went to press it had over $50 billion in outstanding loans.[26]

But, EDC is not required to consider the environmental or human rights implications of its loans. Left-wing activists have long criticized the crown corporation's practices but in 2018 and 2019 EDC received a bout of negative publicity, particularly in the *Globe and Mail*. Environmental groups complained about the $12 billion EDC loaned to oil and gas companies in the first two and a half years of the Liberal government while EDC's top client Bombardier was embroiled in a series of corruption cases.[27] In the most discussed case, EDC loaned US$41-million to support a luxury jet sale to the Gupta brothers who were central to a corruption scandal that toppled South African president Jacob Zuma in 2018.[28] EDC covered 80% of the cost of the businessmen's private jet, which appeared designed partly to help Bombardier gain a lucrative locomotive contract from a state-owned freight company where the Guptas wielded influence. EDC also financed what became a $450 million Bombardier rail contract with South Africa's Transnet SOC.[29]

In the June 2019 exposé "See no evil: How Canada is bankrolling companies accused of bid-rigging, graft and human-rights violation" the *Globe and Mail* Report on Business detailed some controversial EDC deals. According to the story, even when its clients were targeted by law enforcement or court rulings, EDC sometimes continued to offer assistance.

The crown corporation has been exempt from the regulations governing private-sector financial institutions. It wasn't obliged to follow the rules set out by the Office of the Superintendent of Financial Institutions, which supervised federally registered banks, insurers, trusts and lenders.[30]

As part of a mandatory review of EDC's rules, a number of groups called on the Liberals to modify the Export Development Act to compel EDC to screen clients for human rights and environmental considerations and to loosen its privacy restrictions. As this book went to print, it appeared unlikely the Liberals would heed these calls. The government dragged its feet on the mandatory 10-year legislative review that began in 2018. In May 2019 they released a standalone human rights policy for EDC, but it wasn't binding on the crown corporation or its corporate clients. The Steelworkers union described it as "a policy that uses the right words in many places, but includes enough ambiguity and ample room for discretion that it raises concerns and questions about the ability of EDC to place human rights front and centre."[31]

The international trade minister's statements about EDC's response to the negative publicity suggested he would not press for legislative change. In September 2019 Jim Carr told the *Globe and Mail* that EDC had taken steps to clean up its act after a series of embarrassing revelations. "The early evidence, from our perspective, is that mistakes were made, lessons have been learned and they are now being applied," noted Carr. "Compared to where I believe we have been, we're in a better place."[32]

The Liberals' protection of SNC Lavalin reflected their indifference to corruption abroad and the primacy of promoting Canadian corporate interests. In the biggest Liberal scandal during their first term, the Prime Minister's Office interfered in the prosecution of the engineering and construction giant accused of bribing officials in Libya. Former attorney general Jody Wilson-Raybould claimed she was repeatedly pressured to defer prosecution of the Montréal-based company and instead negotiate a fine, which would allow the company to avoid a ban on federal government contracts.[33] Ultimately government lawyers negotiated a $280 million fine with SNC in December 2019.

Facing a 10-year ban on receiving federal government contracts if convicted of bribing Libyan officials, SNC began to lobby the Liberals to change the criminal code in February 2016.[34] The company wanted the government to introduce deferred prosecution agreements (DPAs) in which a sentencing agreement would allow the company to continue receiving government contracts. At SNC's request the government changed the criminal code but Wilson-Raybould resisted pressure from the PMO to negotiate a DPA with the engineering firm.

Cn gov't - an arm of privately owned, global corps.

Before Trudeau went to bat for SNC the firm had either been found guilty or alleged to have greased palms in Libya, Bangladesh, Algeria, India, Kazakhstan, Tunisia, Angola, Nigeria, Mozambique, Ghana, Malawi, Uganda, Cambodia and Zambia (as well as Québec). A 2013 CBC/Globe and Mail investigation of a small Oakville, Ontario, based division of SNC uncovered suspicious payments to government officials in connection with 13 international development projects.[35] In each case between five and 10 per cent of costs were recorded as "'project consultancy cost,' sometimes 'project commercial cost,' but [the] real fact is the intention is [a] bribe," a former SNC engineer, Mohammad Ismail, told CBC.[36]

While Trudeau's interference in the prosecution of SNC highlights corporate influence over politics, it is also a story about a firm at the centre of Canadian foreign policy. "With offices and operations in over 160 countries", SNC has long been a leading corporate face of Canadian foreign policy.[37] Historically, it is not much of an exaggeration to describe some Canadian diplomatic posts as PR arms for the Montréal-based firm.

SNC has been one of the largest corporate recipients of Canadian "aid." The company has had entire departments dedicated to applying for Canadian International Development Agency (CIDA), UN and World Bank funded projects. SNC's first international contract, in 1963 in India, was financed by Canadian aid and led to further work in that country.[38] In the late 1960s the firm was hired to manage CIDA offices in African countries where Canada had no diplomatic representation.[39] In 2006 SNC was bailed out by the Canadian aid agency after it didn't follow proper procedure for a contract to renovate and modernize the Pallivasal, Sengulam and Panniyar hydroelectric projects in the southern Indian state of Kerala.[40] A new state government demanded a hospital in compensation for the irregularities and SNC got CIDA to put up $1.8 million for the project. (SNC-Lavalin initially said they would put $20 million into the hospital, but they only invested between $2 and $4.4 million.)

Even as evidence of its extensive bribery began seeping out in 2013, SNC continued to receive diplomatic support and rich government contracts. SNC and a partner were awarded part of a contract worth up to $400 million to manage Canadian Forces bases abroad; Canada's aid agency profiled a venture SNC co-led to curb pollution in Vietnam; Canada's High Commissioner Gérard Latulippe and Canadian Commercial Corporation vice president Mariette Fyfe-Fortin sought "to arrange an untendered, closed-door" contract for SNC to build a $163-million hospital complex in Trinidad and Tobago.[41] Since 2013 Export Development Canada issued SNC or its international customers upwards of $1 billion in loans.[42] There seems to have been little difference between the approaches of the former Harper Conservative government and the Trudeau Liberals. "Upon seeing SNC-Lavalin's steps to improve its ethics and compliance program and changes it made to its management and governance levels, EDC has facilitated three financing transactions involving SNC-Lavalin since 2017", EDC spokesperson Jessica Draker told the *Globe and Mail* in 2019.[43]

Ottawa's support for SNC despite corruption allegations in 15 countries was not altogether surprising since the company has proven to be a loyal foot soldier for controversial foreign policy decisions.[44] SNC's nuclear division participated in a delegation to India led by International Trade Minister Stockwell Day a few months after Ottawa signed a 2008 agreement to export nuclear reactors to India, even though New Delhi refused to sign the Nuclear non-Proliferation Treaty (India developed atomic weapons with Canadian technology).[45] Describing it as the "biggest private contractor to [the] Canadian mission" in Afghanistan, the *Ottawa Citizen* referred to SNC in 2007 as "an indispensable part of Canada's war effort."[46] During the occupation of Afghanistan CIDA contracted SNC to carry out its $50 million "signature project" to repair the Dahla dam on the Arghandab River in Kandahar province ($10 million was spent on private security for the dam).[47] SNC also constructed and managed Canada's main military base in Kandahar during the war there.[48]

In Haiti SNC participated in a Francophonie Business Forum trip seven months after the US, Canada and France overthrew the country's elected President Jean-Bertrand Aristide.[49] Amidst the coup government's vast political repression, the Montréal firm met foreign installed prime minister Gérard Latortue and the company received a series of Canadian government-funded contracts in Haiti. They also constructed Canada's Embassy in Port-au-Prince.[50] This use of SNC in controversial situations spanned both Liberal and Conservative governments.

Justin Trudeau's ongoing support for SNC Lavalin highlights Liberal Party indifference to corporate corruption in foreign countries. This indifference to, or sometimes active encouragement of, corporate corruption has been especially evident in the mining sector, where Canada is a global giant. The story of the Ugly Canadian Abroad is the subject of the next chapter.

Chapter 8 Notes

1 Trade and investment agreements (https://www.international.gc.ca/trade-commerce/trade-agreements-accords-commerciaux/agr-acc/index.aspx?lang=eng)

2 Omar Alghabra, Canada-Africa Trade : A Platform for Prosperity, Nov 21 2018 (http://www.thepatrioticvanguard.com/canada-africa-trade-a-platform-for-prosperity)

3 Canada-Ukraine Free Trade Negotiations Show table of contents Final Environmental Assessment Report, Jan 2016 (https://www.international.gc.ca/trade-agreements-accords-commerciaux/env/final_ea_canada-ukraine_ee.aspx?lang=eng)

4 Brent Patterson, Trudeau pushes controversial investor-state dispute settlement provision on trip to India, Feb 19 2018 (https://canadians.org/blog/trudeau-pushes-controversial-investor-state-dispute-settlement-provision-trip-india)

5 Martin Lukacs, The Trudeau Formula: seduction and betrayal in an age of discontent, 181

6 Scott Sinclair, A detailed look at the new, decidedly not-so-progressive Trans-Pacific Partnership, Feb 12 2018 (http://behindthenumbers.ca/2018/02/12/backgrounder-new-decidedly-not-progressive-trans-pacific-partnership/)

7 Ibid

8 Martin Lukacs, The Trudeau Formula: seduction and betrayal in an age of discontent, 175

9 Janyce McGregor, Carr to rejoin 'like-minded' for next talks on WTO reform at Davos, Jan 8 2019 (https://www.cbc.ca/news/politics/wto-reform-davos-1.4970104)

10 Julius Bizimungu, WTO reforms may go against the interest of Africa, The New Times, Dec 15 2018 (https://www.newtimes.co.rw/news/wto-reforms-may-go-against-interest-africa)

11 Cameron English, 13 nations say it's time to end 'political posturing' and embrace crop gene editing, Nov 7 2018 (https://geneticliteracyproject.org/2018/11/07/13-nations-say-its-time-to-end-political-posturing-and-embrace-crop-gene-editing/)

12 Robert Arnason, Canada joins support for gene editing, Nov 6 2018 (https://www.producer.com/2018/11/canada-joins-support-for-gene-editing/)

13 Canada joins global partners in support of agriculture innovation and trade, Nov 2 2018, Agriculture and Agri-Food Canada (https://www.newswire.ca/news-releases/canada-joins-global-partners-in-support-of-agriculture-innovation-and-trade-699434161.html)

14 Katelyn Thomas, Le Canada et les norms europeennes sur les pesticides et les OGM, Le Devoir, July 25 2019

15 Mia Rabson, Philippines president gives Canada a week to take back tonnes of trash, or he will 'declare

war' and send it back himself, Canadian Press, April 23 2019 (https://nationalpost.com/news/world/filipino-president-duterte-gives-canada-one-week-to-take-trash-back)

16 Stop sending Canadian trash overseas, environmental activists plead, Aug 2 2019 (https://montrealgazette.com/news/stop-sending-our-trash-overseas-activists-plead)

17 Ainslie Cruickshank, Star Vancouver, Canada opposes ban on 'indefensible' practice of shipping hazardous waste to developing countries, May 10 2019 (https://www.thestar.com/news/canada/2019/05/10/canada-opposes-ban-on-indefensible-practice-of-shipping-hazardous-waste-to-developing-countries.html) ; Kathleen Ruff (https://rightoncanada.ca/?p=4376)

18 "Canada Brand": Violence and Canadian Mining Companies in Latin America, Justice and Corporate Accountability Project of Osgoode Law School, Dec 1 2017

19 Toby Sanger, Canada can help fix broken international corporate tax system, July 3 2019 (https://policyoptions.irpp.org/magazines/june-2019/canada-can-help-fix-broken-international-corporate-tax-system/)

20 Ugo Lapointe, Tax Evasion - Tell The Trudeau Government to Act Now and Close the Legal Loopholes, Oct 19 2018 (https://miningwatch.ca/blog/2018/10/19/tax-evasion-tell-trudeau-government-act-now-and-close-legal-loopholes?__cf_chl_jschl_tk__=3d56ca88760240f89f-e157cdbd35fd68cea300bd-1580533039-0-AfMSm-33RXTZZXuPdoPpU3iZPIrja1DZ-6Ue538qck-VcYJrsQ1mAKgFeXvx8kFsBlN4qjoQA-QJ5XJ3yHHtevpSDRRoECbmFgRGPwHLSx-t8d9N4ViE4UmKpaEcHMiajHKi1a1wtY1eY-HK--29Vd1Y_Q-QubpK3DiYYP3mQX-GA3Z-NOyMl-QcXgxaZdL2uh-FzhsZelki8WvlfV4_ex-LcangR5pEHDVpHmy5xGTCubEPr_wsZd-VF-ZgJDL_oL_sZm8_LSmqXYE8O8yBx8B-W2UYlt2CIAHMVBo-UGxUsarLHiKdjjsRA-fE11IRjNsa1W3FzrA_3A8KdnGRCO0oW_gEo9FJDFTZFrZ_lqnWuash1scCebWd8i1ui9m-PL5lA_9F0BSWg)

21 Janyce McGregor, Fall economic statement sets target of 50 per cent export growth by 2025, Nov 21 2018 (https://www.cbc.ca/news/politics/fall-economic-statement-trade-mcgregor-wednesday-1.4914420)

22 Canada poised to be a leader in cleantech oil and gas innovation, Canadian Trade Commissioner Service, Aug 9 2019, (https://www.jwnenergy.com/article/2019/8/canada-poised-be-leader-cleantech-oil-and-gas-innovation/)

23 Let's Meet at DSEI 2019 (https://info.ccc.ca/dsei)

24 High Stakes for Canada's Infrastructure Companies in P3 Projects, Sept 26 2019 (https://webcache.googleusercontent.com/search?q=cache:8M-R0P1-Nxx8J:https://www.tradecommissioner.gc.ca/canadexport/0001995.aspx%3Flang%3Deng%26wb-disable%3Dtrue+&cd=1&hl=en&ct=clnk&gl=ca&client=safari)

25 Matthew McClearn and Geoffrey York, See no evil: How Canada is bankrolling companies accused of bid-rigging, graft and human-rights violation, June 1 2019 (https://www.theglobeandmail.com/canada/article-export-development-canada-investigation/)

26 Matt McClearn, What does EDC do? A guide to 'Canada's secret trade weapon', June 1 2019 (https://www.theglobeandmail.com/canada/article-export-development-canada-explainer/)

27 Mia Rabson, Liberal government still plans to eliminate fossil fuel subsidies, McKenna says, May 9 2018 (https://ipolitics.ca/2018/05/09/liberal-government-still-plans-to-eliminate-fossil-fuel-subsidies-mckenna-says/)

28 Matthew McClearn and Geoffrey York, See no evil: How Canada is bankrolling companies accused of bid-rigging, graft and human-rights violation, June 1 2019 (https://www.theglobeandmail.com/canada/article-export-development-canada-investigation/)

29 Ibid

30 Ibid

31 Mike Blanchfield, New EDC human-rights policy lacks power, say workers and watchdogs, Canadian Press, May 1 2019 (https://nationalpost.com/pmn/news-pmn/canada-news-pmn/new-edc-human-rights-policy-lacks-power-say-workers-and-watchdogs)

32 Matthew McClearn and Geoffrey York, Trade Minister Jim Carr says EDC must learn from past business 'mistakes', Sept 15 2019 (https://www.theglobeandmail.com/politics/article-trade-minister-jim-carr-tells-edc-to-improve-human-rights-and-anti/)

33 Tonda MacCharles and Bruce Campion-Smith, Jody Wilson-Raybould says she was target of 'veiled threats' over SNC-Lavalin prosecution, Feb 27 2019 (https://www.thestar.com/politics/federal/2019/02/27/jody-wilson-raybould-says-pressure-in-snc-lavalin-affair-was-inappropriate.html)

34 David Cochrane, Inside SNC-Lavalin's long lobbying campaign to change the sentencing rules, Feb 14 2019 (https://www.cbc.ca/news/politics/snc-lavalin-trudeau-bribery-fraud-wilson-raybould-1.5020498)

35 Dave Seglins, SNC-Lavalin International used secret code for 'bribery' payments, May 15 2013 (https://www.cbc.ca/news/canada/snc-lavalin-international-used-secret-code-for-bribery-payments-1.1386670)

36 Ibid

37 Dan Donovan, The Deep State - The Trudeau Government, Lobbyists and the Legalization of Corruption in Canada, Mar 6 2019 (https://www.ottawalife.com/article/the-deep-state-the-trudeau-government-lobbyists-and-the-legalization-of-corruption-in-canada)

38 A history of SNC-Lavalin, Toronto Star, May 25 2013

39 David R. Morrison, Aid and Ebb Tide: A History of CIDA and Canadian Development Assistance, 67

40 SNC-Lavalin Kerala hydroelectric scandal (https://en.wikipedia.org/wiki/SNC-Lavalin_Kerala_hydroelectric_scandal)

41 SNC-Lavalin PAE Inc. to support Canadian military through CANCAP contract, Aug 8 2013 (https://www.newswire.ca/news-releases/snc-lavalin-pae-inc-to-support-canadian-military-through-cancap-contract-512784641.html) ; CIDA Profiles ESSA Joint Venture to Curb Industrial Pollution in Vietnam, Nov 4 2015 (https://essa.com/cida-profiles-essa-joint-venture-to-curb-industrial-pollution-in-vietnam/) ; Patricia Adams, Trinidad and Tobago Taught Canada an Anti-Corruption Lesson Sept 25 2013 (https://www.huffingtonpost.ca/patricia-adams/trinidad-and-tobago-reject-snc-lavalin_b_3985365.html) ; Patricia Adams, SNC-Lavalin Corruption Allegations Abound -- So Why's Canada Promoting the Company Abroad?, Aug 5 2013 (https://www.huffingtonpost.ca/patricia-adams/snc-lavalin-trinidad-and-tobago_b_3701414.html)

42 Geoffrey York and Daniel Leblanc Matthew McClearn, SNC-Lavalin received billions in support from federal export agency, Feb 15 2019 (https://www.theglobeandmail.com/canada/article-snc-lavalin-received-billions-in-support-from-federal-export-agency/)

43 Ibid

44 Dave Seglins, 10 countries where SNC-Lavalin contracts under scrutiny Invoices, budgets list scores of 'illegitimate' project costs, May 15 2013 (https://www.cbc.ca/news2/interactives/snc-lavalin-payments/)

45 No. 17 Minister Day Promotes Canadian Nuclear Technology in India, Jan 21 2009 (https://www.international.gc.ca/media_commerce/comm/news-communiques/2009/386757.aspx?lang=eng) ; Editorial, Canada and India: The nuclear genie, 40 years on, Apr 15 2015 (https://www.theglobeandmail.com/opinion/editorials/canada-and-india-the-nuclear-genie-40-years-on/article23978162/)

46 Andrew Mayeda, Canada's frontline contractors, Ottawa Citizen, Nov 20 2007

47 Paul Watson, Kandahar's parched landscape is a reminder of promises unkept and hopes unfulfilled, Toronto Star, July 14 2012 ; Jessica McDiarmid, Canada spent $10 million for security at Afghan dam project, Mar 13 2013 (https://www.thestar.com/news/canada/2013/03/13/afghanistan_dam_project_9_million_set_aside_for_security_contractors_including_those_in_armed_standoff.html)

48 SNC-Lavalin PAE Inc. to support Canadian military through CANCAP contract, Aug 8 2013 (https://www.newswire.ca/news-releases/snc-lavalin-pae-inc-to-support-canadian-military-through-cancap-contract-512784641.html)

49 Anthony Fenton, The Canadian Corporate Nexus in Haiti, Haiti Progres, May 9 2005 (http://archives-2001-2012.cmaq.net/en/node/21035.html)

50 SNC-Lavalin announces executive changes, Feb 9 2012 (https://www.newswire.ca/news-releases/snc-lavalin-announces-executive-changes-509606951.html)

9. Ugly Canadian Abroad — Mining Exploitation

Canada is a mining powerhouse. With 0.5% of the global population, Canada is home to half the world's mining companies.[1] Present in most countries, Canadian-based or listed firms operate about 4,000 mineral projects abroad, which works out to over 20 per UN member state.[2]

No matter how much Canadians wish they were simply known for hockey or comedians, the mining industry often is the image of Canada abroad. There have been an astounding number of conflicts at Canadian-run mines. Pick almost any country in the Global South — from Papua New Guinea to Ghana, Ecuador to the Philippines — and you will find a Canadian-run mine that has caused environmental devastation or been the scene of violent confrontations.

Canadian-run mines commonly destroyed farmland, harmed endangered species and contaminated drinking water. They also spurred beatings, kidnappings, arbitrary arrests and killings in the communities nearby. Canadian mines often undermined indigenous self-determination and were pushed through despite overwhelming local opposition.

Over the past two decades thousands of articles, reports, documentaries and books have detailed Canadian mining abuses abroad. At least five UN bodies have called on Ottawa to hold Canadian companies accountable for their international operations.[3] In June 2015 the UN Human Rights Committee noted: "The State party [Canada] should (a) enhance the effectiveness of existing mechanisms to ensure that all Canadian corporations under its jurisdiction, in particular mining corporations, respect human rights standards when operating abroad; (b) consider establishing an independent mechanism with powers to investigate human rights abuses by such corporations abroad; and (c) develop a legal framework that affords legal remedies to people who have been victims of activities of such corporations operating abroad."[4]

Nonetheless, the Trudeau regime failed to follow through on their promises to rein in this controversial sector. In fact, the Liberals aggressively supported some of the most retrograde mining firms. When asked about Canada's controversial mining industry during the 2015 election the party responded: "The Liberal Party of Canada shares Canadians' concerns about the actions of some Canadian mining companies operating overseas and has long been fighting for transparency, accountability and sustainability in the mining sector."[5] The statement included explicit support for An Act Respecting Corporate Accountability for Mining, Oil and Gas Corporations in Developing Countries, which would have withheld some diplomatic and financial support from companies found responsible for significant abuses abroad. Similarly, the Liberals released a letter about the mining sector during the 2015 election that noted, "a Liberal government will set up an independent ombudsman office to advise Canadian companies, consider complaints made against them and investigate those complaints where it is deemed warranted."[6]

Trudeau's government waited nearly four years to set up Canada's Ombudsperson for Responsible Enterprise (CORE) to supervise Canadian mining companies' international operations. The ombudsperson had yet to take on a single case by the end of 2019.[7] CORE's initial six-year budget was slightly more than one million dollars annually and the Liberals appointed a former oil lobbyist, Sheri Meyerhoffer, as the initial ombudsperson.[8]

All 14 union and NGO representatives on the government's "multi-stakeholder advisory body on responsible business conduct" resigned in May 2019 after their concerns about the ombudsperson were disregarded. Instead of a robust, independent, position they promised to create in January 2018, CORE "relies on companies' goodwill to voluntarily provide information that it requires in order to do an investigation," said Emily Dwyer, coordinator of the Canadian Network on Corporate Accountability. "It has not been given the basic, minimum kind of mandate and tools that it would need to have any effect."[9]

While the government announced an independent position, they effectively created an advisor to the Minister of International Trade. The ombudsperson must pass its reports by the minister before publication. In another reversal from the government's January 2018 declaration, the ombudsperson wasn't granted the power to compel testimony from mining executives or requisition documents needed to investigate human rights complaints against companies operating abroad. Additionally, the ombudsperson's capacity to deny or withdraw diplomatic or Export Development Canada support from a company found responsible for major rights abuses was neutered.

In April 2019 the chair of the UN Working Group on Business and Human Rights, Surya Deva, criticized the Trudeau government for gutting its promise to rein in Canadian mining abuses abroad.[10] For his part, the UN Special Rapporteur on human rights and hazardous substances and wastes, Baskut Tuncak, said he was "deeply concerned" about environmental practices of Canadian mining companies abroad and that Canada had a "double standard" when it came to regulating the environmental practices of mining companies operating at home versus internationally.[11]

Notwithstanding Liberal promises, it remained extremely difficult to hold Canadian companies accountable domestically for abuses committed abroad. The government failed to adopt legislation modeled on the US Alien Torts Claims Act that would allow lawsuits against Canadian companies responsible for major human rights violations or ecological destruction internationally.

Concurrently, Trudeau continued to place the power of Canadian foreign policy behind the industry. Extractive companies were big beneficiaries of Export Development Canada's services. The

Crown corporation provided tens of billions of dollars in financing and insurance to the extractive sector, including many controversial international projects.[12] To the benefit of mining firms, as noted in the previous chapter, the Liberals demonstrated little interest in establishing human rights and environmental standards for EDC. The Liberals also boosted the Global Affairs run Trade Commissioner Service (TCS), which has supported many mining projects. TCS officials based at Canadian diplomatic outposts assist firms with market assessments, problem-solving, contacting local officials, etc.[13] "The TCS plays a pretty big role," said Ben Chalmers, senior vice-president of the Mining Association of Canada in April 2019. Trade commissioners "stand behind us and give us the additional credibility that being associated with the Government of Canada abroad brings."[14]

Largely designed to protect Canadian mining investment, the Liberals negotiated and signed a number of FIPAs. In a March 2017 release titled "International Trade Minister promotes Canada's mining sector at Prospectors and Developers Association of Canada convention", Francois-Philippe Champagne "announced that the Canada-Mongolia Foreign Investment Promotion and Protection Agreement (FIPA) is now in force. This agreement provides substantial protections for Canadian investors in Mongolia, where there are already significant Canadian-owned mining assets."[15] These investors' rights accords circumscribe governments' capacity to regulate corporations by giving them the right to sue governments — in a private, investor-friendly, international tribunal — for pursuing policies that interfere with their profit making.

The Trudeau government also channeled large sums of aid to international mining. In 2016 the Liberals put up $100 million for international projects titled "Enhanced Oversight of the Extractive Industries in Francophone Africa", "Enhancing Resource Management through Institutional Transformation in Mongolia", "Support for the Intergovernmental Forum on Mining, Minerals, Metals and Sustainable Development", "Enhancing Extractive Sector Benefit

Sharing", "Supporting the Ministry of Mines to Strengthen Governance and Management of the Mining Sector" and "West Africa Governance and Economic Sustainability in Extractive Areas."[16] They ploughed another $20 million into the Canadian Extractive Sector Facility "to promote knowledge generation and improved governance in the extractive sector in Latin America and the Caribbean."[17] The "Skills for Employment in the Extractives Sector of the Pacific Alliance" channeled $16 million into "industry-responsive training systems" in Chile, Colombia, Mexico and Peru where Canadian mining companies dominate mineral extraction.[18] In East Africa the Liberals launched the $12.5 million "Strengthening Education in Natural Resource Management in Ethiopia", which was designed "to improve the employability of people ... in natural resource fields like geology, mining and engineering. It works through universities and technical institutes to improve the quality of programs, align them more closely with the needs of the private sector."[19]

Various other arms of the Canadian state sponsored and promoted international mining initiatives. Throughout the Liberals time in office Global Affairs and Natural Resources Canada has sponsored a Canada Pavilion at the yearly Mining Indaba conference, the largest mining event in Africa.[20] Minister of Small Business, Export Promotion and International Trade Mary Ng attended the February 2020 Mining Indaba conference.[21]

Global Affairs and Natural Resources Canada also supported the annual Prospectors and Developers Association of Canada (PDAC) convention in Toronto. In 2019 Trudeau spoke at the convention and the international trade minister and natural resources minister usually attend the massive mining conference.[22] A release regarding the international trade minister's participation in PDAC 2017 noted Jim Carr will "visit some of Canada's most innovative mining sector companies active in international markets. He will meet with several ministers from countries where Canada has significant mining interests, including Chile, Ethiopia, Guyana, Malaysia,

Mongolia, Peru and Turkey."[23] On the margins of the PDAC convention the Liberals' natural resources minister attended the International Mines Ministers Summit. In 2018 leaders responsible for mining in 27 different countries participated.[24]

Canadian diplomats often hosted or participated in mining forums abroad. Embassy websites, Facebook pages and Twitter accounts also promoted the industry. In her November 2019 "Message from the Ambassador" on Canada's relationship with Burkina Faso, Carol McQueen wrote, "Canadian mining companies are subject to very high standards of corporate social responsibility and respect for the environment. The Canadian Embassy works with these companies, the Burkinabè government and local communities to encourage respect for these standards."[25] Yet, there have been a number of conflicts between Canadian mining companies and local communities in Burkina Faso.[26]

Canadian diplomats regularly visited officials with mining company representatives.[27] In March 2019 Canada's ambassador to Serbia, Kati Csaba, and representatives of Medgold Resources met the president of Bosilegrad to discuss the Vancouver company's copper-gold exploration project in the municipality. According to the embassy's Facebook page, "Ambassador Csaba introduced local authorities to the environmental protection standards followed by Canadian companies, as well as to responsible business practices developed by the Canadian mining industry which position Canada as a global mining leader."[28]

Canadian representatives repeatedly raised mining interests with top government officials. During a December 2017 meeting with Kenyan President Uhuru Kenyatta, who was seeking international legitimacy after winning a controversial election (re-run) boycotted by the opposition, immigration minister Ahmed Hussen promoted Canadian mining and energy interests.[29] Two months earlier Canada's ambassador in Madagascar, Sandra McCardell, pushed extractive interests at a meeting with that country's mining minister.[30]

At the time farmers in eastern Madagascar were in a dispute with Toronto-based DNI Metals over compensation for lands damaged by the firm.[31]

In a similar vein Canada's High Commissioner in Zambia promoted First Quantum Minerals and Barrick Gold, which had been embroiled in various ecological, labour and tax controversies in the copper rich nation that lost billions of dollars to tax dodges by mining multinationals.[32] During an August 2019 visit with President Inonge Wina, Canada's High Commissioner Pamela O'Donnell defended First Quantum and Barrick from criticism regarding their lack of value added production in country. According to 5fm Radio Zambia, O'Donnell responded that First Quantum and Barrick created jobs and contributed significantly to the public purse.[33]

Canadian diplomats also went to bat for half a dozen Canadian mining companies embroiled in a dispute over US$360 million in tax rebates with the Mexican government. "In a string of meetings, Canadian officials have pressed Mexico to fix the problem", noted a June 2017 Reuters story.[34] During a trade mission to Mexico that year Minister of Natural Resources Jim Carr, "raised the matter with Mexico's Secretary of the Economy."[35]

Highly controversial projects received diplomatic support as well. With the local mayor and most of the community opposed to El Dorado's mine in northern Greece, the social-democratic Syriza government investigated whether a flawed technical study by the Vancouver company was a breach of its contract. In September 2017 Canada's trade minister sent a letter to the Greek minister of mines and energy backing El Dorado. François-Philippe Champagne denounced Greece's "troublesome" permit delays.[36] Support for El Dorado prompted Greek anarchist group Rouvikonas to smash the windows and throw paint at the Canadian embassy in Athens in October 2018.[37]

The Trudeau government also threw its diplomatic weight behind Canada's most controversial mining company in the country where it committed some of its worst abuses. Barrick Gold's African subsidiary, Acacia Mining, was embroiled in a major political conflict in the east African nation of Tanzania. With growing evidence of its failure to pay royalties and tax, Acacia was condemned by the president, had its exports restricted and was slapped with a massive tax bill.[38] In May 2017 a government panel concluded that Acacia significantly under-reported the percentage of gold and copper in mineral sand concentrates it exported.[39] The next month a government commission concluded that foreign mining firms' failure to declare revenues had cost Tanzania $100 billion. According to the research, from 1998 to March 2017 the Tanzanian government lost between 68.6 trillion and 108.5 trillion shillings in revenue from mineral concentrates.[40]

The controversy over Barrick's exports led President John Magufuli to fire the minister of mining and the board of the Minerals Audit Agency.[41] Tanzania's parliament also voted to review mining contracts and to block companies from pursuing the country in international trade tribunals.[42]

While the political battle over royalty payments grew, human rights violations continued unabated at Barrick's North Mara mine. A MiningWatch fact-finding mission discovered that "new cases have come to light of serious un-remedied harm related to encounters between victims and mine security and police who guard the mine under a Memorandum of Understanding (MOU) between the companies involved and the Tanzanian Police Force. New cases documented in June 2017 include: loss of limbs, loss of eyesight, broken bones, internal injuries, children hit by flying blast rocks, and by teargas grenades thrown by mine security as they chase so-called intruders into the nearby villages. As in past years, villagers reported severe debilitating beatings, commonly with gun butts and wooden batons. Some are seriously wounded by teargas 'bombs,' or by so-called rubber bullets. Others are shot, including from behind. As in past years there were a number of deaths."[43]

In 2016 a government inquiry reported that the police had killed 65 people and injured 270 during a decade of clashes at the North Mara gold mine. (The company admitted to a slightly lower number while Tanzanian human rights groups estimated as many 300 mine-related deaths.[44]) Most of the victims were impoverished villagers who scratch rocks for tiny bits of gold and who often mined these territories prior to Barrick's arrival. The mine had agreements with local police to provide security at the site, but villagers complained of excessive violence by the officers. The *Financial Times* reported that not a single police officer or security guard working for the company had been killed on duty.[45]

Internal emails uncovered through Access to Information legislation showed that officials in Ottawa and staff at the embassy in Tanzania paid little attention to allegations of human rights abuses at Barrick's mine.[46] Instead, they focused almost entirely on defending the mining powerhouse in its tax dispute with the government.[47]

Amidst the violence at North Mara and an escalating battle over unpaid tax, Canada's High Commissioner set up a meeting between Barrick Executive Chairman John Thornton and President Magufuli.[48] After accompanying Barrick's head to the encounter in Dar es Salaam, Ian Myles told the press: "Canada is very proud that it expects all its companies to respect the highest standards, fairness and respect for laws and corporate social responsibility. We know that Barrick is very much committed to those values."[49] Appointed by Trudeau in mid 2016, Myles — whose "passion for international development began" when he was 17, according to a University of Toronto profile — took a page out of Stephen Harper's playbook.[50] During a 2007 trip to Chile the former prime minister responded to protests against various ecological and human rights abuses at the firm's Pascua Lama project by saying: "Barrick follows Canadian standards of corporate social responsibility."[51]

A Tanzania Business Ethics columnist was not happy with the High Commissioner's intervention. In response, Samantha Cole wrote: "It is so insulting that these Canadians and British still think they can trick us with their fancy nonsense 'spin' politics and dishonesty. What values is Barrick committed to? Have our nation not witnessed with our own eyes killings? rape? arson and burning our homes? destruction to our environment? poison in our water? corruption? fraud? hundreds of legal cases with local Tanzanian companies who are abused, bullied and suffer? and the list goes on. What 'values' is Ambassador Myles boasting about? How dishonest and unethical to stand there and lie about values. He should rather say NOTHING because every country where Barrick operates has a long, long list of illegal activities and crimes."[52]

If they were prepared to openly back Barrick Gold in Tanzania one wonders what exactly a mining firm would have to do to lose Trudeau's support?

In fact, the *modus operandi* of the Liberals has been to rely on people judging its fine sounding words about foreign policy rather than its actions. This is the subject of the next chapter.

Chapter 9 Notes

1 The Honourable Jim Carr, Minister of Natural Resources, delivers the keynote address at the Canada in Conversation event hosted by the Embassy of Canada, Natural Resources Canada, Jun 5 2017 (https://www.canada.ca/en/natural-resources-canada/news/2017/06/the_honourable_jimcarrministerofnaturalresourcesdeliversthekeyno.html)

2 The impact of Canadian Mining in Latin America and Canada's Responsibility, Working Group on Mining and Human Rights in Latin America (http://www.dplf.org/sites/default/files/report_canadian_mining_executive_summary.pdf)

3 Emily Dwyer, Canada's new corporate ombudsperson needs real power, Dec 3 2018 (https://ottawacitizen.com/opinion/columnists/dwyer-canadas-new-corporate-ombudsperson-needs-real-power)

4 "Canada Brand": Violence and Canadian Mining Companies in Latin America Justice and Corporate Accountability Project of Osgoode Law School, Dec 1 2017

5 John Cumming, What the Liberals, Greens and NDP Have to Say on Mining in Canada, Oct 4 2015 (https://www.huffingtonpost.ca/john-cumming/mining-canada-federal-election_b_8235824.html)

6 James Munson, Fulfill mining ombudsperson promise, academics tell Liberals, Mar 14 2017 (http://ipolitics.ca/2017/03/14/fulfill-mining-ombudsperson-promise-academics-tell-liberals/)

7 Jeff Lewis, Canada companies' watchdog to press Trudeau for expanded powers, Reuters, Nov 21 2019 (https://business.financialpost.com/pmn/business-pmn/canada-companies-watchdog-to-press-trudeau-for-expanded-powers)

8 Ibid

9 Ibid

10 Mike Blanchfield, UN official criticizes Canadian delays setting up corporate ethics watchdog, Canadian Press, Apr 30 2019 (https://www.cbc.ca/news/politics/un-watchdog-carr-corporate-ethics-1.5116399)

11 United Nations expert on hazardous waste "deeply concerned" about environmental practices of Canadian mining companies operating abroad, citing Human Rights Clinic's Red Water Report, June 12 2019 (https://www.law.columbia.edu/human-rights-institute/about/press-releases/UN-Expert-On-Red-Water-Report)

12 Richard Poplak, How a Federal Agency Helps Finance Some of the World's Most Corrupt

Regimes, Nov 17 2017 (https://thewalrus.ca/inside-one-of-canadas-most-secretive-agencies/); "Canada is back." But Still Far Behind An Assessment of Canada's National Contact Point for the OECD Guidelines for Multinational Enterprises, Above Ground, MiningWatch Canada and OECD Watch, Nov 1 2016 (https://miningwatch.ca/sites/default/files/canada-is-back-report-web_0.pdf)

13 Ibid

14 Canada sets a world standard for sustainable mining, Apr 3 2019 (https://www.tradecommissioner.gc.ca/canadexport/0003604.aspx?lang=eng)

15 International Trade Minister promotes Canada's mining sector at Prospectors and Developers Association of Canada convention, Global Affairs Canada, News Release, Mar 7 2017 (https://www.canada.ca/en/global-affairs/news/2017/03/international_tradeministerpromotescanadasminingsectoratprospect.html)

16 Project profile — West Africa Governance and Economic Sustainability (WAGES) in Extractive Areas (https://w05.international.gc.ca/project-browser-banqueprojets/project-projet/details/D002411001) ; Project profile — Supporting the Ministry of Mines to Strengthen Governance and Management of the Mining Sector (https://w05.international.gc.ca/projectbrowser-banqueprojets/project-projet/details/D003320001) ; Project profile — Enhancing Oversight of the Extractives Industry in Francophone Africa (https://w05.international.gc.ca/projectbrowser-banqueprojets/project-projet/details/d001596001?Lang=eng) ; Project profile — Enhancing Extractive Sector Benefit Sharing (https://w05.international.gc.ca/projectbrowser-banqueprojets/project-projet/details/D000772001)

17 Canada funds IDB Program for Better Natural Resource Management in the Americas, Mar 31 2016 (https://www.iadb.org/en/news/canada-funds-idb-program-better-natural-resource-management-americas)

18 Project profile — Skills for Employment in the Extractives Sector of the Pacific Alliance (https://w05.international.gc.ca/projectbrowser-banqueprojets/project-projet/details/D002449001)

19 Project profile — Strengthening Education in Natural Resource Management in Ethiopia (https://w05.international.gc.ca/projectbrowser-banqueprojets/project-projet/details/D000284001)

20 Official Canadian Delegation and Canada Pavilion – 2020 Mining Indaba (http://ccafrica.ca/event/canada-pavilion-2020-mining-indaba/)

21 Minister Ng to visit South Africa, Kenya and Ethiopia to deepen Canada's economic engagement in the region, Global Affairs Canada, News release, Feb 1 2020 (https://www.canada.ca/en/global-affairs/news/2020/02/minister-ng-to-visit-south-africa-kenya-and-ethiopia-to-deepen-canadas-economic-engagement-in-the-region.html)

22 PDAC Welcomes Prime Minister Justin Trudeau to World's Premier Mineral Exploration and Mining Convention, Mar 5 2019 (https://www.pdac.ca/communications/press-releases/press-releases/2019/03/05/march-5-2019-pdac-welcomes-prime-minister-justin-trudeau-to-world-s-premier-mineral-exploration-and-mining-convention)

23 Minister Carr hosts Canada Day at Prospectors & Developers Association of Canada Convention, Global Affairs Canada, News release, Mar 4 2019 (https://www.canada.ca/en/global-affairs/news/2019/03/minister-carr-hosts-canada-day-at-prospectors--developers-association-of-canada-convention.html)

24 PDAC-WEF International Mines Ministers Summit 2018 (https://www.pdac.ca/docs/default-source/priorities/public-affairs/imms/pdac-wef-imms-final-report-2018.pdf?sfvrsn=4cc88598_0)

25 Carol McQueen, Message from the Ambassador (https://www.canadainternational.gc.ca/burkinafaso/offices-bureaux/ambassador_msg_ambassadeur.aspx?lang=eng)

26 Yves Engler, Canada as mining superpower (https://www.policyalternatives.ca/Harper_Record_2008-2015/32-HarperRecord-Engler.pdf)

27 Canada supports responsible business in the mining sector, Jan 21 2020 (https://bit.ly/3aytNcu?fbclid=IwAR10q7-QEZGqXag5G7_gqNAaC-TIiVXnJuHzWvBJt4L1NyUgsF4t4HGk7ItU)

28 Embassy of Canada to Serbia, North Macedonia and Montenegro is in Bosilegrad, Apr 9 2019 (https://www.facebook.com/CanadainSerbia/posts/as-part-of-our-commitment-to-supporting-canadian-mining-companies-in-serbia-amba/1064085563789413/)

29 Loise Njeriy, Why Canada eyes Kenya's extractives (https://hivisasa.com/posts/why-canada-eyes-kenyas-extractives)

30 Secteur minier: coopération renforcée avec le Canada, NewsMada, Oct 5 2017 (http://www.newsmada.com/2017/10/05/secteur-minier-cooperation-renforcee-avec-le-canada/)

31 https://www.madagascar-tribune.com/Projet-minier-DNI-METALS-a,23328.html

32 Mark Curtis, Extracting Minerals, Extracting Wealth: How Zambia is losing $3 Billion a year from Corporate Tax Dodging, Oct 2015 (https://www.waronwant.org/sites/default/files/WarOnWant_ZambiaTaxReport_web.pdf)

33 (https://www.facebook.com/5fmZambia/photos/a.361957367201439/2502853133111841/?type=1&theater)

34 Reuters, Mexico owes Goldcorp and five other Canadian miners more than US$360 million: report, June 8 2017 (https://business.financialpost.com/commodities/mining/mexico-owes-goldcorp-and-five-other-canadian-miners-more-than-us360-million-report)

35 Ibid

36 Canada presses Greece on "troublesome" Eldorado Gold delays -Minister, Sept 13 2017 (https://

www.reuters.com/article/eldorado-gold-greece-canada/canada-presses-greece-on-troublesome-eldorado-gold-delays-minister-idUSL2N1LU14I)

37 Canadian embassy in Athens attacked with sledgehammers, red paint, Canadian Press, Oct 22 2018 (https://globalnews.ca/news/4580938/canadian-embassy-attacked-athens/)

38 John Aglionby and Henry Sanderson, Acacia Mining accused of operating illegally in Tanzania, Jun 12 2017 (https://www.ft.com/content/7f53064e-4f7d-11e7-bfb8-997009366969) ; Geoffrey York, Losses mount at Barrick Gold's Africa subsidiary after export ban May 28 2017 (https://www.theglobeandmail.com/report-on-business/industry-news/energy-and-resources/losses-mount-at-barrick-golds-africa-subsidiary-after-export-ban/article35140493/) ; Barrick-owned miner slapped with $190 billion tax bill that would take centuries to pay, Bloomberg News, July 25 2017 (http://business.financialpost.com/commodities/acacias-190-billion-tax-bill-would-take-centuries-to-pay-2/wcm/64143f78-bf2d-4663-ba3f-bb9df09ab885)

39 John Aglionby and Henry Sanderson, Acacia Mining accused of operating illegally in Tanzania, Jun 12 2017 (https://www.ft.com/content/7f53064e-4f7d-11e7-bfb8-997009366969)

40 Ibid

41 Omar Mohammed, Tanzanian President Fires Mines Minister After Minerals Audit, May 24 2017 (https://www.bloomberg.com/news/articles/2017-05-24/tanzanian-president-asks-mines-minister-to-resign-after-audit)

42 Tanzanian parliament to review mining contracts to control exports of copper concentrates, Xinhua, Mar 27 2017 (http://news.xinhuanet.com/english/2017-03/27/c_136159393.htm) ; Catherine Coumans, Anger Boils Over at North Mara Mine – Barrick/Acacia Leave Human Rights Abuses Unaddressed, Mining Watch, July 2017 (https://miningwatch.ca/sites/default/files/2017_field_report_final_-_anger_boils_over_at_north_mara_mine.pdf)

43 Ibid

44 Acacia Mining's Troubles in Tanzania Run Deeper Than Tax, RAID, July 6 2017 (http://www.raid-uk.org/blog/acacia-mining's-troubles-tanzania-run-deeper-tax)

45 David Pilling, Acacia Mining pressed over deaths in Tanzania, Jul 23 2017 (https://www.ft.com/content/40c467e2-66e3-11e7-9a66-93fb352ba1fe)

46 Alastair Sharp, Canada brushed off abuse complaints against Barrick-linked gold miner in Tanzania, emails show, July 10 2019 (https://www.nationalobserver.com/2019/07/10/news/canada-brushed-abuse-complaints-against-barrick-linked-gold-miner-tanzania-emails)

47 Ibid

48 Magufuli sidelines Acacia, opens talks with Barrick, IPPMEDIA, Jun 17 2017 (http://www.ippmedia.com/en/news/magufuli-sidelines-acacia-opens-talks-barrick)

49 Samantha Cole, Is Barrick Gold – Acacia Mining about to STING President Magufuli & the Tanzania Nation?, June 18 2017 (https://tanzaniabusinessethics.wordpress.com/2017/06/18/is-barrick-gold-acacia-mining-about-to-sting-president-magufuli-the-tanzania-nation/)

50 Bianca Quijano, U of T Scarborough alum starts up as Canadian High Commissioner in Tanzania, Oct 28 2016 (http://ose.utsc.utoronto.ca/ose/story.php?id=8880)

51 Alan Freeman, PM sells Canada as third economic option, July 18 2007 (https://www.theglobeandmail.com/news/national/pm-sells-canada-as-third-economic-option/article20399394/)

52 Samantha Cole, Is Barrick Gold – Acacia Mining about to STING President Magufuli & the Tanzania Nation?, June 18 2017 (https://tanzaniabusinessethics.wordpress.com/2017/06/18/is-barrick-gold-acacia-mining-about-to-sting-president-magufuli-the-tanzania-nation/)

10. House of Mirrors
— Judge What I Say, Not What I Do

Early in the Liberals reign Stéphane Dion presented "a guiding principle for Canada in the world". During a major policy speech, the foreign minister claimed "responsible conviction" was the principle motivating the government's international policy.[1] The "responsible conviction" label was a way to distinguish the Liberal brand from the Conservatives. It supposedly also offered a moral-philosophical basis for signing off on the controversial light armoured vehicle sale to Saudi Arabia.

When Chrystia Freeland took charge of foreign policy a year later, she replaced the "responsible conviction" nomenclature with "international rules-based order" (IRBO). On dozens of occasions Freeland, Trudeau and other Liberal officials referred to the IRBO, "international order based on rules" or "international system based on rules". The top stated "aim" laid out in her major June 2017 foreign policy pronouncement was: "First, we will robustly support the rules-based international order, and all its institutions, and seek ways to strengthen and improve them."[2] At the start of 2020 the Global Affairs website's No. 1 priority was "revitalizing the rules-based international order."[3] But, while the IRBO rhetoric was clever branding, designed partly to distinguish the Liberals from Donald Trump's "America First" sloganeering, the Liberals repeatedly violated the IRBO and ignored efforts to strengthen it.

For example, the Royal Canadian Air Force's intelligence and refueling assistance to US forces fighting in Syria violated the IRBO. A military intervention without the country or UN Security Council's approval is a clear violation of international law.

The unilateral sanctions the Liberals adopted against Venezuela, Russia, Nicaragua and others also violated the IRBO. They adopted four rounds of sanctions against Venezuela, which reinforced and legitimated US sanctions that contributed to tens of thousands of deaths. In 2017 the Liberals adopted legislation, modeled after the US Magnitsky Act, empowering the government to freeze individuals' assets/visas and prohibit Canadian companies from dealing with sanctioned individuals. In a sign of Ottawa's growing employment of sanctions as a tool of coercive statecraft, Global Affairs created a Sanctions Policy and Operations Coordination Division in 2018.[4]

But most countries and international law experts believe sanctions are only legitimate when approved by the World Trade Organization or UN Security Council. Economic sanctions outside the framework of the UN charter are generally considered "unilateral" and unlawful. According to the Asian-African Legal Consultative Organization report "Unilateral and Secondary Sanctions: An International Law Perspective", "the imposition of unilateral and secondary sanctions on countries through application of national legislation is not-permissible under international law."[5] Unilateral sanctions also run afoul of the principle of self-determination and people's right to development. In *The International Covenant on Economic, Social and Cultural Rights* a trio of authors note: "Unilateral economic sanctions (as opposed to multilateral UN measures under Chapter VII of the Charter) imposed by one State or group of States on another, to compel the latter to change a particular political or economic policy, could amount to a prohibited intervention and a denial of self-determination."[6] Similarly, the UN Human Rights Council affirmed in 2017 that "unilateral coercive measures are major obstacles to the implementation of the Declaration on the Right to Development."[7]

Beyond sanctions, the Trudeau government openly and aggressively interfered in Venezuela's internal affairs. They coordinated with the opposition and other countries to recognize an obscure opposition politician as president of the country. The UN and Organization of American States prohibit interfering in the internal affairs of another state. Article 2 (7) of the UN Charter states that "nothing should authorize intervention in matters essentially within the domestic jurisdiction of any state."[8] Furthermore, the concept of self-determination is a core principle of the UN Charter and International Covenant on Civil and Political Rights.

When Canada and four other right-wing South American governments brought Venezuela to the International Criminal Court in September 2018 Trudeau portrayed the move as a challenge to the Trump administration's hostility to the court. He described the ICC as a "useful and important way of promoting an international rules-based order."[9] In other words, Trudeau would challenge Washington by showing Trump how the "international rules-based" ICC could undermine a government the US was seeking to overthrow through unilateral sanctions, support for the opposition and threatening an invasion, which all contravene the UN Charter.

The Liberals even claimed their legitimation of US sanctions criminality was a defence of the IRBO. They defended the arrest of Huawei's chief financial officer, Meng Wanzhou, by citing the importance of the "rule of law" and treaties. But, the unilateral sanctions against Iran Washington accused the Chinese telecommunications firm of defying violated international law. By fulfilling Washington's extradition request for Meng the Liberals would legitimate this US illegality.

Then there are climate accords, which are essential to an IRBO worth its salt. Unlike his predecessor, Trudeau didn't sabotage international climate negotiations. But, he openly flouted his commitments under the December 2015 Paris Climate Accord.

Nuclear disarmament is also essential to the IRBO. But powerful allies opposed nuclear arms controls so the Liberals weren't interested in "the international rules-based order" required to curb the existential threat nukes pose to humankind. Trudeau's government refused to join 122 countries represented at the 2017 Conference to Negotiate a Legally Binding Instrument to Prohibit Nuclear Weapons, Leading Towards their Total Elimination.

Despite Dion repeatedly promising to do so, the Liberals failed to ratify the United Nations' Optional Protocol to the Convention against Torture and other Cruel, Inhuman or Degrading Treatment or Punishment (OPCAT).[10] At the start of 2020 some 90 countries had signed OPCAT, which established a mechanism to inspect detention centres.[11] The Liberals also failed to sign the American Convention on Human Rights, which established the Inter-American Court of Human Rights.[12]

The Trudeau government refused to ratify the Basel Ban Amendment, which prohibited rich countries from exporting waste to poor countries.[13] The amendment became binding in late 2019 after it was ratified by 97 countries.

In another sign of their indifference to an IRBO, the Liberals largely ignored international efforts to restrict corporate abuses. The government showed little interest in the OECD's work to curtail 'transfer pricing' and other forms of corporate tax avoidance.

The same can be said for combatting corruption. The Liberals defence of SNC Lavalin highlighted their indifference to corporate Canada's corruption abroad. In 2018 Transparency International downgraded Canada's rating for deterring international corruption from "moderate" to "limited."[14]

The Liberals refused to join the Extractive Industries Transparency Initiative, which seeks to standardize governance in oil, gas and mineral resources. By early 2020, 52 countries were part of this initiative, but not Canada.[15] Is this behaviour characteristic of a country committed to a rules-based international order?

In an October 2019 commentary for Oxfam Canada Ian Thomson noted that the Liberals were "largely absent" from a UN Human Rights Council initiative to develop a legally binding treaty to hold companies accountable for human rights abuses.[16] Launched in 2014, the Transnational Corporations and Other

Business Enterprises project met annually during Trudeau's tenure.[17]

The Liberals failed to ratify dozens of conventions of one of the oldest parts of the IRBO.[18] As this book went to print, they hadn't signed the International Labour Organization's Domestic Workers Convention, which sets minimum conditions for domestic work and recognizes domestic workers' rights to freedom of association. Nor had they ratified the ILO's Violence and Harassment Convention or Indigenous rights convention No. 169, which is legally binding unlike the United Nations Declaration on the Rights of Indigenous Peoples.

Another important component of Trudeau's international branding exercise was "feminist foreign policy". Government officials emphasized feminism/women's empowerment in public statements, diplomatic twitter accounts, Global Affairs websites, etc. The Liberals also highlighted women's role in UN peacekeeping, Royal Canadian Navy deployments and a training mission in Iraq.

Labeling their foreign policy "feminist" began in earnest with the release of a Feminist International Assistance Policy (FIAP) in June 2017. Sixteen months later Freeland convened a first ever Women Foreign Ministers' Meeting with representatives from about 20 countries. At the September 2018 gathering in Montréal Freeland announced that the Liberals would appoint an Ambassador for Women Peace and Security, which Trudeau later said would "help advance Canada's feminist foreign policy."[19]

But, the Liberals' "viewed 'feminist' as a branding tool rather than a realignment of power relations", noted Rafia Zakaria in a *Nation* story headlined "Canada's 'Feminist' Foreign Aid Is a Fraud."[20] The Liberals commitment to feminist internationalism was paper-thin.

In July 2019 Ottawa joined Washington as the only other government to vote against a UN Economic and Social Council resolution stating, "the Israeli occupation remains a major obstacle for Palestinian women and girls with regard to the fulfillment of their rights."[21] As the Liberals touted their "feminist foreign policy", they sold armoured vehicles to the Saudis and deepened ties to other highly misogynistic Gulf monarchies.[22] They also aligned with anti-woman Jihadists against a secular (if repressive) government in Syria.

Disregarding their promise to rein in Canadian mining abuses abroad also undercut the Liberals' "feminist foreign policy". Sexual assault often plagues communities near Canadian-run mines and as the primary caregivers, women are disproportionately burdened by the ecological destruction caused by mining. At the same time, most mining jobs go to men.

Trudeau touted right-wing allies for being pro woman while seeking to get rid of leftist governments with stronger feminist credentials. The PM lauded far right Colombian president Iván Duque for adopting "a gender-equal cabinet." At the same time the Liberals sought to oust a Nicaraguan government in which women held more than half of all cabinet positions and 40 percent of the legislature.[23] Canada's feminist foreign minister also backed the overthrow of a Bolivian government, which adopted a series of legislative measures that greatly advanced women's representation in politics.[24]

A number of repressive, elitist governments claimed the feminist mantle to curry favour with Ottawa. When a parliamentary delegation led by Liberal MP Robert Oliphant, Parliamentary Secretary to the Minister of Foreign Affairs, visited General Abdel Fattah el-Sisi in 2018 the Egyptian president claimed his dictatorial regime promoted women's rights. This hard-to-believe claim appeared in the delegation's post trip report that whitewashed el-Sisi's repression.[25]

In a similar vein, proposed Haitian Prime Minister Fritz William Michel presented a gender-balanced cabinet amidst massive protests in July 2019 calling for President Jovenel Moïse to go. Moïse's appointee sought to align with a stated objective of his second most influential backer, which generated sympathetic Canadian headlines.[26] Along with praise for Moïse, Global Affairs' webpage about "Canada's international assistance in Haiti" focused on gender equity and during a February 2018 visit Minister of International Development Marie-Claude Bibeau launched the first project under FIAP's Women's Voice and Leadership Program (see below).[27] "It's a new president and we want to support him," Bibeau told CBC before leaving on a trip that included a meeting with Haiti's illegitimate president.[28]

In truth, even though it was mainly branding, "feminist foreign policy" rhetoric can help efforts to lessen sexism. As with most forms of oppression, simply raising the subject can be a positive influence. And more concretely, FIAP did direct Canadian bilateral aid towards gender focused initiatives. It channeled $150 million over five years into the Women's Voice and Leadership Program to support local organizations working to advance women's rights. More significantly, FIAP increased the proportion of the bilateral aid budget devoted to initiatives with gender equity as a primary target from 2% to 15% over five years.[29] At the same time, practically all of Canada's bilateral international assistance initiatives were supposed to integrate gender equality and the empowerment of women and girls.

But, FIAP didn't include any new aid, which was at its lowest proportion of GDP in half a century.[30] A year after the release of FIAP Finance Minister Bill Morneau hyped "the largest new investments in international assistance in over a decade", but aid was still set to decline as a share of GDP.[31] In "Canada's Feminist International Assistance Policy: Bold Statement or Feminist Fig Leaf?" Stephen Brown and Liam Swiss wrote, "while the feminist aid policy will buttress the Liberal government's feminist credentials, it will also provide a convenient fig leaf for the lack of political will to expand aid funding and decidedly unfeminist policies in other areas."[32]

(As I've detailed elsewhere, the primary objective of Canadian overseas assistance has long been to advance Western interests, particularly keeping the Global South tied to the US-led geopolitical order.[33] Aid has also been designed to help Canadian companies and to co-opt internationalist minded young people into aligning with Canadian foreign policy. While most individual aid projects offer some social benefit, they've also helped justify the imprisonment of Haiti's constitutional prime minister, rewrote Colombia's mining code to benefit corporations, assisted Filipino landlords blocking much-needed land reform with violence, etc.[34])

Two days before launching FIAP the Liberals announced their defence policy review, which included a plan to increase military spending by 70% over a decade.[35] The government committed $62 billion more to the military — already five times the aid budget — over 20 years.[36] "Billions for the military and a lump of coal for foreign aid", noted the *Globe and Mail*'s Campbell Clark.

The Canadian Forces is a highly patriarchal institution. Women represented 15.4% of military personnel in 2018.[37] In 2015 former Supreme Court judge Marie Deschamps found a "culture of misogyny" in the CF "hostile to women."[38] Her officially sponsored investigation concluded, "the overall perception is that a 'boys club' culture still prevails in the armed forces."[39] Four years later Deschamps told a House of Commons defence committee there had been little progress in eliminating sexism within the CF.[40]

Along with increasing military spending, the Liberals promoted the arms industry and their international sales. A male-dominated sector, Canadian weapons were sold to a number of violent, misogynist, governments. The Liberals deployed Canadian Forces on a number of aggressive missions. In Iraq, they boasted about killing a person with a three-kilometer sniper shot. A purveyor of violence, the Canadian military was the institutional embodiment of 'toxic masculinity'. A genuine "feminist foreign policy" would seek to rein in — not expand — the CF.

But a "feminist foreign policy" was only one piece of the Liberals 'talking left and acting right' agenda. Foreign Minister Freeland repeatedly framed her support for the military and US Empire in leftish ways. In a major 2017 foreign policy speech Freeland claimed that increasing military spending was an assertion of Canadian sovereignty. After calling for "a substantial investment" in the CF, Freeland said, "to rely solely on the U.S. security umbrella would make us a client state."[41] But, Washington constantly pressured Ottawa to increase military spending. Paul Cellucci revealed that when he was appointed US Ambassador to Canada in 2002 his only instruction was to press for increased military spending while Donald Trump repeatedly pressured Ottawa to increase spending on the CF.[42]

An honest analysis of the CF reveals that it isn't currently oriented towards protecting Canada from aggression, but rather towards expanding the US-led empire. The depth of the Canada-US military alliance is such that if US Forces attacked this country it would be extremely difficult for the CF to defend our soil!

On another occasion, Freeland deflected questions about nakedly interventionist policies with more leftish rhetoric. Asked about Chavismo's continued popularity and Ottawa's interference in Venezuela's internal affairs after a Lima Group meeting in Toronto, Freeland said, "Canada has never been an imperialist power. It's even almost funny to say that phrase: we've been the colony."[43] Few indigenous people would agree that Canada was simply a "colony". Or, for that matter, Haitians.

Extending the left nationalist framing, Freeland noted, "one of the strengths Canada brings to its international affairs" is that it doesn't engage in "regime change."[44] Freeland's claim that Ottawa doesn't engage in "regime change" was laughable (Libya 2011, Haiti 2004, Congo 1961, etc.). Basically, what Freeland was saying is that it may walk and quack like a regime-change-promoting duck, but Ottawa's bid to overthrow Venezuela's government was actually just a cuddly Canadian beaver.

This deception and hypocrisy would be laughable, except for the real-world consequences. Economic exploitation, militarism, trampling of human rights, interference in other countries internal affairs and environmental destruction have been enabled rather than minimized by Justin Trudeau's rhetoric. Both Conservative and Liberal Party governments have followed a similar foreign policy path. Why? How can Canadians change this? The conclusion will offer some thoughts on these subjects.

Chapter 10 Notes

1 Stéphane Dion: On 'responsible conviction' and Liberal foreign policy, Mar 29 2016 (https://www.macleans.ca/politics/ottawa/stephane-dion-how-ethics-inspires-liberal-foreign-policy/)

2 Address by Minister Freeland on Canada's foreign policy priorities, Global Affairs Canada, June 6 2017 (https://www.canada.ca/en/global-affairs/news/2017/06/address_by_ministerfreelandoncanadasforeignpolicypriorities.html)

3 Plans at a glance and operating context (https://www.international.gc.ca/gac-amc/priorities-priorites.aspx?lang=eng)

4 Milos Barutciski, Matthew Kronby, Robert Dawkins and Josh Scheinert, Administration of Canada's Sanctions Regime Gets A Welcome Makeover, Oct 26 2018 (https://www.mondaq.com/canada/Government-Public-Sector/748908/Administration-Of-Canada39s-Sanctions-Regime-Gets-A-Welcome-Makeover)

5 Unilateral and secondary sanctions: an international law perspective (http://www.aalco.int/52ndsession/EXECUTIVE%20SUMMARY.pdf)

6 Idriss Jazairy, Ethics & International Affairs, Vol 33, Issue 3, Fall 2019 (https://www.cambridge.org/core/journals/ethics-and-international-affairs/article/unilateral-economic-sanctions-international-law-and-human-rights/77DF5AD157ED1BFBA3952C9235171CCB/core-reader)

7 Idriss Jazairy, Unilateral Economic Sanctions, International Law, and Human Rights (https://www.cambridge.org/core/services/aop-cambridge-core/content/view/77DF5AD157ED1BFBA3952C9235171CCB/S0892679419000339a.pdf/unilateral_economic_sanctions_international_law_and_human_rights.pdf)

8 Westphalian model (http://www.westarctica.wiki/index.php/Westphalian_model)

9 UN court asked to investigate Venezuela, Sept 27 2018 (http://www.jamaicaobserver.com/international/un-court-asked-to-investigate-venezuela_145331?profile=1032)

10 Standing up for human rights and those who defend them, Global Affairs Canada, Dec 10 2016 (https://www.canada.ca/en/global-affairs/news/2016/12/standing-up-human-rights-those-defend-them.html)

11 CHAPTER IV HUMAN RIGHTS 9. b Optional Protocol to the Convention against Torture and Other Cruel, Inhuman or Degrading Treatment or Punishment New York, Dec 18 2002 (https://treaties.un.org/pages/ViewDetails.aspx?src=TREATY&mtdsg_no=IV-9-b&chapter=4&clang=_en)

12 Bernard Duhaime, Ten Reasons Why Canada Should Join the ACHR, Revue générale de droit, Vol 49, 2019

13 Ainslie Cruickshank, Star Vancouver, Canada opposes ban on 'indefensible' practice of shipping hazardous waste to developing countries, May 10 2019 (https://www.thestar.com/news/canada/2019/05/10/canada-opposes-ban-on-indefensible-practice-of-shipping-hazardous-waste-to-developing-countries.html) ; Kathleen Ruff (https://rightoncanada.ca/?p=4376)

14 Geoffrey York, Matthew McClearn, See no evil: How Canada is bankrolling companies accused of bid-rigging, graft and human-rights violation, June 1 2019 (https://www.theglobeandmail.com/canada/article-export-development-canada-investigation/)

15 (https://eiti.org)

16 Ian Thomson, 5 things Canada's next government should do to curb corporate abuses of human rights, Oct 16 2019 (https://www.oxfam.ca/blog/5-things-canadas-next-government-should-do-to-curb-corporate-abuses-of-human-rights/)

17 Binding treaty (https://www.business-humanrights.org/en/binding-treaty)

18 Ratifications for Canada 37 Conventions and 1 Protocol (https://www.ilo.org/dyn/normlex/en/f?p=1000:11200:0::NO:11200:P11200_COUNTRY_ID:102582)

19 Prime Minister names first Ambassador for Women, Peace and Security, June 12 2019 (https://pm.gc.ca/en/news/news-releases/2019/06/12/prime-minister-names-first-ambassador-women-peace-and-security)

20 Rafia Zakaria, Canada's 'Feminist' Foreign Aid Is a Fraud, Feb 11 2019 (https://www.thenation.com/article/archive/feminist-aid-canada-womens-economic-empowerment/)

21 Cnaan Liphshiz, UN body passes resolution accusing only Israel of women's rights violations, July 26 2019 (https://www.timesofisrael.com/un-body-passes-resolution-accusing-only-israel-of-womens-rights-violations/)

22 Rafia Zakaria, Canada's 'Feminist' Foreign Aid Is a Fraud, Feb 11 2019 (https://www.thenation.com/article/archive/feminist-aid-canada-womens-economic-empowerment/)

23 Christine Wade, Revolutionary Drift: Power and Pragmatism in Ortega's Nicaragua, Aug 13 2015 (https://www.worldpoliticsreview.com/articles/16456/revolutionary-drift-power-and-pragmatism-in-ortega-s-nicaragua)

24 Alice Campaignolle, Irene Escudero, and Carlos Heras, In Bolivia, A Backlash Against Women in Politics, Nov 19 2018 (https://nacla.org/news/2018/11/19/bolivia-backlash-against-women-politicsen-bolivia-una-reacción-violenta-contra-las)

25 Ahmed Abdelkader Elpannann, Why is Canada ignoring the horrendous human-rights violations in Egypt?, July 3 2018 (https://nationalpost.com/opinion/why-is-canada-ignoring-the-horrendous-human-rights-violations-in-egypt)

26 Yves Engler, Trudeau 'feminizes' support for corrupt and repressive Haitian president, July 31 2019 (https://yvesengler.com/2019/07/31/trudeau-feminizes-support-for-corrupt-and-repressive-haitian-president/)

27 Canada's international assistance in Haiti (https://www.international.gc.ca/world-monde/issues_development-enjeux_developpement/priorities-priorites/where-ou/haiti.aspx?lang=eng) ; Minister Bibeau announces support to Women's Voice and Leadership initiative in Haiti, Global Affairs Canada, News Release, Feb 19 2018 (https://www.canada.ca/en/global-affairs/news/2018/02/minister_bibeau_announcessupporttowomensvoiceandleadershipinitia.html)

28 Kathleen Harris, Helping Haiti: Bibeau begins 3-day visit focused on improving health, empowering women, Feb 18 2018 (https://www.cbc.ca/news/politics/haiti-bibeau-health-women-1.4539678)

29 Canada launches new Feminist International Assistance Policy, Global Affairs Canada, News Release, June 9 2017 (https://www.canada.ca/en/global-affairs/news/2017/06/canada_launches_newfeministinternationalassistancepolicy.html)

30 Justin Trudeau and Canadian Foreign Policy, Canada Among Nations 2017, 26

31 Richard Nimijean, Introduction: Is Canada back? Brand Canada in a turbulent world, Jul 23 2018 (https://www.tandfonline.com/doi/full/10.1080/11926422.2018.1481873)

32 Stephen Brown and Liam Swiss, Canada's Feminist International Assistance Policy: Bold Statement or Feminist Fig Leaf?, Oct 2017

33 Yves Engler, The Black Book of Canadian Foreign Policy, 158-161

34 Ibid, 105/129

35 Justin Trudeau and Canadian Foreign Policy Canada Among Nations 2017, 26

36 Daniel Leblanc and Steven Chase, Ottawa Lays Out $62-Billion in New Military Spending over 20 Years, June 7 2017 (https://www.theglobeandmail.com/news/politics/ottawa-lays-out-62-billion-in-new-military-spending-over-20-years/article35231311/)

37 Kathleen Harris, Military looks at foreign recruits to boost ranks, May 25 2018 (http://www.cbc.ca/news/politics/caf-military-foreign-recruits-1.4675889)

38 Stephanie Levitz, Military's sexualized culture hostile to women: inquiry, Canadian Press, April 30 2015 (https://www.ctvnews.ca/canada/military-s-sexualized-culture-hostile-to-women-inquiry-1.2352263)

39 External Review into Sexual Misconduct and Sexual Harassment in the Canadian Armed Forces - Culture of the CAF Marie Deschamps, C.C. Ad.E., External Review Authority, Mar 27 2015 (https://www.canada.ca/en/department-national-defence/corporate/reports-publications/sexual-misbehaviour/external-review-2015/culture-caf.html)

40 Military slow to fix sexualized culture, Canadian Press, Feb 8 2019 (https://www.theglobeandmail.com/canada/article-canadian-military-slow-to-fix-sexual-assault-problem-former-judge/)

41 Address by Minister Freeland on Canada's foreign policy priorities, Global Affairs Canada, June 6 2017 (https://www.canada.ca/en/global-affairs/news/2017/06/address_by_ministerfreelandoncanadasforeignpolicypriorities.html)

42 Murray Dobbin, Harper's Taste for War PM's pride tied to military muscle, U.S. approval, Sep 25 2006 (https://thetyee.ca/Views/2006/09/25/Afghanistan/) ; Teresa Wright, Trump sends letter to Trudeau calling for increase in NATO defence spending, Canadian Press, Jun 22 2018 (https://www.cbc.ca/news/politics/trump-letter-trudeau-nato-1.4719198)

43 Oct 26 2017 (https://twitter.com/compartycanada/status/923754580642549761) ; Resolving the Venezuelan Crisis, Streamed live on Oct 26, 2017 (https://www.youtube.com/watch?v=e5RQsHU-uKU8&feature=youtu.be&t=59m52s)

44 Ibid

11. It's the System Dummy— Conclusion

Economic, cultural, racial and geopolitical forces explain the continuity between Liberal and Conservative foreign policy. Power is concentrated in the hands of very few wealthy people who dominate our economic system. Both the Liberals and Conservatives depend on the 1% of Canadians to fund their election campaigns. Both parties, and every government that is not willing to change the economic system, come up against and acquiesce to the power of the establishment. That establishment includes the wealthy, corporate Canada, think tanks, the dominant media, and other institutions of power.

Leaders in various fields, corporate Canada is highly transnational. For example, the world's largest privately held security company, GardaWorld had 80,000 employees operating across the globe in 2019. The Montréal-based firm followed US/Canadian troops into numerous countries and worked for western corporations in different hotspots. Another Montréal company, SNC Lavalin, is among the largest engineering companies on the planet. With projects in dozens of countries, SNC benefited greatly from Canadian diplomacy and aid. SNC was a member or sponsor of the Canadian Council on Africa, Canadian Council for the Americas, Canada Arab Business Council, Canada-ASEAN Business Council, Conseil des Relations Internationales de Montréal and other foreign policy lobby/discussion groups. Brookfield Asset Management is one of the largest private-equity titans. The Toronto-based company had $500 billion in assets under management and owns businesses in over 30 countries.[1] It was also a member of the Canadian Council for the Americas, Canada-United Arab Emirates Business Council and other internationally focused lobby groups. CAE is among the world's largest flight simulation firms. The Montréal based company works with militaries around the world.

Then there are the banks. Ranked among the world's 60 largest, Canada's 'big five' are major international players.[2] Scotiabank, for example, operates in more than 30 countries.[3] A number of stories highlighted Scotiabank's concerns about protests against inequality in Chile at the end of 2019.[4] The Trudeau government's support for unpopular billionaire president Sebastián Piñera was likely influenced by the Toronto-based bank's interests in the country. On the other hand, Scotiabank, which began operating in Venezuela just before Hugo Chavez was elected, had frosty relations with the Bolivarian government. The bank's perspective almost certainly contributed to Ottawa's hostility towards Caracas. In January 2020 Scotiabank CEO Brian Porter took the unusual step of penning "A call to action on Venezuela" in the *National Post*.[5] The op-ed urged governments to "seize assets of corrupt regime officials" and use the proceeds to give "support to the democratic movement in Venezuela." Porter applauded the Liberal government's "moral clarity by unambiguously condemning the Maduro regime's abuses." It also praised their "tremendous courage and leadership in the hemisphere and on the world stage."[6]

Canadian banks expanded their operations in Latin America to do more business with Canadian mining clients.[7] Engineering and law firms have also gone global in search of business with Canadian mining firms.[8]

Of course mining provides the starkest example of Canada's dominance of a rapacious industry. With 0.5% of the world's population, half of all mining companies are currently based in Canada or listed on Canadian stock exchanges.[9] Canadian corporations operate thousands of mineral projects abroad. There have been many indications of the industry's political influence. Dion's chief of staff, Julian Ovens, worked in the mining industry for 14 years. He was head of strategy for BHP Billiton in Saskatoon until November 2015 when he moved into the foreign minister's office.[10] Ovens subsequently became chief of staff to the international trade minister.

The mining industry thwarted legislation to constrain their abuses abroad. According to a report titled "Lobbying by mining industry on the proposed Canadian Ombudsperson for Responsible Enterprise (CORE)", the two main industry associations met government officials hundreds of times between when the government announced it would establish an ombudsperson and its presentation of what turned into a largely powerless position.[11] Between January 2018 and April 2019 the Mining Association of Canada and Prospector and Developers Association of Canada lobbied the federal government on 530 occasions.[12] They met officials in the Prime Minister's Office 33 times. The industry lobbying campaign was likely even greater since individual mining companies also organized dozens, if not hundreds, of visits.

Mining interests likely influenced the Trudeau government's push to oust the Venezuelan and Bolivian presidents. A number of Canadian companies clashed with Caracas over its efforts to gain greater control over gold extraction. Crystallex, Vanessa Ventures, Gold Reserve and Rusoro Mining all had prolonged legal battles with the Venezuelan government. In 2016 Rusoro Mining won a $1 billion claim under the Canada-Venezuela investment treaty and Crystallex was awarded $1.2 billion under the treaty, which it struggled to recover.[13]

In 2012 Evo Morales nationalized Vancouver-based South American Silver's operations in central Bolivia. Ottawa protested the move.[14] Executives of other Canadian mining companies criticized Morales and they repeatedly expressed fear over "resource nationalism" in the region.[15]

The Canadian mining industry was highly dependent on neoliberal capitalist reforms. Benefiting from the privatization of state-run mining companies and loosened restrictions on foreign investment, Canadian mining investment in Latin America has exploded since the 1990s.[16] No Canadian mining firm operated in Mexico or Peru at the start of the 1990s yet by 2010 there were nearly 600 Canadian mining firms in those two countries.[17] Foreign mining companies often made staggering profits. One study found that the three biggest gold mining companies operating in Latin America — all Canadian — earned US$15 billion from 15 mines between 1998 and 2013, which worked out to a 45 per cent rate of profit.[18]

Any government that reversed neoliberal reforms was a threat to the more than one hundred billion dollars Canadian mining companies had invested in the Americas.[19]

Other elements of Canadian capital also depended on neoliberalism. SNC Lavalin, CPCS Transcom and other consulting/engineering firms benefited from governments around the world shifting to public-private partnerships. Ditto for infrastructure giant Brookfield Asset Management. Financial liberalization also benefited Canadian banks.

In short, important segments of corporate Canada have been tied to extreme capitalism.

Other structural and cultural forces explain Liberal foreign policy. Efforts at rapprochement with Russia, for instance, were stymied by the organized Ukrainian community. Founded in 1940, the Ukrainian Canadian Congress (UCC) regrouped six provincial councils and 20 branches. It claimed to speak on behalf of 1.2 million Canadians of Ukrainian descent. Among its backers were some wealthy individuals, including billionaire Ottawa Senators owner Eugene Melnyk, who was part of UCC's advisory council.[20] A number of MPs of Ukrainian background had ties to the group, including minister Freeland who "opposed any warming of relations with Russia."[21] When the now defunct *Embassy* published the "Top 80 Influencing Canada's Foreign Policy" UCC President Paul Grod was listed.[22] In *Canada is Not Back: How Justin Trudeau is in Over His Head on Foreign Policy*, Jocelyn Coulon, who was a member of Trudeau's International Affairs Council of Advisers and then an adviser to Dion, described how the UCC sabotaged efforts to lessen tension with Russia. "Dion's determination to restore relations with Russia quickly came up against pro Ukrainian pressure groups", he wrote.[23]

The Israel lobby has been even more powerful. Together the United Jewish Appeal/Combined Jewish Appeal of Toronto, Montréal, Winnipeg, Windsor, Calgary, Edmonton, Hamilton, London, Ottawa, Vancouver and Atlantic Canada raised over $100 million annually and had about $1 billion in assets.[24] For half a century UJA Toronto has organized an annual Walk with Israel and the Montréal branch organizes an annual Israel Day march. Many thousands march each year. The lobbying arm of the UJA/CJA, the Centre for Israel and Jewish Affairs has over 40 staff and a $10 million budget.[25] In addition, B'nai B'rith has a handful of offices across the country. For its part, Friends of Simon Wiesenthal Center Canada's budget is $7-10 million annually.[26] These groups work closely with StandWithUs Canada, CAMERA, Honest Reporting Canada and other Israeli nationalist political organizations. Dozens of registered Canadian charities, ranging from the Jewish National Fund to Christians United for Israel also engage in at least some pro-Israel campaigning.

Between 2013 and 2020 the chief fundraiser for the Trudeau Liberals was Stephen Bronfman, scion of an arch Zionist family.[27] Canadian billionaires Larry Tanenbaum, Gerald Schwartz, Mark Scheinberg, David Cheriton, Daryl Katz, Sylvan Adams, Seymour Schulich as well as the Azrieli, Zekelman, Reichmann and Sherman families, all backed Israel. Sometimes that support has been quite aggressive.

In "A Story of Failed Re-engagement: Canada and Iran, 2015–2018" University of Ottawa professor Thomas Juneau highlighted the Israel lobby's role in deterring the government from re-establishing diplomatic relations with Iran: "Initially, Cabinet and most caucus supported re-engagement. Dion, who was actively lobbied by Bombardier (whose headquarters were in his riding) and the Montréal Chamber of Commerce, was especially keen. Other senior ministers such as Freeland (International Trade) and Harjit Sajjan (Defence) also supported. With time, however, opposition within caucus grew. It was led by Michael Levitt, the influential MP for York-Center and chair of the Canada-Israel Interparliamentary Group, and also included Anthony Housefather (MP for Mount-Royal). These MPs had support from former minister Irwin Cotler, who had long argued for harsher policies towards Iran."

Juneau continued, "other interviewees also highlighted the differences in organization among pressure groups. Between the tabling of the motion [to oppose reengaging with Iran] and the vote four days later, groups opposing reengagement, such as the Center for Israel and Jewish Affairs, rapidly launched an effective campaign to pressure MPs. Groups favoring reengagement, however, such as the Iranian Canadian Congress, were unable to match these lobbying efforts."[28]

For a movement defending open racism and colonialism the Israel lobby wielded a unique and powerful stick: The ability to play victim and smear those advocating for justice as racist.

The Liberals ousted high-profile Imam Hassan Guillet as a candidate to run for the party in 2019 after B'nai B'rith attacked him for challenging Israeli expansionism.[29] The winner of the Saint-Leonard-Saint-Michel riding nomination gained global notoriety for his sermon at the memorial for the victims of the 2017 Québec City mosque attack, but when B'nai B'rith twisted his pro-Palestinian statements to imply he was anti-Semitic the Liberals dumped their star candidate.

Similarly, when members of the extremist Jewish Defence League attacked peaceful pro-Palestinian activists protesting a presentation by Israeli military reservists at York University, Trudeau sided with the thugs crying anti-Semitism. Following a statement by B'nai B'rith, CIJA and the Israel lobby's point person in the Liberal government, Michael Levitt, Trudeau denounced "anti-Semitism" by pro-Palestinian demonstrators.[30]

On some issues there's no ruling class consensus or particularly powerful lobby group. For example, the foreign policy power structure has been divided over China. Corporate Canada and elements of the Global Affairs bureaucracy generally preferred greater ties with Beijing while the military/security sector sought conflict. This split offers a window into the divergent structures of the foreign policy establishment.

The Canadian business class is well integrated with their US counterparts through parallel stock ownership, corporate boards, Florida residency, etc. They generally view the world and profit from it in a similar way to their US counterparts. Still, corporate Canada had extensive ties in China independent of their US colleagues.

Also well integrated with their US counterparts, Canada's military/security institutions had limited ties to their Chinese counterparts. Since 1949 China has largely been considered an enemy. Additionally, the military, CSIS and Communication Security Establishment tend to be more xenophobic with latent Sinophobia feeding their anti-China campaigning.

Another factor explaining the dynamic was the scope of Washington's dominance over military/security affairs, which is more pronounced than over economic affairs. Fear of being cut off from their powerful US ally motivates the Canadian military/security agencies' anti-China position. Simultaneously, corporate USA is more divided on China than the country's military/security establishment. Like their Canadian counterparts, many US businesses see money to be made in China and focus on short-term profits rather than world domination.

The military and associated industries are powerful political players. With the largest public relations machine in the country, the Canadian Forces (CF) promotes its worldview through a history department, university, journals, war commemorations and hundreds of media relations officers.[31] Backed by the CF and arms firms, the Canadian Global Affairs Institute, Royal Canadian Military Institute, Conference of Defence Associations and Royal Canadian Legion promote a militarist worldview. So do a number of academic initiatives financed by the military.

The CF has various mechanisms to influence the people supposed to oversee it. The CF coordinates an Air Force Day and Navy and Coast Guard Day on Parliament Hill while the Canadian Forces Parliamentary Program embeds MPs in operations and the Canadian Leaders at Sea Program takes influential individuals on "action-packed" multi-day navy operations.[32] Representing over 900 corporations, the Canadian Association of Defence and Security Industries (CADSI) has 20 staff at an office near Parliament Hill.[33] With a new Liberal government in place, CADSI put on a full court press. The association's 2016 report described: "An intense engagement plan that included hundreds of engagements with targeted decision makers, half of which were with Members of Parliament, key ministers and their staffs, including the Prime Minister's Office. From one-on-one meetings, to roundtables, to parliamentary committee appearances, to our first ever reception on Parliament Hill, we took every opportunity to ensure the government understood our industries and heard our message."[34]

The influence of the military lobby was on display with the lack of debate over the Liberals' hundred-billion-dollar naval vessel purchase, the largest single taxpayer expense in Canadian history. Ditto with the 2017 defence policy's unquestioned acceptance of NATO, NORAD and the Five Eyes.

The latter alliance highlights the intersection between militarism, geopolitics and white supremacy. While claiming to be anti-racist, the Liberals promoted the Five Eyes intelligence arrangement. Their 2017 defence policy noted, "building on our shared values and long history of operational cooperation, the Five-Eyes network of partners, including Canada, the United States, United Kingdom, Australia and New Zealand, is central to protecting Canada's interests and contributes directly to operational success." But, the partnership oozes of white supremacy. Settler colonialism and empire unite an alliance that excludes wealthier non-white nations (Japan and South Korea) or those with more English speakers (India and Nigeria). It's not a coincidence that the only four countries (Canada, Australia, New Zealand and the US) that originally voted against the United Nations Declaration on the Rights of Indigenous Peoples (UNDRIP) in 2007 are part of the Five-Eyes.[35]

Alongside 'Anglosphere' racial solidarity, Washington greatly influences Canadian foreign policy. Donald Trump has pressured the Liberals to take more hawkish positions. Trudeau feared the US president's instability, particularly amidst negotiations over NAFTA. Since the original 'free trade' agreement with the US in 1989 Canadian businesses have become more dependent on southern trade. The captains of industry feared that Trump's push to renegotiate NAFTA would disrupt highly profitable investment/trade patterns.

Just after Chrystia Freeland was named new foreign minister — six weeks into Trump's presidency — a US embassy official in Ottawa dispatched a cable to the State Department in Washington entitled "Canada Adopts 'America First' Foreign Policy." Uncovered by Communist Party researcher Jay Watts through a freedom of information request, the largely redacted cable also noted that Trudeau's government would be "Prioritizing U.S. Relations, ASAP" and that Trudeau promoted Freeland "in large part because of her strong U.S. contacts."[36]

The US-based Grayzone's Ben Norton wrote an article based on the cable linking it to Canadian policy on Venezuela, Syria, Russia, Nicaragua, Iran and elsewhere.[37] A number of left-wing websites reposted Norton's article, I wrote about it and RT International invited me on to discuss the memo. But, no other media mentioned a memo that would no doubt have embarrassed Freeland and the broader foreign policy establishment.

While the blackout was media wide, the lack of reaction by one of the most left-wing commentators afforded space in a corporate daily was particularly striking. Previously *Toronto Star* columnist Heather Mallick described Freeland as "likely winner of Canadian of the Year, should that prize exist."[38] In other columns she called Freeland "Canada's famously feminist Foreign Minister", a "brilliant and wonderful Liberal candidate" and lauded "a stark, extraordinary speech [Freeland delivered] in Washington on Wednesday after receiving a diplomat of the year award at the Foreign Policy forum."[39]

While she praised Freeland, Mallick was hostile to Donald Trump. I emailed Mallick to ask if she'd seen the embassy cable, whether she planned to write about it and if she considered it ironic that US officials thought her "Canadian of the Year" was pursuing an 'America First' policy. She didn't respond to two emails, but subsequently praised Freeland again.

Another revealing foreign policy story ignored by the media concerned heavily-armed Canadian troops dispatched to the Port-au-Prince airport.[40] On February 15, 2019, the Haiti Information Project videoed/photographed Canadian soldiers patrolling the Toussaint Louverture airport in the midst of a general strike calling for the president to resign.[41] I wrote a story about the deployment, wondering what they were doing in the country (the Haiti Information Project suggested they may have helped family members of President Jovenel Moïse's unpopular government flee the country). I was in contact with reporters at the *Ottawa Citizen* and *National Post* about the photos, but no media reported the special forces' presence in Haiti. More generally, the dominant media downplayed the scope of anti-government protests in Haiti, which directly targeted Canadian policy.

The dominant media also ignored explosive leaks from the Organisation for the Prohibition of Chemical Weapons showing the Organization's management misled the public about a purported chemical attack in Douma, which the Liberals blamed on Bashar al-Assad and cited to support US, Britain and France bombing Syria.

I wrote a story about it in December 2019 but couldn't find a single major media report about leaks from an organization Canada promoted and heavily funded.

Isolating Canada from world opinion on Palestinian rights was another issue the media largely ignored. More than a dozen times a year the Liberals voted against UN resolutions upholding Palestinian rights backed by most of the world. The dominant media basically only covered the subject when the Liberals shifted their vote. In an indication of this dynamic, a December 2019 *National Post* story was headlined "Trudeau accused of breaking promise to stand by Israel, following vote on UN resolution."[42] The 700-word article concluded with the most salient fact: Only Israel, Micronesia, the US, Marshall Islands and Nauru voted against the motion. While the Israel lobby and some Liberal voters in the Jewish community backed Canada's position at the UN, the broader public was uncomfortable with Israeli expansionism and Canada isolating itself from world opinion.[43] But the media's failure to cover the issue meant the overwhelming majority of Canadians had no idea how the Liberals voted.

The dominant media all but ignored Liberal support for the UAE, Kuwait and other Gulf monarchies as well. Ditto for their support of unconstitutional Honduran President Juan Orlando Hernandez.

While the media largely avoided discussing a series of unjust, embarrassing, international policies, they took a different tack with Venezuela. After two decades of attacks against Hugo Chavez and Nicolás Maduro the corporate media began to cheerlead the federal government's push for regime change in Venezuela. CTV News host Don Martin cheerfully began an interview after a February 2019 Lima Group meeting in Ottawa by stating "the Lima summit has wrapped and the object of regime change is staying put for the time being" and then he asked Freeland "is Maduro any step closer to being kicked out of office as a result of this meeting today?"[44] Later in the interview Martin applauded the US and Canada's bid "to put the economic pincers around it [Venezuela's economy] and choking it off from international transactions."

The media largely relied on government statements/officials when covering Canada's role in Venezuela. Even when they sought out nongovernmental voices they were generally individuals connected to the government. Former ambassador in Caracas, Ben Rowswell, was far and away the most cited non-governmental voice on Canada's role in Venezuela. Rowswell put a liberal gloss on naked imperialism and, despite repeatedly claiming the Venezuelan president's violation of the constitution two years earlier provoked Ottawa's campaign, Rowswell had been involved in efforts to oust Maduro since 2014.[45]

Irwin Cotler, a lawyer for hard-line opposition leader Leopoldo López, was also quoted on multiple occasions. The former Liberal minister had been criticizing the Chavez government since at least 2009 when Venezuela broke off diplomatic relations with Israel in response to its killings in Gaza.[46] At a May 2018 press conference promoting a report seeking to have the International Criminal Court investigate Maduro's government, Cotler claimed the Venezuelan "government itself was responsible for the worst ever humanitarian crisis in the region."[47] (Worse than the extermination of the Taíno and Arawak by the Spanish? Or the enslavement of five million Africans in Brazil? Or the 200,000 Mayans killed in Guatemala? Or the thousands of state-murdered "subversives" in Chile, Argentina, Uruguay, Brazil, Peru? Worse than the tens of thousands killed in Colombia, Honduras and Mexico in recent years?)

The Venezuelan NGOs most quoted in the Canadian media — Foro Penal, Provea, CODEVIDA, Observatorio Venezolano de la Conflictividad, Observatorio Venezolano de Prisiones, etc. — backed the opposition and had ties to the Canadian embassy in Caracas.

The only obviously immoral foreign policy decision extensively covered from a critical lens was the LAV sale to Saudi Arabia. But, the dominant media still relayed government claims that arm sales were frozen despite Canada transferring over $2 billion worth of weapons to the monarchy in 2019. They also minimized the extent to which Canadian weapons were used in the devastation of Yemen.

In addition to distortions, omissions and pandering to power, some in the dominant media seemed to be acting more like fawning sycophants than serious journalists. Their portrayal of Freeland was often downright embarrassing. *The Walrus* headlined a March 2018 article "Chrystia Freeland Wants to Fix the Twenty-first Century" while a November 2019 *Hill Times* story noted, "Freeland has been an ardent defender and champion of international liberalism and a rules-based international order."[48] The proof? Well, she said so.

A long *Globe and Mail* profile just before the October 2019 election was maybe the most shameful. Written by the paper's five senior international correspondents, the two-page spread headlined "For Chrystia Freeland, the political is personal" began: "There are two reactions you get when you ask around the globe about Chrystia Freeland and Canadian foreign policy under her leadership. She's either one of the last, best hopes of the liberal world order — or she's an out-of-touch idealist who is risking trade by starting diplomatic fights that Canada can't hope to win." Presumably, the *Globe's* top-flight international investigative team failed to find anyone who believed Freeland promoted pro-US, corporate and militarist policies.

With such a compliant media perhaps it is no surprise that the NDP demonstrated little interest in challenging the dominant media's depiction of international affairs. Nor did Green leader Elizabeth May stray far from the liberal establishment worldview. To slightly varying degrees they supported the Liberals on NATO deployments and militarism, as well as the thrust of Ottawa's policy towards Ukraine, Syria, Rwanda, Nicaragua, Haiti and Venezuela. As I detailed in *Left, Right: Marching to the Beat of Imperial Canada*, NDP MPs have long been absorbed into the Ottawa foreign policy swamp.

A vice-chair of the anti-Palestinian Canada Israel Interparliamentary Group, NDP defence critic Randall Garrison "is a passionate advocate for the Canadian military", according to the Canadian Defence Review.[49] Representing a riding that includes the Esquimalt naval base, Garrison held his 2015 election night party and other events at the Esquimalt Legion.[50] Part of the Canadian NATO Parliamentary Association, Garrison criticized the Liberals' 2017 announcement that they would increase military spending by 70 per cent over the next decade on the grounds more money wasn't invested immediately. Garrison bemoaned that "all we have is promises for future [military spending] increases" and in another interview said "the money you're proposing will not keep pace with the rate of inflation."[51] A proponent of Canada leading a NATO battle group to Latvia, Garrison also criticized the Liberals for failing to immediately follow its defence policy's recommendation to upgrade a multi-billion dollar early-warning radar system used by the North American Aerospace Defense Command (NORAD), which is a military alliance that has drawn Canadian personnel into supporting US belligerence.[52]

For her part, the NDP foreign critic through the Liberals' first term in office, Hélène Laverdière, was a Canadian diplomat for more than 15 years, even winning the Foreign Minister's Award for her contribution to Canadian foreign policy.[53] In 2016 she spoke to the notorious anti-Palestinian American Israel Public Affairs Committee (AIPAC) lobby organization and participated in a ceremony put on by the head of the explicitly racist Jewish National Fund during a visit to Israel.[54]

It's not just in Israel where Laverdière aligned with the US Empire's machinations. Laverdière supported deploying troops to the Russian border and repeatedly called for more sanctions on that country.[55] She demanded Canada take tougher action against the Assad regime and released a June 2018 statement — with NDP Critic for International Human Rights Cheryl Hardcastle — "unequivocally condemning the 'shoot-to-kill' policy of President Ortega's government ... Nicaraguan authorities continue to use a policy of state repression, including the use of excessive force, extrajudicial killings, pro-government armed squads, and control of the media in order to stop protests."[56] On a number of occasions, the NDP foreign critic demanded Ottawa do more to undermine Venezuelan President Nicolás Maduro. After the Liberals went all in to overthrow Maduro she agreed with the Liberals' recognition of Juan Guaidó as president of Venezuela.[57]

The leader of the Greens was close to Trudeau's long-standing foreign-policy adviser Irwin Cotler. In May 2019 Elizabeth May attended a press conference organized by Cotler calling on Canada to impose sanctions on 19 Iranian officials and to follow the Trump administration in listing the country's Revolutionary Guard as a terrorist organization.[58] May's support for ramping up Canadian hostility towards Tehran took place amidst increasingly bellicose moves by Washington. May also participated in at least three press conferences organized by Cotler to call for the release of the leader of Venezuela's hardline Voluntad Popular party Leopoldo López.[59] The Harvard-educated López endorsed the military's 2002 coup against President Hugo Chavez and was convicted of inciting violence during the 2014 "guarimbas" protests that sought to oust President Nicolás Maduro (Cotler joined López' legal team). According to a series of reports, López was the key Venezuelan organizer of the plan to anoint his protégé Juan Guaidó interim president of Venezuela and on April 30, 2019, he escaped house arrest to join Guaidó in a failed coup bid.

Extra-parliamentary opposition to Liberal foreign policy was largely confined to small international solidarity and peace groups. With the exception of Trudeau's climate and mining policies, labour unions, NGOs and other more influential progressive organizations provided limited pushback. Canada's largest private sector union offers a stark example of indifference to the Liberal pro corporate and empire foreign policy. Unifor invited Freeland to address their August 2019 convention. Inviting the foreign minister to their convention was part of the union's controversial embrace of the Liberal Party (Trudeau also spoke). But, it also reflected a coldness to the injustices Canada contributed to abroad. In a search at the time of the convention I couldn't find a single Unifor statement that directly criticized Freeland or Canadian foreign policy (the union was a member of Common Frontiers, which did criticize Canadian policy in Venezuela and Honduras).

As for supposed "non-governmental organizations" that are supposed to be independent of government? An umbrella group representing dozens of major development NGOs, the Canadian Council for International Co-operation (CCIC) often cheered Liberal foreign policy. In September 2018 the CCIC co-organized a conference titled "Is Canada Back: Delivering on Good Intentions?" Publicity for the event with the Canadian Association for the Study of International Development noted: "Inspired by Justin Trudeau's 2015 proclamation 'Canada is Back', we are presenting panels that illustrate or challenge Canada's role in global leadership. Are we doing all that we could be doing in the world?"[60] Formulating the question this way ignored the government's arms sales to Saudi Arabia, backing for brutal mining companies, NATO deployments, antagonism towards Palestinian rights, efforts to topple the Venezuelan government, failure to end Canada's 'low level war' on Iran, backing for an unpopular Haitian president, refusal to support nuclear weapons controls, promotion of military spending, etc.

In November 2019 CCIC co-organized a Summit on Canada's Global Leadership. The event included Chief of the Defence Staff Jonathan Vance, Minister for International Development Karina Gould, Trudeau advisor Bob Rae, former CSIS director Richard Fadden, former head of the Canadian International Development Agency Margaret Biggs and others.[61] Describing himself as a lobbyist for greater aid, CCIC CEO Nicolás Moyer said in an interview before the Summit on Canada's Global Leadership that it was important to bring together different sectors of Canadian foreign policy because "there is no path which leads towards increased federal commitments to ODA [overseas development assistance] which can exist without a strong ambition for Canada's role in the world. We need champions in other sectors that also want an ambitious and impactful foreign policy."[62] Willing to include the military as part of his grand foreign policy coalition, Moyer added, "it's why I am looking forward to discussions at the summit, for example between Chief of the Defence Staff Jonathan Vance and Canada's Ambassador for Women Peace and Security Jacqueline O'Neill." Instead of challenging unjust Liberal policies, the CCIC largely shilled for the liberal (aid) arm of Canadian foreign policy.

So, unfortunately the scope of opposition to Trudeau foreign policy has been limited. But a few groups I engaged with offer a glimmer of hope and an indication of the sort of campaigning required to change foreign policy culture.

Through bold activism Solidarité Québec-Haïti pushed back against Liberal party imperialism. In Summer 2019 members of the group interrupted two press conferences (and a barbecue) by Minister of La Francophonie and Tourism Mélanie Joly to call on the Liberals to stop propping up a repressive, corrupt and illegitimate president in Haiti. Solidarité Québec-Haïti also directly questioned Liberal MP Emmanuel Dubourg, Minister Jean-Yves Duclos and former International Development Minister Marie-Claude Bibeau over the government's policy in Haiti.

On August 18 a member of Solidarité Québec-Haïti interrupted Trudeau at a press conference to ask why Canada supported a corrupt, repressive and illegitimate president in Haiti. On September 30, 2019, 15 Haitian community members and allies occupied Trudeau's election office for a little over three hours. The Solidarité Québec-Haïti activists called on the PM to stop backing Moïse and withdraw from the so-called Core Group. The *Montréal Gazette* published a good article on the sit in, which was picked up by a half dozen outlets. Part of it was translated into French and published by

La Presse, Journal Métro, Ricochet and *Telesur* all ran their own articles on the office occupation. A few days later *Le Devoir* published a good article promoting our demand titled "Le Canada appelé à lâcher le président haïtien Jovenel Moïse." A slew of Haitian news sites and community radio programs covered the occupation. As with previous Solidarité Québec-Haïti actions, the occupation received substantial attention on social media.

As a follow-up to the occupation of his office two days later, we organized a last-minute rally outside a community boxing ring where Trudeau put on his gloves for a photo-op. Ten of us chanted loudly "Jovenel repressif, Trudeau complice". The PM's large RCMP detail called the Montréal police, which dispatched a dozen officers who arrested organizer Marie Dimanche. The arrest generated some corporate media attention and significant buzz within the Haitian community. A week later Solidarité Québec-Haïti organized a 40-person rally outside Trudeau's electoral office, which was covered by Global, TVA and other news outlets. We also attempted to disrupt Trudeau's final election rally, which prompted Radio Canada to describe 10 of us chanting "Canada out of Haiti".

Alongside these efforts, Solidarité Québec-Haïti organized an "open letter calling on the Canadian government to stop backing a corrupt, repressive and illegitimate Haitian president." About 150 writers, musicians, professors and activists signed, including David Suzuki, Roger Waters, Linda McQuaig, Amir Khadir, Will Prosper, Tariq Ali, Michele Landsberg and Yann Martel. It was published by many media outlets and referenced in a number of stories.

A month after the election Solidarité Québec-Haïti organized a demonstration. Two hundred marched on a cold November day chanting "solidarity with the Haitian people" and "no to Canadian imperialism in Haiti."

Disruption Network Canada was another initiative that challenged Liberal foreign policy. It sought to mobilize activists to confront politicians through peaceful, direct action. In 2019 members

of Disruption Network Canada and Mouvement Québécois pour la Paix interrupted a dozen speeches/press conferences by Liberal ministers/prime minister to question their militarism, anti-Palestinian positions, climate policies, efforts to topple Venezuela's government, etc. We interrupted:
- a Université de Montréal talk by Foreign Minister Chrystia Freeland to criticize Canada's effort to overthrow Venezuela's government;
- a corporate luncheon with Defence Minister Harjit Sajjan to condemn increased military spending, arms sales to Saudi Arabia and NATO deployments;
- a press conference by Justice Minister David Lametti to challenge his promotion of a Bombardier surveillance plane sale to the UAE and Canada fueling the war on Yemen;
- an event by Environment Minister Catherine McKenna to criticize spending tens of billions of dollars on heavy carbon emitting fighter jets and naval vessels amidst the climate crisis;
- press events by Transportation Minister Marc Garneau and Prime Minister Trudeau on their anti-Palestinian positions.

A number of these actions garnered corporate media attention. Clips of almost all of them were widely viewed on social media.

In order to show politicians, the media and even many progressives that some of us are hostile to Canadian foreign policy we need to raise our voices and be disruptive in the cause of international solidarity. People are often reluctant to demonstrate their international solidarity because they think their voices will not be heard. In my experience these people crave signs of resistance. And acts of resistance generally beget more such acts.

With the dominant media refusing to cover critical perspectives on important international issues, we need to find other ways to put forward our message and push back against government policies. We also need to give the decision-makers a bit of a headache and inspire like-minded individuals to act. Disrupting ministers and politicians at public events can be a high impact form of international solidarity and is an example of much needed direct-action democracy.

***

The overall lesson to be learned from this book should be that people must look past the rhetoric offered by politicians to describe what Canada is doing around the world. Just because the Liberals say more progressive things than the Conservatives doesn't mean their governments are, in fact, more progressive. Grassroots organizations that speak truth to power are essential to inform Canadians about what is being done in our name across the planet. We can't only rely on corporate media outlets for information about international affairs. And when we know our government is doing something wrong we must speak up, make noise, disrupt — that is the only way our voices will be heard above the demands of entrenched power.

Conclusion Notes

1 (https://www.brookfield.com)

2 List of largest banks (https://en.wikipedia.org/wiki/List_of_largest_banks)

3 Doug Alexander, Scotiabank CEO urges assistance for troubled Venezuela in National Post op-ed, Bloomberg News, Jan 28 2020 (https://business.financialpost.com/news/fp-street/scotiabank-ceo-seeks-assistance-for-troubled-venezuela-in-op-ed)

4 Geoff Zochodne, Scotiabank's strategic foray into Latin America hits a snag with Chile unrest, Nov 22 2019 (https://business.financialpost.com/news/fp-street/scotiabank-chile-unrest)

5 Brian Porter, A call to action on Venezuela, Jan 27 2020 (https://nationalpost.com/opinion/opinion-a-call-to-action-on-venezuela)

6 Ibid

7 Yves Engler, Mining Peru, Dec 23 2010 (https://www.counterpunch.org/2010/12/23/mining-peru/)

8 Grahame Russell, Canadian Companies Mining With The Genocidal Generals In Guatemala (https://rightsaction.org/mining-with-genocidal-generals/)

9 The Honourable Jim Carr, Minister of Natural Resources, delivers the keynote address at the Canada in Conversation event hosted by the Embassy of Canada, Natural Resources Canada, June 5 2017 (https://www.canada.ca/en/natural-resources-canada/news/2017/06/the_honourable_jimcarrministerofnaturalresourcesdeliversthekeyno.html)

10 Colin Robertson, Staffing the Foreign Minister's Office, April 27 2016 (http://www.colinrobertson.ca/?p=1603)

11 Charlotte Connolly, Lobbying by mining industry on the proposed Canadian Ombudsperson for Responsible Enterprise (CORE), July 24 2019 (https://justice-project.org/wp-content/uploads/2019/07/2.-Report-on-Lobbying-by-Mining-Industry-july-24-fin.pdf)

12 Ibid

13 Claudia Maria Arietti López, Venezuela to pay US$1 billion for expropriating Canadian mining company's investment, Dec 12 2016 (https://www.iisd.org/itn/2016/12/12/venezuela-to-pay-us1-billion-for-expropriating-canadian-mining-companys-investment/) ; Martin Dietrich Brauch, Venezuela ordered to pay US$1.202 billion plus interest to Canadian mining company Crystallex for FET breach and expropriation, Aug 10 2016 (https://www.iisd.org/itn/2016/08/10/crystallex-international-corporation-v-bolivarian-republic-of-venezue-

la-icsid-case-no-arb-af-11-2/)

14 Yves Engler, Stephen Harper's Endless Campaign for Mining Profits, Nov 22 2012 (https://thetyee.ca/Books/2012/11/22/Harper-Mining-Profits/)

15 Hal Weitzman, Bolivia's Morales vows to nationalise mining industry in La Paz, May 8 2006 (https://www.ft.com/content/feff7e00-ded6-11da-acee-0000779e2340#axzz3k2pQcSbH) ; Gabriel Friedman, 'Obsession' with world class assets leads Barrick Gold where others fear to tread, Nov 6 2019 (https://business.financialpost.com/commodities/mining/asset-quality-always-overrides-jurisdiction-obsession-with-world-class-assets-leads-barrick-gold-where-others-fear-to-tread)

16 Malavika Krishnan, Canadian Mining in Latin America: Exploitation, Inconsistency, and Neglect, June 11 2014 (http://www.coha.org/canadian-mining-in-latin-america-exploitation-inconsistency-and-neglect/)

17 Yves Engler, Mining Peru, Dec 23 2010 (https://www.counterpunch.org/2010/12/23/mining-peru/)

18 Todd Gordon and Jeffery R Webber, Canadian capital and secondary imperialism in Latin America. Canadian Foreign Policy Journal, Volume 25, Issue 1, 2019

19 Canadian Mining Assets Information Bulletin, Feb 2019 (https://www.nrcan.gc.ca/mining-materials/publications/19323)

20 Kathryn Blaze Carlson, Sens owner Melnyk urges Canadian action on Ukraine, Mar 21 2014 (https://www.theglobeandmail.com/sports/hockey/sens-owner-melynk-urges-canadian-action-on-ukraine/article17626045/)

21 Jocelyn Coulon, Canada is Not Back: How Justin Trudeau is in over his head on foreign policy, 149 ; Canada: marking 125 years of Ukrainian settlement, Jan 21 2017 (http://www.ukrweekly.com/uwwp/canada-marking-125-years-of-ukrainian-settlement/)

22 Ukrainian Canadian Congress (https://en.wikipedia.org/wiki/Ukrainian_Canadian_Congress)

23 Jocelyn Coulon, Canada is Not Back: How Justin Trudeau is in over his head on foreign policy, 149

24 Fred Waks takes the reins of the Jewish Foundation of Greater Toronto, UJA Federation of Greater Toronto, Dec 13 2012 (https://jewishtoronto.com/news-media/fred-waks-takes-the-reins-of-the-jewish-foundation-of-greater-toronto/) ; Beryl Wajsman and Joel Ceausu, Federation CJA unveils art exhibit honoring visionaries, The Suburban, Dec 14 2016 (http://www.thesuburban.com/news/city_news/federation-cja-unveils-art-exhibit-honoring-visionaries/article_0f35e64c-457c-5a2d-a6d7-69381a01359e.html)

25 Andrew Cohen, Canadian Jews need to ask lobby group some tough questions, Feb 13 2018 (https://ottawacitizen.com/opinion/columnists/cohen-canadian-jews-need-to-ask-lobby-group-some-tough-questions)

26 Friends of Simon Wiesenthal Center for Holocaust Studies (https://www.charitydata.ca/charity/friends-of-simon-wiesenthal-center-for-holocaust-studies/890666761RR0001/)

27 Jane Taber, Trudeau taps millionaire Stephen Bronfman to help fill Liberals' war chest, Aug 28 2013 (https://www.theglobeandmail.com/news/politics/stephen-bronfman-to-lead-trudeaus-fundraising-campaign/article13999238/)

28 Thomas Juneau, A story of failed re-engagement: Canada and Iran, 2015–2018, Canadian Foreign Policy Journal, Jan 2019

29 Ex-Liberal candidate Guillet says Liberals knew about social media posts before ousting him, Canadian Press, Sept 4 2019 (https://montreal.ctvnews.ca/ex-liberal-candidate-guillet-says-liberals-knew-about-social-media-posts-before-ousting-him-1.4577683)

30 Dimitri Lascaris, Justin Trudeau Sides With Pro-Israel Thuggery At York University, Nov 23 2019 (https://dimitrilascaris.org/2019/11/23/justin-trudeau-sides-with-pro-israel-thuggery-at-york-university/)

31 Yves Engler, A Propaganda System: How Canada's Government, Corporations, Media and Academia Sell War and Exploitation

32 Jane Taber, When parliamentarians go to war, Oct 22 2010 (https://www.theglobeandmail.com/news/politics/ottawa-notebook/when-parliamentarians-go-to-war/article1381081/) ; Department of National Defence and Canadian Armed Forces Parliamentary Program (https://www.canada.ca/en/department-national-defence/programs/parliamentary-program.html)

33 Caroline Phillips, Overhauling defence lobby group just the start for Ottawa's Christyn Cianfarani, Ottawa Business Journal, Apr 3 2019 (https://obj.ca/article/overhauling-defence-lobby-group-just-start-ottawas-christyn-cianfarani)

34 Mike Greenley, CADSI Annual General Meeting, Report of Chair of CADSI Board of Directors, Mar 29 2017 (https://www.defenceandsecurity.ca/media/speech&s=48&v=e5e4c1604be58d-78f97ae608140c3349)

35 United Nations Declaration on the Rights of Indigenous Peoples (https://www.un.org/development/desa/indigenouspeoples/declaration-on-the-rights-of-indigenous-peoples.html)

36 Ben Norton, 'Canada Adopts America First Foreign Policy,' US State Dept boasted in 2017, with appointment of FM Chrystia Freeland, Grayzone, July 5 2019 (https://thegrayzone.com/2019/07/05/canada-adopts-america-first-foreign-policy-us-state-department-chrystia-freeland/)

37 Ibid

38 Heather Mallick, Chrystia Freeland plays a winning hand, Dec 11 2018 (https://www.thestar.com/opinion/star-columnists/2018/12/11/chrystia-freeland-plays-a-winning-hand.html)

39 Mallick Heather, Toronto's McQuaig and Freeland pay a price for being female, Nov 18

2013 (https://www.thestar.com/opinion/commentary/2013/11/18/torontos_mcquaig_and_freeland_are_running_while_female_mallick.html) ; Heather Mallick, Chrystia Freeland dares to look at a dark American future, June 15 2018 (https://www.thestar.com/opinion/star-columnists/2018/06/15/chrystia-freeland-dares-to-look-at-a-dark-american-future.html)

40   15 Feb 2019 (https://twitter.com/HaitiInfoProj/status/1096629898762829824?fbclid=IwAR37Azm-bxaJX_1b0v5p2d-FDWhN2DE2M-nGGqRKSTP-0Co9phPD88zZW9fGo)

41   15 Feb 2019 (https://twitter.com/HaitiInfoProj/status/1096630200463290368?fbclid=I-wAR1a1r59Qdyyz5EAB_xREqvwGIYRl66kQw-CxJs-dHDl9vRozGgRTMfmstXs)

42   Stuart Thomson, Trudeau accused of breaking promise to stand by Israel, following vote on UN resolution, Dec 18 2019 (https://nationalpost.com/news/trudeau-accused-of-breaking-promise-to-stand-by-israel-following-vote-on-un-resolution)

43   2017 Survey: On Israel-Palestine, Canadian Gov't is out of Touch (https://www.cjpme.org/survey) ; Eight-in-Ten (79%) Canadians Believe We Should Not Take Either Side in Israeli - Palestinian Conflict (https://www.ipsos.com/en-ca/eight-ten-79-canadians-believe-we-should-not-take-either-side-israeli-palestinian-conflict)

44   Canada helping Venezuelans 'reclaim democracy': Freeland, Feb 4 2019 (https://www.youtube.com/watch?v=_ajmQyYco3w)

45   Yves Engler, Canada's meddling in Venezuela: the case of Ben Rowswell, May 24 2019 (https://yvesengler.com/2019/05/24/canadas-meddling-in-venezuela-the-case-of-ben-rowswell/)

46   Yves Engler, Canada escalates its hypocritical attack on Venezuela, Oct 17 2018 (https://yvesengler.com/2018/10/17/canada-escalates-its-hypocritical-attack-on-venezuela/)

47   OAS panel on Venezuela grilled by Max Blumenthal for hypocrisy and bias, May 29 2018 (https://www.youtube.com/watch?v=hAT8c9G-tinY&app=desktop)

48   Neil Moss, Mending global relationships, defending economic interests Champagne's top tasks, say foreign policy analysts, Nov 22 2019 (https://www.hilltimes.com/2019/11/22/mending-global-relationships-defending-economic-interests-champagnes-top-tasks-as-canadas-top-diplomat-say-foreign-policy-analysts/225461)

49   Yves Engler, NDP MP Refuses to Withdraw from Canada-Israel Interparliamentary Group, Aug 22 2018 (http://www.palestinechronicle.com/ndp-mp-refuses-to-withdraw-from-canada-israel-interparliamentary-group/)

50   Kendra Wong, NDP Randall Garrison takes Esquimalt-Saanich-Sooke after tight race, Oct 19 2015 (https://www.vicnews.com/news/ndp-randall-garrison-takes-esquimalt-saanich-sooke-after-tight-race/)

51   Murray Brewster, More soldiers, ships and planes for military in Liberal defence, Jun 7 2017 (https://www.cbc.ca/news/politics/liberal-sajjan-garneau-defence-policy-1.4149473) ; Murray Brewster, Liberals planning $600M down payment on defence strategy, Jun 20 2017 (https://www.cbc.ca/news/politics/dnd-budget-boost-1.4170340)

52   Lee Berthiaume, Trudeau will face pointed questions on Canada's NATO role at Poland summit, Canadian Press, July 7 2016 (https://www.thestar.com/news/canada/2016/07/07/trudeau-will-face-pointed-questions-on-canadas-nato-role-at-poland-summit.html) ; Marco Vigliotti, Conservatives, NDP call on Liberal government to match rhetoric with action on NORAD cooperation, Nov 27 2017 (https://www.hilltimes.com/2017/11/27/conservatives-ndp-call-liberal-government-match-rhetoric-action-norad-cooperation/126680) ; Yves Engler, NORAD is a relic of the Cold War and it's time to end it, May 11 2018 (https://rabble.ca/blogs/bloggers/yves-englers-blog/2018/05/norad-relic-cold-war-and-its-time-end-it)

53   Hélène Laverdière (https://en.wikipedia.org/wiki/Hélène_Laverdière)

54   Yves Engler, Why is Canada's NDP supporting Israeli racism?, May 25 2017 (https://electronicintifada.net/content/why-canadas-ndp-supporting-israeli-racism/20576)

55   Canada to deploy troops to Ukraine in training role, Apr 14 2015 (https://www.ctvnews.ca/canada/canada-to-deploy-troops-to-ukraine-in-training-role-1.2326288) ; Lee Berthiaume, Canada under pressure to strengthen Ukraine crisis response, Dec 23 2014 (http://ottawacitizen.com/news/politics/canada-under-pressure-to-strengthen-ukraine-crisis-response)

56   NDP Statement on the Situation in Nicaragua, June 4 2018 (https://www.ndp.ca/news/ndp-statement-situation-nicaragua)

57   Yves Engler, Mainstream media boosts Trudeau's popularity over Venezuela, Feb 13 2019 (https://yvesengler.com/2019/02/13/mainstream-media-boosts-trudeaus-popularity-over-venezuela/)

58   Joseph Brean, Victims of Iranian state violence urge Canada to sanction regime's top ministers, May 9 2019 (https://nationalpost.com/news/canada/victims-of-iranian-state-violence-urge-canada-to-sanction-regimes-top-ministers)

59   Yves Engler, Green leader May supports same old pro-imperialist foreign policies, May 15 2019 (https://canadiandimension.com/articles/view/green-leader-may-supports-same-old-pro-imperialist-foreign-policies)

60   (https://ccic.ca/conference-2018/)

61   Speakers / Conférencier(ières) (https://globalleadershipsummit.ca/speakers/)

62   Eva Salinas, Five questions with… humanitarian Nicolás Moyer, head of the CCIC, Nov 22 2019 (https://www.opencanada.org/features/five-questions-with-humanitarian-Nicolás-moyer-head-of-the-ccic/)

Also Available From Black Rose Books

Left, Right

Marching to the Beat
of Imperial Canada

BY YVES ENGLER

Paperback: 978-1-55164-663-3
Cloth: 978-1-55164-665-7
Ebook: 978-1-55164-667-1

Also Available From Black Rose Books

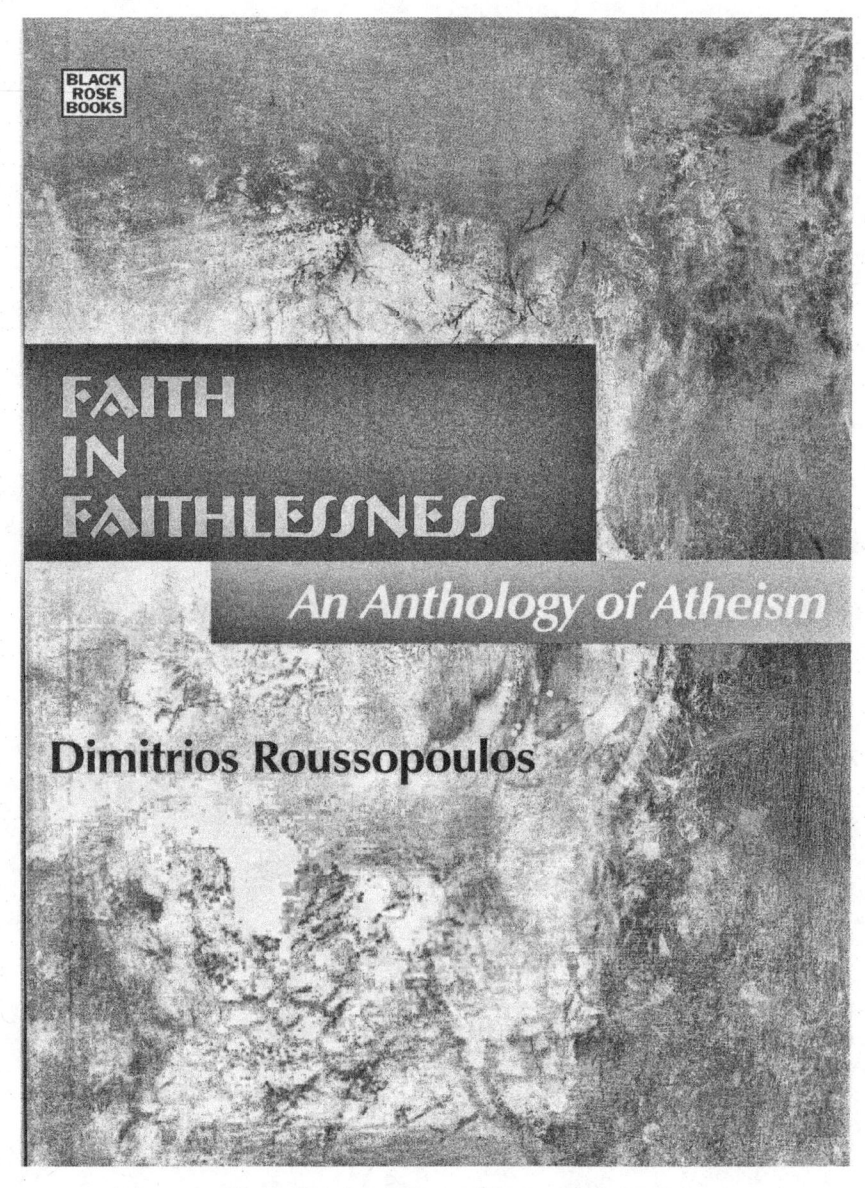

FAITH IN FAITHLESSNESS
An Anthology of Atheism

Dimitrios Roussopoulos

Paperback: 978-1-55164-312-0
Cloth: 978-1-55164-313-7

Coming in Spring 2020 From Black Rose Books

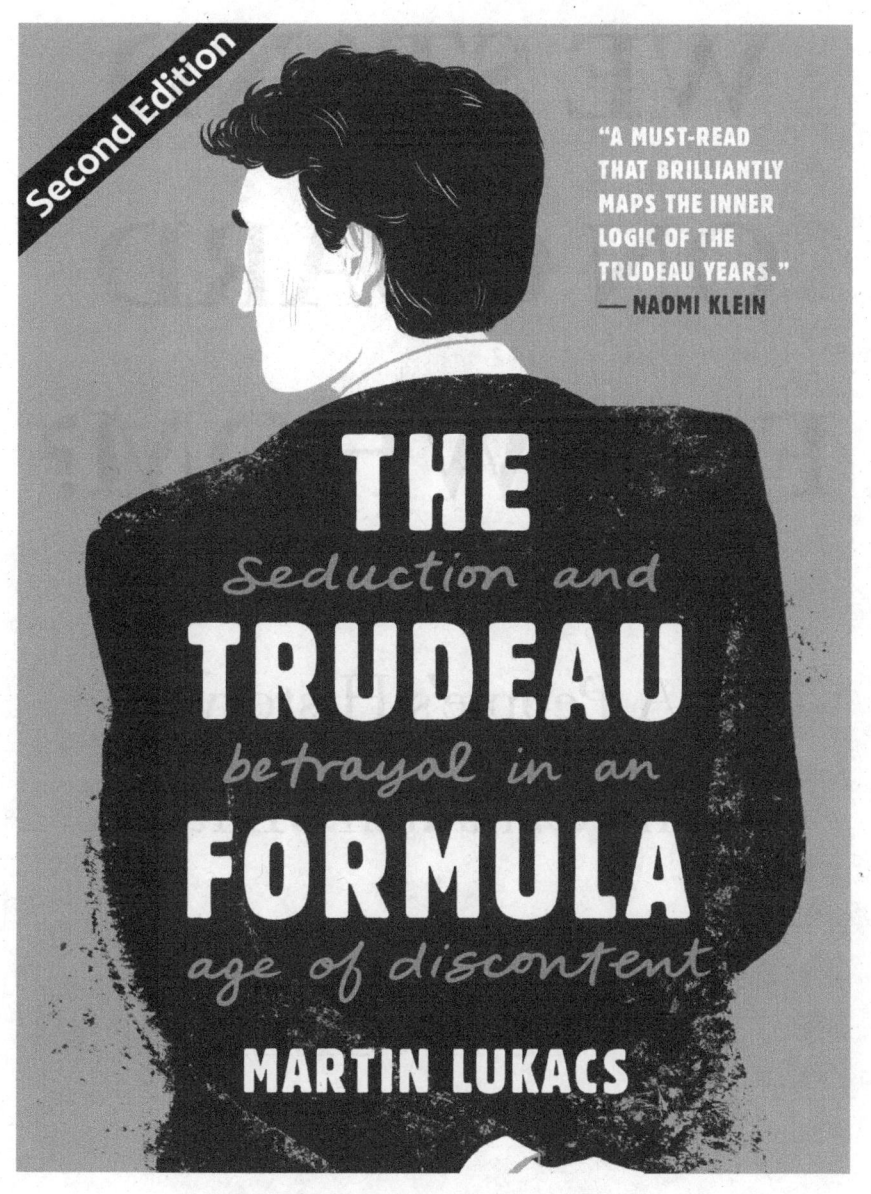

THE TRUDEAU FORMULA
Seduction and betrayal in an age of discontent

Second Edition

"A MUST-READ THAT BRILLIANTLY MAPS THE INNER LOGIC OF THE TRUDEAU YEARS."
— NAOMI KLEIN

MARTIN LUKACS

Paperback: 978-1-55164-754-8
Cloth: 978-1-55164-756-2
Ebook: 978-1-55164-758-6

Coming in Fall 2020 From Black Rose Books

WE STAND ON GUARD FOR WHOM?

A People's History of the Canadian Military

YVES ENGLER

Paperback: 978-1-55164-755-5
Cloth: 978-1-55164-757-9
Ebook: 978-1-55164-759-3

COMPETING FOR
ELVIS